WALKING
BY DAY

Donald Hutchins

CPR Prompt Corporation - Springfield, Massachusetts

For permission to reproduce selections from this book write to:
Permissions, CPR Prompt Corporation, 60 Brookdale Drive
Springfield, Massachusetts 01104

Hardcover   ISBN   0-9666102-0-2
Paperback   ISBN   0-9666102-1-0
Library of Congress Catalog Card Number: 98-96492

Printed in the United States of America

JACKET DESIGN BY KRISTIN MORIARTY WHITE

*For Rachel Carson with the hope
that we can right the course*

Contents

I. A Fable for Tomorrow

There was once a summer home in the heart of the Berkshire Hills where human life seemed to live in harmony with its surroundings. The family that summered in that home was blessed with caring parents, four active children and a golden retriever. Their waking hours were filled with sounds of laughter and talk of golf scores. After dinner things were somewhat quieter. This was the season and place where the family really came together. Dad was home at night and the poor television reception in the mountains allowed more time for conversation, Monopoly and the endless jigsaw puzzle. In Dickens' words, this was the best of times.

Outside the home a few potted plants shared the ground with wild flowers and laurel. There was just enough grass to place mowing on the list of family chores. As a summer cottage, the height of the grass was of no real significance until just before summer-resident parties.

Some would argue whether it was the quiet mornings or those

summer parties that are best remembered. Both stamped indelible impressions on the children's minds. The parties were unique in that there were no barriers, such as age or interests, which divided the family in the winter. They remembered the footballs that flew over the heads of young girls mimicking steps seen at Jacob's Pillow the night before and neighbors questioning whether the Red Sox would win a World Series in their lifetime.

Then a strange blight crept over the family and that summer home began to change. This was not Ibsen's dysfunctional family blight, but a malady caused by outside forces. Some evil spell had settled on the community. The summer home now stood neglected with no signs of life except the trampled grass where the crowd had stood for the auction.

Bobby Hutchins was not sure what he would tell his dad. Maybe it would be best to say nothing. Each year he visited the summer home to capture the old memories. It gave him something to talk about with his father and filled those lulls that had become so difficult to bridge as his father became more and more withdrawn.

At times he would convince himself that this withdrawal was part of the aging process or because his mother had died and broken the family bond. In truth Bobby knew that it had all started with the "Judgement." Those damage payments had sapped his father's lust for life. Oh, the spirituality remained and he knew his father was at peace with God, but he felt that his dad had already left this world for a better place.

His dad had no zest for golf, paddle or those Florida vacations that once commanded great attention. Jenny said it was because mom was gone, but Bobby knew the truth, his dad could not afford those things anymore.

On his way to this abandoned summer home, Bobby saw indications of this same decay. There was no life in the mill buildings that lined the banks of the Westfield River. The buildings' hopes for revival were crushed, as the commercial lenders became suspicious that pollution would be found under the buildings' foundations. It was no different for the factory buildings in Westfield and Pittsfield that lay abandoned after risk assessments indicated the possibility of pollutants. Now they joined those state lists of unproductive assets called brownfields, while developers ripped away at the virgin fields and forests to provide new factory sites in the suburbs.

Bobby's recent conversations with a real estate broker came to mind. This friend was frustrated by the long delays these risk assessments had brought to his industry. The broker bemoaned the fact that, because of environmental red tape, many sales never materialized and those closings his firm did complete were taking three months longer than in the past. He saw lawyers getting rich as he floundered to keep his head above water.

Bobby had also read about farms that lay fallow in the Midwest because young farmers could not find financing to purchase the farms of older farmers that were retiring. Seems that very few farms could pass the rigid tests required under the federal environmental law called CERCLA. That's not surprising when you consider that almost every farm once stored gasoline, pesticides, oils and fertilizers that could spill into the soil. This accounting of pollutants does not even include animal and human waste plus such substances as anti freeze and household cleaners, which never left the farms. Regional banks purchased the small local banks, which once had done farm financing, and the lenders invoked the same environmental standards as they had for any business client. When they drilled those test wells and sent water samples to the labs, tests from many farms showed toxic substances in the ground water in violation of the drinking water quality standards that applied. The worst part was that not only did the young farmers lose their financing and not buy the farms, but the conditions were reported to state environmental departments that forced the farm owners to start expensive remediation programs to clean the toxins from tons of soil.

Perhaps it was the chorus of robins, catbirds, jays, and wrens;

perhaps the warm sun and bright colors of the fall leaves on the trees that made Bobby recoil at the injustice as he stood by the abandoned summer home. He sighed and said to himself, "Where are the priorities in America? Are not human lives more important than trees and insects? Why is it that families and jobs are being liquidated while nature blooms?"

Bobby spent much of his leisure time working with youngsters at Special Olympics. He understood that being sensitive to other humans took effort. He was not naive and realized that many people preferred the constant and undemanding love of pets and potted plants than to interacting with other humans. But, why must laws made by communities of people be so insensitive and cruel? Laws above anything else should champion the glory of humanity.

Bobby thought back to the squabbles that he and his brothers had as children. His mother would say, "Just tell them that sticks and stones will break my bones but words will never hurt me." Unfortunately, she was wrong. In the end it was words like strict, joint and several that had brought his father down and precipitated the lawsuits.

Other words in phrases that Bobby revered in grammar school had also failed his family; such as the phrases corporate limited liability and innocent until proven guilty. In the real world, his dad was assumed guilty as the courts begrudgingly gave him the opportunity to prove his innocence.

These CERCLA laws were written in such a way as to deny owners of small companies any hope of distancing themselves from damage claims. A convicted federal corporate tax evader has a better chance than his father did to divorce himself from such damage claims. Bobby wondered if all the small manufacturers and distributors across America were aware that the limited liability shield did not apply to corporate owners under CERCLA.

Bobby's family, once so cohesive, is now scattered with no place to call home. After losing his business, Bob's dad continued to defend himself against the tort actions that followed him personally. The next victim was the summerhouse and acreage that had once been valued at 1/4 million. The auction sale, organized by the damaged parties, brought the plaintiffs only a small portion of the true value because of the "fire sale" conditions and the large percentage paid to the lawyers.

No one thought that when Bobby's mother died, it would expose her estate to the environmental damage claims. One might expect that his father's lawyers would have protected those funds that his mother had received as inheritances years ago, however this contingency was never considered. For his father to lose a wife and to have the courts claim her estate seemed a terrible injustice to Bob. He knew that his father had given up on life when his dad allowed his mother's inheritance to be seized without putting up a fight.

No witchcraft, no enemy action had silenced this family and forced them to abandon their worldly possessions. The family had not done it to themselves; the law had done it to them.

This family does exist, as do a thousand counterparts in America. Their spring is silent because they have given up. They have had no voice to tell America what these laws have done to them. Bobby's family was one of the first families in the United States to be involved in environmental litigation. Many of our best Americans have been dispossessed as they entered their retirement years and thousands more will meet the same fate in the future. Many will never know until they attempt to sell their farms or businesses and the buyers drill test wells as part of the financing. At that time, waiting for those environmental lab test results, can only be compared to waiting for biopsy tests taken for cancer.

This grim specter has crept upon us almost unnoticed. Do we not wonder why so many buildings sit idle along bus lines where buses could easily and economically bring inner city workers to them? Is it better to have developers displace birds and animals by building factories in the countryside? Why has America built a new caste society and placed lawyers at its aegis?

I wish that this were, "*A fable for tomorrow*," and just as Rachel Carson's fabled silent spring, never become a reality. Unfortunately for America, we are past the point of this being a fable. This is frighteningly real and taking place across the country on a daily basis.

One of those thousands of silenced voices belongs to me. Bob is my nephew and this book is an attempt to explain.

II.   A Midsummer Night's Dream

A number of years ago, as the litigation marched into the discovery phase, I had trouble sleeping. When I lay awake some nights, I would fight endless battles in the courts of my mind.

At one point, I read that the way to fight insomnia was to get out of bed and read or watch TV, anything to get your mind off your troubles. Fortunately for me, this idea worked.

In time I learned to walk downstairs, turn on the TV to any channel, lie on the sofa and listen to the TV. Within minutes I would fall asleep. Sometimes, I would wake, listen to a little more in a groggy state and either fall back to sleep on the sofa or go upstairs to bed where I would immediately fall to sleep.

I assume that the quiet sounds from the TV focused my mind on a late night comedian, ball game or old movie just enough to remove me from my problems. As my mind emptied, tenseness would leave me and I'd fall off to sleep. Of course many times this sofa sleep resulted in a few aches and back pains the next morning

A phenomenon of this television-induced sleep was a surrealistic menagerie of dreams, television and reality. They mixed to the point where I was unaware if I dreamed about something or had heard it on television. This may be a form of lunacy, however this confusion did not bother me at all. I didn't think about it except on the rare occasion when I started to talk about something and realized that the thought may have come from the television's witches caldron of sounds and graphics and not from the everyday life I was leading.

I remember vividly one particular occasion where I spent most of the day observing a former supplier being deposed. For those not initiated in such legal procedures, let me tell you that a deposition must be the most boring and frustrating experience known to man. At those times that I have been deposed, or at depositions that I have observed, a witness sits down with a stenographer and is interrogated by lawyers representing the various parties involved. After taking an oath, the witness is asked question after question by the opposition lawyers. Later, a friendlier lawyer asks many of the same questions in an effort to blunt some answers, smooth inconsistencies and correct answers that the witness totally blew.

When I am deposed, I consider even a simple question like, "Where do you reside?" as some convoluted attempt to trick me. I also find that at times I hear a voice answering, but it is not my voice, sort of a distant echo that stops when I close my mouth.

A short way through a deposition I usually become comfortable to the point where I am concerned that the questioner understands my answers. Realizing that these lawyers could use my expertise, I become an instant educator. Generally my attorney will then ask for the opportunity to stop the session and advise me, "Just answer the question." At that point, I become annoyed that my attorney won't allow me to educate the fools and set the record straight.

The average Joe, including me, ends the testimony with feelings of could have, should have and why didn't I? The most sobering part comes some weeks later when the deposed is asked to review the deposition. After the embarrassment of reading an abundance of hesitations such as "ah," "you know," "like," the witness is overjoyed that the technical sections show him or her to be quite knowledgeable.

To get back to my story, let me say that on that particular day I watched a former supplier to my Company being deposed. I was totally frustrated by his statements, but as an observer I could do nothing. As part of his testimony, he vaguely recalled carrying a small sample container of a solvent called perchloroethylene to one of our plants in the spring of 1979.

He was not sure of the plant's location or to whom he delivered the container or the date and time. His confusion was not surprising considering he was speaking of an event that he thought took place almost 20 years earlier.

With one vague recollection, he supplied sufficient testimony to potentially cost my Company millions of dollars. While his testimony would be impeached by my lawyers at a later date, it gave the opposition's legal staff renewed life.

Later, on the evening of that deposition, my son, Erik, complained about a homework assignment, "It was so dumb!...Who cared about ancient Greece?...Why do I have to learn about those gods and their stupid myths?"

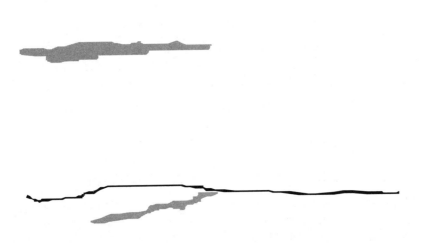

III.   Looking For the Lawyer God

I was in the middle of the bar scene from the movie, *Star Wars*. It was truly weird seeing those strange animal like creatures. I pressed on because I knew that I could lose the only chance I had to find the legal gods. Next, I ran through a tunnel-like opening in a wall and then I burst out on the most calming scene that I ever experienced.

Everything was abnormally quiet. The building in front of me was tall and very modern. There was a large fountain in front and steps leading to a double entrance. The entrance on the right led to a major bank. The one on the left to the lobby of an office tower. The lobby exuded elegance with fixtures of shiny brass and walls of polished black marble. A polite security guard waited to direct me to one of the tower's elevators.

He seemed to know instinctively what I was looking for. He said, "Thirty-fourth floor," and pointed to an elevator. There were no other passengers, so I had an opportunity to look at a reflection of myself in the elevator mirror. I appeared messed up, sweaty, with my cloths wrinkled after all I had gone through to get there.

Then I remembered having felt the same way rushing into law offices in Boston and New York City. I have often thought that visiting such big city law offices is like playing in the opposing team's ballpark. The advantage always goes to the host lawyer.

I was surprised that there weren't any secretaries riding the elevator all dressed up but wearing sneakers. Every time I visit office towers in New York City, the appearance of women in the law offices and on the streets are two different worlds. In the law office, legal secretaries are subdued, gracious and dressed for a tea dance. Outside the office, their outfits remain the same except for the footwear, which becomes either boat shoe or Nike as they stand in their sneakers and eat a street vendor's pretzel for lunch. I find this contrast of secretaries working in palaces looking like princesses and then eating quickie lunches for sustenance, just another aberration of the legal profession.

When the elevator door opened, the receptionist sitting directly ahead simply smiled politely and said, "We have been expecting you." She led me to a conference room that had a fantastic view of what might have been Boston harbor.

She asked if I would like coffee and then directed me to a small table in a corner with a magnificent silver coffee service and beautiful china. I answered that I was fine even though I would have loved a black coffee and a muffin.

She encouraged me to sit down and then she left. I felt more comfortable walking around the room and looking out the window at the view. Besides, there were twenty upholstered chairs around the huge conference table and I was not sure where I should sit.

I waited and waited wondering all the time if the receptionist let them know that I was there. I wasn't surprised to be waiting because I had spent an excessive amount of time waiting for lawyers during the past few years in the same type of conference rooms. I have found that appointment times are only approximations in most law offices.

To my relief the door opened and a good looking, well-dressed woman entered the conference room. I liked her instantly. She put out her hand and as I shook it she said, "I understand that you have been looking for me." I wanted to say, "Baby, I've been looking for you all my life." However I was smart enough to reply, "Yes, I am," but then I heard words coming from my mouth, "I may have been looking for you, but I don't know why."

She just smiled and quietly pointed to a seat. She pulled out a seat next to me and we sat down together. The next thing I knew I blurted out, "Are you a goddess of law?" Her expression changed. It was as if a cloud passed over. In an almost apologetic manner she replied, "There are no legal gods. Throughout history, no culture has had mythological legal gods. Doctors have their serpents and farmers fertility gods. Someday, we will be important enough to a civilization to be recognized. Everyone knows that lawyers are already the topic of more television series in America than doctors."

At that point, she recovered her composure and her smile returned. Now I was embarrassed for asking the question. I prayed that she would not hear about the popularity of *ER* and *Chicago Hope* and the fall of *LA Law* in the ratings. But again I stupidly mumbled, "Well then, who are you?"

It was then that she told me that her mother was Demeter and her father was Hypnos. Her parents hoped that she would enter the Arts as a muse, but during the women's movement, she rebelled and entered law school at Hellenic University. She passed the Olympian bar exam with such high marks she was chosen to descend to Earth and clerk for a Supreme Court justice in Washington. She found that time the most stimulating in her career because of rulings on civil rights, school busing and sex discrimination. As a muse, it was her calling to increase the respect of lawyers in America. Simply to listen to earthlings talk of young lawyers marching arm in arm with Martin Luther King stimulated her. She saw this as an opening to have law recognized in the courts of the gods so that one day, there would by myths, totems and sculptures of a legal god intertwined with those of Apollo,

Athena, Ares and Eros. Perhaps she could be the first goddess of law. No she didn't want that. With her background, fighting for her place in law school, she truly wanted to be the god of law. She felt that gender should be deleted from the vocabulary of the deities.

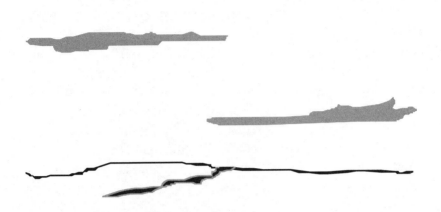

IV.   The Muse

My hostess went on to say, "We all know that Zeus is the ruler of the gods. Much of his time during the last century has been spent shaping up Ares, the god of war. Zeus's constant vigil has forced Ares to downsize his operations from wars to police actions. Ares crept into Korea and Vietnam in the last three decades by calling them police actions. Only after Zeus counted casualties did he realize that he'd been had, that war by any other name is still war.

"Zeus is sort of a purist when it comes to authorizing the creation of new gods. In his opinion, to rise from muse to god, a divine being must not only achieve greatness, but also work in a field that has meaning to earthlings. To him love, light, medicine, poetry, war, hunting, childbirth, etc. are all godlike endeavors. There is even Hephaestus, the god of metalworking. However, throughout the universe, law has never proved sufficiently important to the lives of earthlings to have them conceive of a lawyer god.

"As a muse living in Washington in 1962, I was not involved in the Divine Court and had never met Zeus. My dream that I could do something to give lawyers divine recognition was known only to me.

"In 1962 everything changed. I was her muse when Rachel Carson wrote a book called, *Silent Spring*. At first, *Silent Spring* found little recognition in America, although it did receive an enthusiastic response in our Divine Court. The reason for such acclaim was that Rachael Carson entitled the first chapter, "A Fable for Tomorrow." Zeus was thrilled with Ms. Carson's concept because fables, myths, vedas and fetishes had long been out of fashion in America. Now he saw fertile ground to resurrect his realm."

At that moment, something must have awakened me as I lay sleeping cramped up on the sofa. The TV set was pumping out an old John Wayne movie. I started to get up but must have fallen back to sleep. All I remember is the Muse getting deeper into her story.

The Muse continued where she had left off, "Zeus needed one of his divine beings to work this opportunity furnished by Rachel Carson's fable. This was years before Lucas introduced his *Star Wars* trilogy and mythology was in the doldrums. Sir Edward Burnett Tylor, the English anthropologist, had taken human form in the 1800's to push the idea that myths accounted for unexplained occurrences in dreams. Since then, most of Zeus's efforts to bring life to the old gods had not been successful. That's when I got the call.

"As the only divine being stabled in Washington, D.C. in the 1960's, I was asked to watch over Rachel Carson and to help spur recognition of the many environmental problems. I'm proud to say I did a great job and her book, *Silent Spring* became the springboard for impressive changes on earth.

"By the late 1970's, I had promoted environmental concerns and educated a generation of young people. The prophecy of silenced voices in spring, as described in Chapter I of *Silent Spring* never happened. In my opinion, the laws I encouraged which removed DDT and other dangerous pesticides from the market were a major factor in the improvement of the environment in America.

"I was called back to the Heavens for a *Recognition Feast* toward the end of the 1970's. The *Feast* is like your Academy Awards ceremony except we don't waste time on commercials. Actually, Dionysus throws better post *Recognition Feast* parties than you will ever see in Hollywood.

"For me, the *Recognition Feast* was a bummer. While the gods of love, agriculture and growing things praised my work for the environment, no divine being mentioned my legal triumphs. There was not a god who appreciated the fact that lawyers framed the laws that would banish DDT. Nor did they recognize that earthly lawyers had marched arm in arm with environmentalists and fought those chemical companies that wished to continue the status quo.

"I was depressed when I realized that I would never be the lawyer god and that lawyers would never get the recognition they deserved. When the parties ended, I ran off with Dionysus and spent the next year on the 'Dark Side.'

"At the time the 'Dark Side' was just getting started, the Vaders hadn't found it yet and it was sort of like Miami Beach in the 1980's. But, for me, it was a great place to be depressed and miserable. Many misdirected people hung out there.

"Pluto is the god of the Underworld and he would jet into the 'Dark Side' on the weekends. During that year, I got to know him pretty well. We had some real sick conversations.

"When I told him of my dashed hopes to become the first lawyer god, he told me of others who had gone before me and almost made it. He explained that Americans historically had considered lawyers as professionals that helped with real estate transfers or wills. Those that were ambitious went into politics and became senators or presidents where they usually were guided by Ares, the god of war or he himself, the god of the Underworld. He said Washington, Lincoln, Roosevelt, and Johnson were in Ares' camp while Kennedy went with Ares during the day and joined his stable at night.

"The assumption in the heavens was that to achieve the status of lawyer god in mythology, a muse would need to raise legal recognition to the same realm as love, war, agriculture or healing. A lawyer god would need to hurt people, feed them and become involved in almost every facet of their lives.

"We sent a muse down in 1913 to get things started. He developed a concept called the income tax that was a dandy. The best part was that he was able to write the income tax law in such a way that it was impossible for people to understand. In my opinion, he should have become a deity on the spot but with the First World War, Ares made a comeback and that little sucker muse was called back. It was only in the years that followed that we recognized in the heavens that income tax could cause more pain and suffering than most wars. The bottom line was that small, two man law offices grew to become law firms with tax departments and tax specialists. More importantly, lawyers were beginning to learn how to make money.

"My biggest disappointment was the muse we sent down to help gain stature for patent attorneys. You would think that if lawyers have both a law and engineering degree, they would be admired in America. The patent muse created patent law firms and gained permission for them to advertise early in the century. However, the patent muse didn't come close to becoming a god. After he totally screwed up the U.S. Patent Office and got it out of sync with most other patent offices in the world, he didn't gain recognition. Of course, he did manage to raise patent legal fees considerably and extract vast sums from Kodak and Polaroid, which enhanced the status of many patent attorneys.

"There have been others who almost made lawyer god. They really pushed the envelope. The muse that came up with divorce law is a good example. That muse was real creative.

"First, he took marriage that had always been negotiated by parents or tribal custom and induced Nineteenth Century poets to write of romantic love as the most important ingredient of marriage. Even though Hestia and Artemis scoffed, he convinced

18

whole generations that love and marriage were synonymous. If you didn't have romantic love, you had no marriage. Artemis kept sending the word down to earth that she was the goddess of hunting and childbirth and Dionysus kept talking fertility trash, but in the end the little muse convinced Americans that a legal marriage should be bound with love. Therefore, if there was no love in the marriage, a lawyer could call on one partner to dissolve the marriage.

"That marvelous little muse almost made lawyer god but he was called back to the heavens to answer charges of missed alimony payments. Seems that his divine wife read some of those Nineteenth Century novels, fell in love with a Titan and divorced him. That muse is still complaining about how much that divorce cost him.

"There have been others. Because no one dies in the heavens, I am amazed that one of our guys conceived of estate planning. Those Americans really bought into that program. When he first told us, no one could believe he could sell it. Actually, he had done an apprenticeship with that muse that invented the income tax. He had inside information on how oppressive that tax would become so he knew that lawyers could show people how to shield both income tax and inheritance tax. While there may be a lawyer god some day, I'm sure there will never be an insurance god. I think if that ever happened, the estate-planning muse should get the job. But the insurance people are held in less esteem in America than are the lawyers. Truthfully, they don't have a prayer even though they put three or four unrecognizable letters after their name to appear professional."

I stopped my hostess at that point to ask where she was going with all this stuff. Yet by now she was really into it and kept on talking.

She went on to say that she left the "Dark Side" after that year, with renewed vigor. Remembering Pluto's words, she returned to Earth with a new plan. She would do as he said and raise the image of lawyers in America.

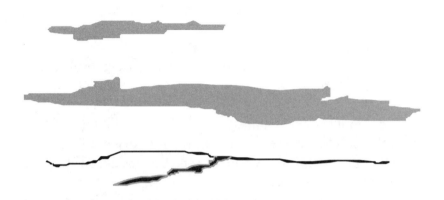

V.   A Raising

My hostess continued, "I did not fully understand Pluto or Underworld terminology and from my legal training at Hellenic University, I interpret things quite literally. I assumed that Pluto meant raise from the heavenly meaning to rise, to elevate, to increase, so I started to promote that image in the American legal community.

"I planted photographs in architectural journals to encourage lawyers to leave their gloomy, stained-wood offices and move to a higher plane. You will recall that in the 50's and 60's, most lawyers were housed in ancient offices near courthouses and county clerks. Their hanging artwork was generally a matted Currier and Ives lithograph. Their rates ranged between twenty and forty dollars per hour and a will was a flat $100.00. This was before the estate-planning muse began to connect.

"The other fixtures in these law offices were Royal typewriters and anything covered with green felt. I suppose the secretaries with the silver blue hair could also be called fixtures.

"When I returned to earth and Washington, I sat on lawyers' shoulders like an angel and encouraged four new concepts:

1. Follow the banks into high rise buildings.
2. Raise your rates in relation to the height of the buildings.
3. Lose the Currier and Ives.
4. Always place yourself higher than the eye level of your client.

"Did I do it? You're damned right I did. Revolution, let's call it revolution. Name one law office you know that didn't shadow a bank's move to the luxury high rise and become a repository for the paintings of local artists.

"Between 1960 and 1980, thousands of lawyers' wives became the art world's greatest patrons as they spruced up their husbands' digs. The logos Herman Miller, Haworth and Steelcase challenged that of Gucci in law offices throughout the land as decorators started to till this virgin territory.

"The fourth thing I mention was my coup de malloc or masterstroke as we say in the heavens. I mused my lawyers to know that they should always place themselves higher than the eye level of their clients. You should understand that lawyers historically have been administrators in most earthly societies. At times, they rose to judicial levels, but generally a law degree allowed lawyers to be, 'Of service to others,' in the United States before the 60's.

"I had a slight head start in that lawyers had learned to place a judge above others in the courtroom. It was also good that attorneys stood before seated juries and witnesses were asked to sit after they are sworn in.

"What a retched situation that lawyers had no uniform in America. At least in Great Britain, they could gain respectability by using a wig. It really killed me to see some lawyers in plaid coats with leather at the elbow. By 1960, IBM had cornered the gray flannel suit so I had to look further than clothes to make the man or in this case to make the model American lawyer.

"I actually got lucky by pushing for relocation to modern office towers. The banks jumped deeper into real estate. They would use the new law office conference rooms for closings. The lawyers supervised and ran the closings placing the clients and bank officers in a subservient role. Legal secretaries learned to mark the pages needing signatures with little red check marks and the clients and bank officers would sign the stack of contracts as indicated by these check marks. The law offices even became clients of banks and investment houses when lawyers learned to act as transfer agents and trustees of funds.

"While I did not help with the invention, my hero was Mr. Wang who brought the first word processors to law offices. If muses understood kissing, I would have kissed Wang in the 1970's. Because of Wang, every lawyer could write a contract or a will just by filling in the spaces and following the bouncing ball.

"I also placed my imprimatur on the Washington law boutiques. Under my mantle, they created the legislation, lobbied legislatures, helped pass legislation, interpreted the law during seminars and wrote master contracts which could be purchased and downloaded by any attorney willing to pay the freight.

"To put all these things together was my greatest challenge. I realized that it would not be possible to give lawyers sufficient education to understand the contracts that they were now capable of writing. Therefore, I was forced to give them the appearance of knowing what they were doing.

"My solution was a divinely inspired subconscious finishing school for lawyers. From the 1960's, I established lawyer behavior models, which I displayed on television, movies and print. These white, Anglo Saxon, male lawyer role models were displayed in dark, well-tailored suits and only in frantic meetings were they allowed to strip down to a white shirt and tie. Never could they roll up their sleeves and short sleeves were definitely off limits.

"I then devised a facial expression, which combined the sympathy of a clergyman with the superiority of a prep school headmaster. I prescribed this for use by lawyers in situations where pathetic laymen could be stoically admonished for being pathetic laymen.

"Guess what? From 1960 to the present, my plan has worked beautifully. The results have been beyond my wildest dreams. In America, surveys show an ambiguity: On the one hand, people would rather visit their dentist than a lawyer, while at the same time, they would encourage their children to enter the legal profession.

"Now many Americans prefer appointments with their therapists rather than their lawyers because an hour with the therapist costs about one half that of an hour with a lawyer. Plus the therapist does not bill for every telephone call and photocopy.

"I was happy because after fifteen years of effort, I had raised the profile of lawyers close to that of Apollo's doctors, Ares' soldiers, Demeter's farmers and Hestia's housewives. I was certain that upon my return to the heavens for my review, I would be named the lawyer god.

"I returned to the heavens in triumph. Along the procession route were banners that read:

> 'All hail American lawyers.'
> 'Raise your sons and daughters to be lawyers.'
> 'A few good men but many great lawyers.'
> 'Put your trust in lawyers.'

"At the end of the procession stood Recognition Hall. Here Zeus would recognize my work and raise me to the podium as a deity.

"When the crowd quieted, Zeus, the ruler of the gods, made his grand entrance. Having watched the last few Super Bowl halftimes, I was ready for some quality pomp; I mean his clouds were real, not those make believe kind that come from a smoke gun.

"Within a few short minutes, Zeus was on the podium. He greeted the crowd in that regal deep voice. As I strained to hear those words that would make me the lawyer god, Zeus hesitated, then he started to snicker, within seconds he was laughing. My god, he was almost human! I realized that he was breaking up with laughter. When he finally composed himself he said, 'My gods, you've got to hear this one. Bacchus broke me up with this joke coming over. A priest, a doctor and a lawyer died and went to the gates of heaven where they met Saint Peter. Saint Peter said to the priest, "We have many vehicles in heaven, which one would you like?" . . . . . .

"I didn't even hear the rest of what Zeus said. All I heard was Zeus telling a lawyer joke. I had heard these before when I was in Washington. I did not find lawyer jokes funny at all.

"Even now, I choke-up when I think of my embarrassment. Why had Bacchus told Zeus that lawyer joke and why did Zeus think it was so funny?

"When he finished the punch line, one of the Centaurs to my left reared up and yelled, 'Zeus, how many lawyers does it take to screw in a light bulb?' I didn't wait for the answer, that horse's ass got the whole Court telling lawyer jokes. The way Zeus was laughing, I knew that I had not raised lawyers to a godly level. In those fifteen years I spent on Earth, the lawyer jokes increased with the increases of legal fees. Rather than guide lawyers to respect, I had raised them to high places, high buildings and high fees. Rather than honoring me as the lawyer god, lawyers were making money their god.

"At that point, I wandered again to the 'Dark Side.' I swore that I would not listen to Dionysus again. That's when I turned to Hades, the god of the Underworld."

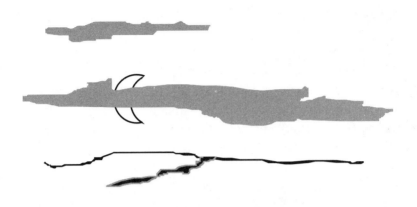

VI.   Hades

"You mortals have really done a job on Hades and the Underworld. Somehow Hades became confused with the Christian idea of hell. Perhaps Dante focused that concept for you mortals when he wrote *The Inferno*.

"As a muse, I've had very little exposure to your Christian concepts so your worldly ideas of judgement, fire and brimstone are foreign to me. As a mortal and Christian, you know very little about our Underworld. Listen to me and you will learn that the Underworld is a very stimulating place. Actually I think most Americans would relate to our Underworld much more easily than to Zeus and our other gods. To understand our Underworld, you should think of California or better yet, Californians.

"The older gods get upset when new ideas come out of the Underworld, but within about ten years, these ideas are accepted all over heaven. I don't know if it's the climate or the muses in Hades which incubate the latest fashions and thoughts. Maybe its because they have more cults. Just last year, all the muses in one cult poisoned themselves and waited for a meteor to fly by to take them to Earth and a better life. Damn fools, the poison only made them sick. Now, they're really upset that they are immortal and can't kill themselves. Guess you can't please every deity.

"Well, as I was saying, I was still determined to become the lawyer god and felt that I could pick up some ideas from Hades. After I raised their position in America, lawyers became a mockery both in the heavens and on Earth. My efforts had given American lawyers a pompous attitude, a high fee structure and an arrogance that brought them ridicule.

"I waited a few years until the late 1970's and things only got worse. On Earth, it became politically incorrect to tell Polish and gay jokes so everyone turned to lawyer jokes.

"It was also evident that big payoffs like the tobacco and breast implant settlements would reward a few attorneys handsomely, but I needed grunt work for the less talented attorneys. I needed something that would be mind numbing for lawyers which the general population wouldn't understand.

"To make things worse, my work in influencing America had encouraged females to become lawyers. Because law school is the most profitable graduate program, the number of law students was increasing yearly and legal rates had started to peak.

"I decided it was time to take another shot at becoming the lawyer god. I had been on R and R long enough. My only problem was that I had no clue as to where to start. That's when I called on Hades.

"Hades is chameleon in appearance. By that I mean, he is like OJ's defense team, he can change appearance, attitude, skills and color as required. He can be boringly technical, cold and cunning or a good old boy. There can be an audience of one or hundreds and he'll work the crowd.

"When I went to him with my problems, he was warm and understanding. I think he knew all about me because before I could say very much he said, 'Honey, think about it, are you ready to be a god? Are you willing to make the sacrifice?'

"I did not understand what he was trying to tell me. That's

when he said, 'Wake up and smell the roses! There are only a few gods. Each god represents a very important part of mortal life. Aphrodite the goddess of love has an effect on most people's lives. She may overdo it at times, but generally love is important.

'The god Asclepius may look like a snake, but that appearance gives him a bad rap. As a serpent he can lose his skin and grow it anew, so mortals think of him as a healer. Could any mortal think of lawyers as healers?

'Ares, the god of war, causes misery to people on Earth. War can ruin civilizations and mortal life, and disrupt economies on a massive scale. I believe the misery caused by lawyers is simply an annoyance.

'Demeter is the goddess of growing things. This to mortals is food. Do lawyers supply food for anything other than controversy? Let's face it, you made a bad choice when you determined to become the lawyer god. Lawyers have little effect on mortal lives. Most mortals could live long and productive lives without lawyers.

'You have been deceived living in Washington. In Japan and other countries, there are comparatively few lawyers. In America, most divorces are amicable until the lawyers step in, then the mistrust percolates. Why do you think that do-it-yourself divorce books have become so popular as have books on preparing wills and real estate transfers?'

"As Hades talked, I realized that he was right. It was almost impossible to take people whose specialty was arranging words and have them make a critical difference on mortal life. To make matters worse, lawyers had no real opinion or position on issues; they simply took the side of anyone who could pay their fees.

"Then Hades caught my attention when he said, 'Why don't you go back to the game plan that got you so far in the past, the environment? Very few earthlings concerned themselves with DDT and insecticides before you became Rachel Carson's muse and she wrote *Silent Spring*. The environment may be the hot button for America. Think about it and see what you can come up with.'

"I reminded Hades that I had influenced lawyers, legislators and common Americans to pass environmental laws. That those laws written in the 1960's and 1970's had been successful in the U.S. and the most harmful pesticides had been removed from the market. Rivers were becoming less polluted and a generation of students had been taught to respect the environment.

"These were wonderful accomplishments and my efforts were never rewarded. What more could I do with the environment so that lawyers would be recognized for their influence on environmental laws and I could be named lawyer god.

"Hades laughed, then he asked, 'Do any law firms have environmental specialists? Do lawyers make much money practicing environmental law?'

"I thought about it. Hades was right. When laws banned DDT, chemical companies complied and such pesticides were taken off the market. The early environmental legislation caused no controversy or confrontation between parties. These laws produced very little law work and resulted in embarrassing small fees for law firms. Steel companies constructed smoke scrubbers on smokestacks, for example, and scrubbers required simple permits but no litigation. There was only a minimum of environmental litigation because penalties for non-compliance were in the form of fines from federal and state governments. The environment was definitely a dead end for lawyers in the 1970's. The dead end for me was surely at hand as I realized that there was no need for a lawyer god. I hated to think about failing and reverting to my mother's hopes that I become a poetry muse. I needed a hook, a wrinkle or anything that would revitalize my quest to be the lawyer god.

"What could I do as part of the environmental movement that would disrupt lives, cause dissension and terrorize mortal souls like war, love, healing and fire. In a flash, it came to me as one word, *remediation*."

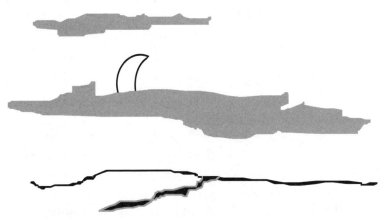

VII.   Remediation

This muse continued by saying, "Just as Odysseus had confused the Trojans, I rolled my horse inside the walls of the U.S. Congress in 1980. It was easy. This horse was named Superfund and it was filled with an armed battalion called *Remediation*. Never was pain so stealthily hidden.

"While I am sure that there are some who would feel that the 1980 Superfund law was not divinely inspired, I suggest to you that Congress lacked the cunning and foresight to create such a document. I am the author and I am the lawyer god. Mr. Hutchins, you are here today to authenticate this miracle. I have been waiting for you to testify to my genius for eight years. It is time to go before the tribunal."

We didn't walk to another room. It was more like one side of the conference room morphed into a gigantic court. I remained seated and swiveled around to view the courtroom.

The Muse stood up and walked toward a high podium where Zeus was standing. He was godlike, strong and muscular and resembled Arnold Swartzanager. A white sash dropped from one shoulder to form a robe, which draped from his waist to the floor. He truly looked like the ruler of the gods.

From another side, a short figure walked toward Zeus' podium. I could have sworn it was Danny Divito. As crazy as it sounds, it was as if the movie, *Twins*, was taken place before my eyes.

Zeus looked down, waved his muscular arm and said with a booming voice, "The Muse has petitioned to become a god...er... the lawyer god.

"The Muse will be cross-examined by the court eunuch called Jester. Please excuse this inconvenience, but we downsized the court when we merged with Jupiter two thousand years ago and haven't budgeted for this kind of tribunal. I am sure the Jester will handle this very well."

I didn't know what was happening, but my quick impression was that the Muse would roll over this Jester like a steamroller. I could see Zeus study the Muse's body and it looked like he'd welcome this muse as a god in a New York minute.

Then Zeus broke in with some opening comments. After these words, he said, "Muse, you claim that after the early successes of the 1960's and 70's, the environmental movement had become complacent and that you revitalized it. Muse, what say you to this?"

"Honorable Zeus, Chapter One of Rachel Carson's book, *Silent Spring*, tells the fable about towns in America losing their singing birds, beautiful flowers and honey bees due to the use of DDT. This caught the imagination of people in America so Congress banned DDT and other insecticides from the market. Encouraged by this success, environmentalists then directed their attention to other serious pollution problems such as oil spills, toxins and waste disposal. The Environmental Protection Agency was established which brought fifteen federal programs under a single management organization.

"Unfortunately, the success of these programs led to complacency and environmental lobbies in Washington became concerned with losing momentum and funding. My first success was to rejuvenate the environmental movement by publishing sensational stories such as Love Canal near Buffalo and a dioxin incident in

Seveso, Italy. When these sensational stories grabbed headlines and citizens became fearful that their bodies were being poisoned by unknown toxins, it was easy to persuade congresspersons that something dramatic and politically expedient should be done by the government."

Zeus nodded in agreement and said, "Jester; I'll give her that claim. History has shown Love Canal and Seveso to be overreactions by the American press. The early fears never materialized. I'll admit the Muse did a good job stirring up public sentiment with very little scientific fact to back up the stories. That's one for you, Muse."

All I heard from the Jester had been mumbling sounds. Now and again he'd pump his finger in the air, but he did not interrupt Zeus. Finally, the Jester replied in what sounded like a New York City taxi driver's accent, "Ah, big deal, do we intend to honor her for her beautiful body or for what she has accomplished? Hey, I like you, Muse, I mean shaved head or not, you could really light my fire. But, let's face it, every writer has a muse. The environmental movement started when you got into Rachel Carson's ear and she wrote *Silent Spring*. In my book that makes you a muse and not a god.

"To become a god, you have to have a profound effect on mortals' lives. You have to be the answer for puzzles that humans don't understand. Mortals have to feel pain or joy when you enter their souls.

"Lawyers could be removed from earth tomorrow and it wouldn't change things. They're called mouthpieces and used by mortals as tools to put the screws to one another. As the Jester, I could do that myself. There's nothing to it.

"Now gods are gods. They're the man! Or in some cases, they're the woman...well I mean, you know what I mean.

"Actually, they're the god. Look at Ares, the god of war. He has really gotten into the lives of people. Ares has caused misery, death and destruction to the lives of mortals. I mean, you gotta admire a guy like that.

"Then there's Aphrodite, the goddess of love. What can be more miserable than love, I mean that's bad stuff. Bad or good, these mortals sing about love. Some country singers sound forlorn, no matter what kind of love they're singing about. Good love or bad love, their man can be here or gone, they sound the same. Even Clinton's wife made that sound when she said, 'Stand by my man.'

"I've seen 'made men' go whacko with love at least in the movies. Even Rocky went nuts for a little mousy broad in that movie, what was it, *Rocky I, II*, or *III?* No, it must have been just *Rocky* because by *II*, she was seeing a shrink and having a facelift or something the mortal broads do.

"And fertility, that's the god Dionysus. He'll blow your mind. I mean, half the mortals don't want kids and the other half are taking all those pills to have them. I mean this guy, Dionysus, takes the action on either side. He's got pills for making babies; he's got pills for preventing babies. He takes the action both ways like a bookie."

By this time, I could see Zeus starting to agree with the little guy. There are no streets in the heavens, but to me he was street smart. With a few words, he had cut the legs out from under the Muse.

When I looked over, her head was still high. The Jester hadn't upset her. I suppose years of working with the women's movement in heaven had given her confidence.

She simply looked at the Jester, then looked up at Zeus and said, "I have created a chaos on Earth. It has cost more than most wars. It has entered deeply into mortals' lives to cause bankruptcy. It has stolen their land and earthly assets. It has caused dissension between friends and neighbors. It has left acres of property unusable. It has forced industry into virgin lands in the countryside. The chaos I created is a true enigma. It makes no rational sense and it has caused disputes among people and governments sufficient to enrich many of the lawyers in America. And just like the fertility god, this pill of wrath can bring fortunes to lawyers playing both sides.

"When I helped the legal fraternity write the Comprehensive Environmental Response, Compensation and Liability Act of 1980 (CERCLA) and called it 'Superfund,' I created more mischief than the gods have seen since the glory days of ancient Greece."

"I object, I object," the Jester jumped back in. Now, he was not mumbling, his voice was high and squeaky. "There is no proof of what the Muse says. She's just talking politics. In America, every four years candidates campaign against the trial lawyer's associations and money going to the lawyers rather than to victims, but that's just a political thing. After the elections, it always blows over. Then you never hear about it again.

"Hey, in America people die early deaths from gang shootings, drug wars and family violence. Tobacco is a proven killer. Federal moneys go to efforts to straighten out these problems, there's no money left for cleanups. Besides, they're getting all these big companies that polluted to clean their messes up. I think it's good to go after those bastards that spilled the stuff.

"Besides on *60 Minutes* or *20/20* or one of those shows that tells it right, I saw that they got methods on earth to clean that crap out of the ground. I heard that maybe bacteria would eat the solvents.

"You know they're back to swimming and boating in the Great Lakes and most of the rivers have been cleaned up. They must have done something at that Love Canal because I never hear about it. I mean, today you never read about those cancers in Pennsylvania or on California farms. Whatever happened in Woburn, MA. I mean, I know that the lawyer won a lawsuit and Harr wrote a book, *A Civil Action.* — Well, I guess the book was more about litigation than pollution cleanup. Did you read it Zeus? Well, you know what I mean, this little lawyer went up against those firms that charge the big fees and he won.

"Well, I don't know what the kids got for their suffering or if they ever straightened that Woburn situation out, but it was fun to read how this little guy won the lawsuit and got some big cash from those perpetrators.

"Anyway, I never heard of as much misery and frustration like war can cause. This here muse is blowing smoke. She's got no proof."

Again, the muse raised her head confidently. She said to Zeus, "I have proof of my miracle. I guided legislation through Congress that made no sense. I hid remediation in a disguise called 'Superfund' much better than Ares did with that dumb Trojan horse. He is blunt; I am subtle. Mr. Hutchins is my proof. When you hear Hutchins' story, you will acknowledge my gifts. I put nonsense ahead of reason, falsehood in front of truth, fear above faith and had my message carried to Congress by some of the brightest lawyers in America.

"My messengers were liberals and conservatives, young and old, rich and poor. I got them all to march lock step into Congress carrying my torch. They did it not only willingly, but also with enthusiasm. Many that carried my message continue to carry it today. They fear that by looking at the truth, they may give back something to that faction which they call big business.

"The early environmental laws were good. They did their job. America's springs, summers, winters and falls have become far less polluted and less hazardous. Rachel's prophecies of silent springs never came to American towns.

"The parts of the Superfund law that deal with remediation are my coupe de maine. Mr. Hutchins is a small businessman who has been made insolvent by the Superfund law. His story is a microcosm of what is happening all over America. The truth will make me the lawyer god. Hear my words and follow the money."

The Jester broke in with a little smile and said, "I thought that to environmentalists green meant trees and leaves. Now you're telling me to follow the money. Are you saying follow the green stuff, follow the money?"

The Muse replied, "That green money will prove my case. Mr. Hutchins, tell Zeus your story."

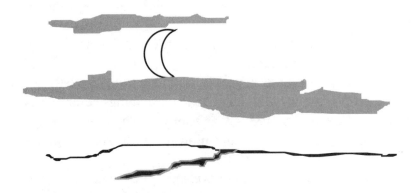

VIII.   My Story

I thought I'd be nervous, but I wasn't. I suppose I had lived with this thing for so long it was a relief to find someone who would listen. My story just started to flow, "Looking back, I realize now that in 1990 I was in a zone, like the feeling when you're having a good round in golf. You don't realize its purity until it's over and you try putting it together again. The worst thing to do when you're in that zone and driving the ball well hole after hole is to think about it and ask why. What are you doing differently?

"Never try to answer those questions or you'll lose it. Never dissect your swing on the golf course. If you think about it, everything will go to hell. Experience tells me that much of life is luck or chance. While we instruct our youngsters that hard work will lead to success, that's not always accurate. Call it good fortune or God's blessing, whatever it is plays a very big role.

"Well, anyway, my brother and I own a small machine shop and for many years, we had made a very good living. By 1990, I had been at Hutchins Tool, a business my father had started, for over thirty years."

The Jester laughed and said half under his breath, "You should have gotten a life."

I turned to him and said defensively, "It was a life, and a good life. I had a nice home, three boys doing well in school and I was healthy. True, I wasn't traveling to Europe and skiing in the Rocky Mountains every winter, but I had done those things before I was married. Therefore in 1989, I was happy to play a little tennis, coach my sons' hockey teams and allow my wife to run the house and be at home to raise our children.

"Oh, there were times I might have speculated what I could do in a large corporation or in a better business climate, but when a family business is handed down, there are a lot of perks in the early years. If you start your career with assets, you learn to protect what you have. I assume a small business is like a family farm. With time, the owner and the business can not be differentiated. You are the business and the business is you. Experts of business schools would scoff, but I'll guarantee small business will outlast all the models and business practices promoted by business schools during the last 50 years. Methods like 'Just in Time' and 'Kaizen' will be forgotten while the small business providing a product or service will plod on."

I could see that the Jester, from his heavenly perch, knew very little about American business. I felt better defending my life and answering the little bastard. It was only later that I realized that most deities in Greek mythology were bastards so I could have called him that to his face and he would not have understood my profanity.

I continued my story by again addressing Zeus, "Hutchins Tool is located in Springfield, Massachusetts. While we originally made tools and dies, our work has migrated toward the machining of aircraft and medical parts on highly sophisticated computer controlled machine tools. Our specialty is CNC Swiss screw machining and electrical discharge machining (EDM).

"EDM is rather different in that we can machine very hard metal parts using a shaped electrode as a tool. During the process,

38

electric sparks jump the gap and the spark vaporizes a small amount of the metal being machined. The thousands of sparks vaporize small portions of the work and a cavity is created. As a result, the cavity takes the inverse shape of the electrode. If the electrode is in the shape of a doll's body, the cavity in the workpiece becomes a cavity with a form of the doll's body. This is the way we would cut the cavity for a plastic mold used for producing a doll's body shape.

"You should also be aware that almost all machine tools are lubricated with oil and that petroleum based lubricants are used as coolants to help in the cutting of metal. It is also very common to find solvents, such as alcohol, in manufacturing plants for cleaning purposes to dissolve such substances as oil, paints, inks and grease. As a matter of fact, it would be difficult to find a home, farm, office or school in America that did not use some sort of solvent.

"While environmentalists may find oils and solvents to be dirty words, it is impossible to maintain a modern society without them. Unless somebody is living in the wilderness surviving on berries and roots, they are probably involved with automobiles, airplanes or boats that require oils as lubricants."

At that point, the Jester broke in and said, "I expect that those green peace people couldn't chase the whalers if they didn't use oil and diesel fuel in their boats. Some muse should go to Earth and sell them Cupid's wings."

Because I agree with many of the green peace goals, I ignored the Jester and went on with my testimony. "As I have said, it was 1990 and both my Company and I were in a zone. Things were going well and while we were working long hours, I was at peace with the world. Therefore, I was not alarmed when we received a certified letter addressed to my father from the Massachusetts Department of Environmental Protection. Although my father was 90 years old and not active in the business, we kept his title as President as a tribute to him. The letter read:

September 27, 1990

Certified Mail, Return Receipt

Arthur Hutchins, President
Hutchins Tool & Engineering Co, Inc.
60 Brookdale Drive
Springfield MA, 01104

   Re: Request for Information Pursuant to M.G.L. c. 21E,
        1 Panama Street, East Longmeadow, Massachusetts

Dear Sir:

   The Massachusetts Department of Environmental Protection (The "Department") is investigating the release of oil and/or hazardous materials at a property located at 1 Panama Street, East Longmeadow, Massachusetts (the "site").

   Information available to the Department indicates that there have been one or more releases of oil and/or hazardous materials at or from the site, the prevention and mitigation of which is governed by M.G.L. c.21E. You are being asked to supply certain information as set forth in this request because you have been identified as a current or former occupant of a building located at the site.

   Pursuant to the Department's authority to conduct information gathering activities and to investigate, sample and inspect records, conditions, equipment, practices and property in accordance with M.G.L. c.21E, sections 4 and 8, you are directed to provide to the Department, by no later than twenty-one days after your receipt of this letter, responses to the information solicited in Exhibit "A", which is attached hereto and incorporated herein by reference.

   Your response to this request should include evidence that you have conducted a detailed and timely investigation of the facts

40

surrounding the subject matter of this request. Sources of such information should include, but are not limited to: business records; past and current company publications, reports, letters and memoranda; environmental audits; and interviews with past and current employees.

Failure to respond to this request within the time allotted above, or the submission of false or misleading information in such a response, may subject you to legal action, including but not limited to civil administrative penalties assessed by the Department.

Complete responses to this request should be sent to the undersigned, with a copy to Stephen Richmond, Deputy General Counsel, at the address on the letterhead above. Should you have any questions about this request, please do not hesitate to contact Mr. Richmond (413) 784-1100.

Thank you in advance for your cooperation in answering the questions set forth in this request.

Sincerely yours,

Stephen F. Joyce
Regional Engineer

cc w/o enclosure:

Louis S. Moore, Esq.
Anna Symington
Stephen M. Richmond, Esq.

"As enclosures to the letter there was a glossary of terms and a sheet with ten questions. No space was provided after the questions to write answers. This should have alerted me to the idea that the DEP was going through a bureaucratic exercise and was not expecting full answers to what they were asking.

"I looked upon this letter from the Massachusetts DEP as a

simple information gathering exercise. We had leased a small part of the Panama Street property during the 1970's so I assumed the DEP was gathering background data. The questions related to the date of our lease, employees on the site, type of operation and uses of oils or solvents.

"During the next week, I had our office staff gather whatever information we had that would help answer the questions. Because it was from eleven to sixteen years since the lease, only the personnel records were available.

"Out of curiosity I decided to call Steve Peroulakis, a former employee of Hutchins Tool who was currently a tenant at Panama Street, to find out what the DEP questions were all about."

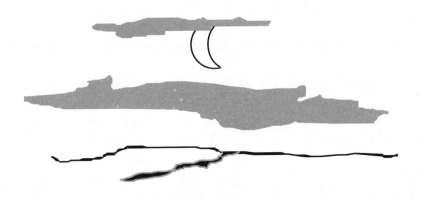

IX.   Steve

My testimony continued as I said, "Years ago, I had a job-opening at Hutchins Tool for a part-time draftsman so I contacted Springfield Technical High School. I had graduated from Tech, so I knew the school would send me a bright kid that could learn our system. They sent me Steve Peroulakis.

"Steve's family had emigrated from Greece a few years earlier. Although he had some problems with English, Steve did a good job for us for a number of years until he left for college."

The Jester broke in again. "No question he was good, he was Greek. We are all good."

At that point, Zeus banged the podium with his fist and shouted, "Zeus is ruler of all gods and all nations." He then threw a thunderbolt at the Jester, which zapped him pretty good. It blew away the Jester's robe and left him standing naked except for a leaf in place of his genitals. He didn't seem embarrassed, only stunned. It was obvious that this kind of thing had happened to him in the past. He pulled his scorched garment around his body and under his breath he mumbled words which sounded like a curse.

I was startled and saw that the Muse had a big smile on her face as Zeus raised his head in dominance. I became more guarded in what I would say to these gods as I went on with my story, "After a few years, Steve dropped out of college and asked me for a machining job in our EDM Department. He was happy to work all the hours we could give him both at night and on the week-ends. He eventually married and continued to work hard and to put in long hours.

"In 1973, we were awaiting the arrival of two expensive numerically controlled lathes. To make room for this equipment, we leased a 2500 sq. ft. section of a 7500 sq. ft. building on Panama Street in East Longmeadow, Massachusetts. We sent four people to the site: John Bosini, our most highly qualified grinding machine operator, Paul Benson, an engineer, and Steve Peroulakis plus Al Courchesne, both of whom operated the EDM machines. This was a small, one shift, temporary answer to our space needs. However, what started as a temporary solution, spanned the years from 1973 to 1979, the year we took occupancy of our new building.

"Steve acted as a group leader or foreman over the EDM machines at the Panama Street building. After a few years, Courchesne left the Company and a few more employees were hired. The maximum number of Hutchins' employees was reached just before we left this Panama Street site in 1979, when we peaked at five.

"In late 1980, Steve purchased a used EDM machine and placed it in his garage. When asked why he wanted a machine at his home, he said that he thought he could fix it up and resell it at a profit.

"On March 30, 1981, six months after our discussion about the EDM machine in his garage, Steve left Hutchins Tool and solicited many of our customers for his new company, Precision EDM, Inc. which he founded as a competitor to Hutchins Tool. Soon, Steve returned to the same Panama Street site, which Hutchins Tool had left in 1979.

"Because Hutchins Tool had wired this space for our machine shop needs, it was a perfect place for Steve to rent for his new operation. Doing business as Precision EDM, Steve was very successful and captured many of our old customers and much of the available EDM business.

"When these things happened, I was not concerned with the competition because EDM was only a small portion of our business. Other areas were growing much faster and showed more promise. As a businessman, I was never happy to lose a skilled employee and even more upset if the former employee became a competitor. However, like many things, you learn to accept these situations and live with them.

"So you can see that it was with some concern that I called Steve on October 2, 1990 to ask about the questionnaire from the DEP. As someone who currently leased space in that Panama Street building, I hoped that he could enlighten me as to why the DEP was gathering background information.

"When Steve came to the phone, he showed no hesitation in answering my questions. He spoke with the slight Greek accent that I remembered and seemed almost relieved to tell me the story.

"He told me that around February of 1989, Arden Thompson, who had constructed the Panama Street building in 1972 and had continued to own it since that time, decided to divide the building into three sections. His plan was to sell each section as a business condominium. The first tenants he approached were Steve and his partner Bob Valerie, another former employee of Hutchins Tool."

The Jester having recovered from being stunned by the thunderbolt, but still standing half-naked, snorted and said, "This is getting incestuous just like the heavens. You mean to tell me all these Precision employees once worked for Hutchins. Then they returned to Panama Street to open their own business and solicited Hutchins Tool's customers. Probably took the old price books with them."

Now Zeus laughed and said, "Hey, Muse this is better than the

Oedipus story. These earthlings better learn to get it together. Go on, Mr. Hutchins with your story."

I continued, "Steve then compared the cost of a mortgage for the condominium space to what he was paying for rent and decided to buy his section of the building. Of course, he then had to apply to a bank for a mortgage. As part of the mortgage financing, the banks in Massachusetts had added what they referred to as a 21E investigation as a requirement for obtaining mortgages. Steve didn't know about 21E when he started to purchase the building, but he sure does now.

"In 1983, the Massachusetts Legislature passed Massachusetts General Law Chapter 21E, the Massachusetts Oil and Hazardous Material Release Prevention and Response Act (MGL Chapter 21E). The part of the act that applied to Steve's financing is an environmental site investigation that the banks require so that they do not get stuck by placing mortgages on polluted properties. When the mortgage applies to a manufacturing plant, the loan officer demands the drilling of test wells at the site to determine if there is hazardous material in the ground water.

"In the case of Steve's agreement to purchase the Panama Street property, hazardous material was found in the ground water when water samples were sent to a testing laboratory. As a result, the bank disqualified the mortgage application and Steve did not buy the property.

"Unfortunately for Mr. Thompson, he lost the sale and he also had to report the test results of the groundwater from the wells to the Massachusetts Department of Environmental Protection (DEP). The environmental specialists who do this testing are required by regulation to report results found in 21E investigations.

"Suffice to say that Mr. Thompson reported the results as required and was left with no sale and a problem. He eventually retained Attorney Lou Moore to deal with the Massachusetts DEP at the suggestion of his personal attorney. Attorney Moore had given notice to the legal community that environmental law was his legal specialty.

"This phone call to Steve was moving from the casual to the concerned level because I remembered seeing that an Attorney Moore had been copied on the questionnaire that the DEP had sent to Hutchins Tool. Even so, I was not prepared for Steve's next comment. He told me, with a tone of embarrassed hesitation, that Attorney Moore had spent some time with Thompson, Steve's partner Bob Valerie and himself and he had sent Steve an affidavit to sign. When I asked what kind of affidavit, Steve said, "You know, about my dumping solvent out in back of the building when I worked for you. When I gasped and said, 'When did you do this Steve?' he said, 'Oh, It wasn't right, I didn't sign the affidavit that Attorney Moore sent for me to sign.'

"Fortunately, I had enough composure to say to Steve, 'If you still have that affidavit, could you send me a copy?' To my surprise, he said, 'Ok, what's your FAX number? I'll FAX it right over.'

"I said thanks and ended the telephone conversation. Within minutes, I was reading a FAX copy of the Affidavit written by Attorney Moore's office staff, which Steve refused to sign because it was, 'Not right.' It read:

September 26, 1990

Mr. Stylianos G. Peroulakis
Precision E.D.M., Inc.
1 Panama Street
East Longmeadow, MA 01028

Dear Mr. Peroulakis:

I'm enclosing herewith a revised Affidavit in accordance with our telephone conversation this afternoon. Please return the signed Affidavit to me.
Thank you for your cooperation in this matter.

Louis S. Moore

47

AFFIDAVIT OF STYLIANOS G. PEROULAKIS

I, Stylianos G. Peroulakis, on oath depose and say that:

1. *I am the president and owner of Precision E.D.M., Inc. which has its place of business at 1 Panama Street, East Longmeadow, Massachusetts.*

2. *I was formerly employed as a machine operator for Hutchins Tool & Engineering Company, Inc. ("Hutchins") from the late 1960s to 1981.*

3. *I have personal knowledge of the facts contained herein.*

4. *Hutchins leased a portion of the building known as 1 Panama Street, East Longmeadow, Massachusetts (the "Site") from about 1973 to about 1977 or 1978.*

5. *During the above-mentioned period, Hutchins operated a machine shop at the Site. During the period of its operations at the Site, Hutchins used a cleaning fluid for machine parts. This fluid was a very heavy liquid with a strong odor. We referred to it as perchloroethylene.*

6. *This solvent was regularly delivered by tank trucks and deposited into barrels in the shop for later use. The solvent was then used to clean or degrease machine parts. Approximately 55 gallons of this solvent was used in a typical week. The use of perchloroethylene as a solvent in this volume went on for most of the years I was employed by Hutchins at the Site.*

7. *The standard practice for disposal of used solvent was to empty 5 gallon buckets into the floor drain in the shop. However, there was a metal residue or sludge, which would accu-*

48

mulate at the bottom of the solvent barrel. Because of this, the floor drain would occasionally become clogged and over-flow. On such occasions, used solvent would be disposed on the ground at the rear of the building. I recall an area of approximately ten feet by fifteen feet where the grass would die after the occasions when used solvent was disposed of on the ground.

8.   *This disposal of used solvents onto the ground occurred regularly over the period during which I was employed by Hutchins at the Site, as the floor drains would become clogged quite often and Hutchins provided no alternative method of disposal.*

Signed under the pains and penalties of perjury this _____ day of September, 1990.

_____
Stylianos G. Peroulakis

COMMONWEALTH OF MASSACHUSETTS

HAMPDEN S.S.
September _____, 1990

Then personally appeared the above-named Stylianos G. Peroulakis and acknowledged the execution of the foregoing in-strument to be his free act and deed, before me,

_____
Notary Public
My Commission Expires:

Then for the first time, the Muse approached Zeus. She was excited and said to him, "May I speak, I mean that's the first of the miracles. Did you get it? Let's stop. I don't want you to miss it."

"You heard Mr. Hutchins mention General Law, Chapter 21E in Massachusetts. That's the environmental remediation law for Massachusetts. In most states, the remediation laws are named something else, have different signing dates, but they are almost exact copies of the federal Superfund law.

"Historically, most social legislation comes from the grass roots level in America. The pressure is from below at the state level and not centralized. In the past, states have had 'right to work' and 'minimum wage' laws long before similar federal laws were enacted.

"If people experienced some of the Superfund provisions on the state level prior to 1980, they would have learned that this was not workable legislation because it caused too much confrontation between parties. I had to take momentum from the environmental movement that was hot in 1980 and concentrate it at the national level to force through Superfund. I didn't have time to muse in fifty states.

"My subtle arts persuaded congresspersons that they must take the initiative and include tort provisions in the 1980 law. My agents went right past the state capitals and directly into the halls of Congress.

"The enthusiasm for cleaning up Love Canal was so high it was like selling apple pie and motherhood. No one dared to stand up and say, is this legislation right or workable? There was no right or wrong. The only question was who would pay for remediations? Congress had a simple answer that seemed to satisfy everyone. As part of the CERCLA, the U.S. Government provided a fund of money that would be used for remediations. Congress passed this 'Super-funded law' with little dissension."

"Muse," said Zeus, "you're way ahead of me. First you are talking about Massachusetts law Chapter 21E and then the federal Superfund law. I know that they're not the same. Let's stick with one or the other."

"That's my point," said the Muse. "The first miracle is that we caught a lot of little fish with the big fish. Take a look at the state laws that govern remediation, they are almost direct copies of CERCLA. CERCLA of 1980, which the journalists called Superfund, provided 1.6 billion dollars to clean up hazardous waste sites and prosecute violators. However the federal government did not intend to administer the law. They encouraged the states to write their own laws and delegated much of the administration of the environmental regulations to state agencies like the Massachusetts DEP.

"In 1983, Massachusetts passed Chapter 21E and provided little or no funding to clean up Massachusetts' sites. This same pattern of under-funding state laws mimicked the under-funding of the federal Superfund law. No one realized when these laws were written; that there was not enough money in the world to clean up all the sites that would fall under the provisions of these laws.

"As a result, the federal government depended upon states to establish departments to carry out these laws. However, with very little state funding to back them up, these state agencies were only able to go through the motions.

"My plan was diabolically cunning. I realized that if I got the Feds, that the states would fall all over themselves getting in line. Hell, we never even sent a muse to Boston to lobby them. All they needed was a word processor and a copy of the federal law.

"Most of the elected officials in the statehouses had no knowledge of environmental science so they simply copied the lists of hazardous materials published by the federal agencies. There was no independent thought or testing in the states, so that today some suspected hazardous agents may remain on a state list after being dropped from the federal lists."

The Jester jumped into the argument. "Pretty unbelievable, but no miracle. It was just a good hustle, like Butch Cassidy and the

Sundance Kid. You parlayed a little fear from Love Canal into a situation where people were ready to sift all the sands on earth looking for something that could harm them if they drank it. Big deal, without a muse people put smoke in their lungs and drugs in their veins. It's no miracle to panic the American population into looking for needles in a haystack. Zeus, she can say what she wants, but in my neighborhood that's no miracle."

Zeus answered, "Maybe yes, maybe no. What more can Hutchins tell us? Hutchins story is starting to sound like a Greek tragedy. I always like the part where the innocents suffer."

My answer to Zeus came out as I continued, "I never expected to suffer. Neither my Company nor me was guilty of anything. Panama Street had been leased to over 25 different outfits since Thompson built it. Machine shops, furniture strippers, oil distributors and a refrigeration service once occupied the building. Precision EDM had run two shifts averaging ten people doing production EDM since 1983. How could anyone prove that Hutchins Tool was responsible?

"Looking back, I'll agree that I was naïve. I grew up in a simpler time. I was taught that government was organized to help people, things should be fair to all citizens and that if you worked hard and were honest good things would come to you. I didn't know that when the DEP sent its questionnaire regarding our lease of floor space years ago, that it was the tip of an iceberg that would sink me and my business."

Now the Muse interjected, "If I could have a minute, I want to tell you about my night with Asclepius. While Mr. Hutchins may not know him, he had a tremendous effect on this tragedy. Asclepius, who is sometimes depicted as a serpent, is the god of healing."

X.   Asclepius

The Muse now held the floor. When she spoke of Asclepius, she took on the look of a seductress. I sensed that we weren't hearing everything about her relationship with him. There's something sensual about women and snakes. While most women will squeal and run from them, some are overly attracted to them. For example, they speak about Eve being enticed by the Serpent.

The Muse started by saying, "After my time on Earth acting as a muse for Rachel Carson's writings and my aborted early attempts at becoming the lawyer god, I was in a depressed state. Asclepius was my physician and he had me on a health maintenance program. He knew my body better than I did.

"As the god of healing, he selected two plagues which would be incubated in the 1960's so that massive healing programs could begin in the 80's and 90's and right into the millennium. Historically, these plagues have given the medical field good exposure and placed medicine high in mortal's esteem. Oh, there have been a few blunders, such as blood letting not doing much for a plague in the middle ages, but throughout history healers like Pasteur, Jenner and Curie have received very favorable press.

"Asclepius conceived of two new plagues. One was a deficiency sickness and the other something he was calling karkinos. Physicians had received great acclaim in the past curing scurvy as a deficiency disease and Asclepius felt that his latest plagues would give mortals massive problems that healers could solve. I'll have to admit learning Asclepius' strategy gave me insight into how he kept medicine paramount in the minds of mortals.

"Unfortunately, lawyers come up a little short when it comes to positives, so I needed a different hook. I realized that if I had a plague for lawyers to conquer, it would improve their image and enhance my chances to become the lawyer god. In desperation, I had to use all my charms to persuade Asclepius to give me one of his two healing programs. I think he realized that there was nothing I could do to enhance the legal profession through healing programs because lawyers are not healers. But Asclepius offered to let me use karkinos, one of his new plagues, in an exchange of favors."

At that moment, the Jester chimed in, "Exchange of favors, do I sense some indiscretions? Did you and Asclepius smoke a little of that lust dust that Bacchus spread around Yale Law School? Or possibly you smoked but didn't inhale. I get all that earthly stuff confused."

Zeus laughed and the Muse went on with her story by saying, "At one of my last healing sessions I learned that the translation of karkinos in English is cancer; this was the break that I needed. For our promotion work we extended the meaning to, 'Any cancer producing substance,' and passed it along to my contacts in the word foundries. By extending the meaning from cancer to also cancer-producing substance, we could develop fear not only for the disease but also for anything that might cause the disease. Within months we had the American press using the words cancer and carcinogen interchangeably.

"In the hands of Asclepius, the healing god, his deficiency plague, which became known as AIDS, would be treated as an illness. As such, the researcher starts with the disease and works back to the cause or causes. Because Asclepius introduced AIDS to the world, rational, scientifically based, research procedures have been followed by public health services. As a matter of fact, privacy laws have restricted almost any investigation of the transmitters of AIDS and such transmitters have not been considered liable under tort law. For example, the gay airline steward said to have brought some of the original AIDS strains from Africa to Southern California has never been held responsible, nor has the airline where he worked or the hotels where he transmitted the AIDS virus to victims.

"If you contrast this to karkinos, you will see how I convoluted common sense in America. By translating the word karkinos into English as carcinogen, I was able to change the discipline from healing to litigation. Rather than a researcher starting with a malignant tumor, I influenced thinking in America so a researcher would start with a suspected agent and try to create cancer in rats. Sort of an inverse scientific experiment; prior to this a researcher would start with the cancer and trace back to the source. I feel that the confusion I spread was a brilliant maneuver and should help to earn me the title, lawyer god."

At that point, the Jester interjected. "Hey, slow down, give some examples that I can understand. What's this cause and effect crap?"

Realizing that he was not understanding her logic, the Muse started again, "Jester, If you think like a healer you look at the symptoms and illness. Healers that do clinical research, try to work back from the disease to trace the route taken by the cause. For example malaria was traced step by step back to the mosquito which was the carrier."

The Jester jumped in again, "Hey divine one, don't you realize that those researchers on earth have used that procedure to trace back certain forms of lung cancer to tobacco and a number of skin cancers to sun exposure?"

"Ok, ok," said the Muse, "I agree that is the way the healers are finding the causes of cancer, but that's where I came in. I remembered what the gods had done to kindle the witch trials in Salem.

First, you create fear and suspicion so those earthlings are look-ing for a scapegoat. Then you panic earthlings into believing that the scapegoat is at the root of the problem. Do witches cause miscarriages? Watch the play, *The Crucible,* and you'll find that it was difficult to prove that a person was not a witch after she had been accused. In the same way, I knew that it would be impossible to prove that a substance was not karkinos or cancer causing.

"I am the muse that panicked Americans into believing that many, many substances cause cancer. I suggested that the way to cure cancer was to test any substance that anyone would suspect could cause cancer. I made sure that the tests would be tedious and time consuming and the results questionable. I knew that earth-lings would not approve of testing humans, so I brought in an animal that mortals have always hated, the rat.

"Then I directed moneys to laboratories that implanted chemi-cal substances into millions of rats and looked for signs of tu-mors. Any suspected agent was fair game, from trichloroethyl-ene to shoe polish.

"This was a very hard sell because some mortals in Washington had enough sense to realize that many cancers could already be traced back to such things as sunlight, tobacco-smoke and radia-tion. It was obvious that the money would be better spent on research for cancer cures.

"As a guarantee that these rat researchers would build a huge list of carcinogens, I had my congresspersons and lobbyists write quotas into the CERCLA legislation. I had Congress mandate that within 6 months of CERCLA passage, there would be at least 100 hazardous substances on the list and later 100 per year for three years. You can see that pressure was on the Agency for Toxic Substances and Disease Protection (ATSDP) to go full-speed ahead. If they had reasonable doubts about a substance, it was called hazardous."

"Get real," said the Jester, "not even the most dimwitted mor-tals would believe that they could vote a quota for scientific research. I can just hear the pep talk from the lab director. Gentlemen I know that this lab has been able to discover only a limited number of verifiable carcinogens through our research over the past 10 years, but I want you to meet our quota of 100 cancer causing substances by March 31St."

The Muse answered, "You got it Jester. Now you've got to see my hand in all this. Of course, I had panic and fear on my side. There is strong sentiment in America that considers big business an enemy of the people. When this was mixed together with words like pollution, contamination and waste, I had myself a campaign. Webster's Dictionary in the 1970's defined pollution as defilement and impurity. These are words that earthlings find disgusting.

"If there was no Love Canal, I would have created it. It was wonderful for my cause because Love Canal brought all of the mortals' prejudices together: Large corporations, pollution and fear, all in one package.

"Believe me, I never could have caused this panic with scare tactics about sunlight or tobacco smoke, because most earthlings loved the sun and nicotine. But those faceless brutes in the big corporations were an easy mark."

The Jester butted in, "Yea, yea, yea, so you say, but isn't most of the hazardous waste dumping done by big business?"

The Muse answered, "Years after I got this thing moving humans realized that most trash and waste is produced by average citizens and is deposited in municipal facilities. There is also an abundance of waste created by the military and other government agencies. Fortunately for my campaign, most Americans wanted to believe that industry produced the largest volume of waste. In truth, it is America's industries that have the most advanced recycling programs because it is in their best interest to reclaim and reuse raw materials.

"It was also my good fortune that positive stories like industry's advances in recycling never made the news. However, I saw to it that any newspaper story on the environment that could include the words G.E., PCB, oil spill, Mobil Corp, etc. would find a warm welcome with the editors."

Now the Jester spoke up, "I've got to hand it to you Muse that was some move. You got Americans to fear things they could not see, taste or feel in substances that they didn't eat, drink or touch. How did you cause that fear? Were people dying in the streets or massively deformed at birth? I remember that in the Middle Ages there were plagues that caused mortals to panic."

The Muse answered, "Crazy as it sounds, that wasn't happening. Earthlings quickly learned that most of the birth defects came from drug abuse, medications, alcohol, tobacco, physical abuse and medical tragedies. It is only the truly mysterious birth defects where there are no answers that are attributed to environmental factors.

"Most Americans do not know their neighbors. They are generally uninformed about the percentage of certain illnesses in their neighborhoods. If a family has a child with leukemia, information that another child with a similar sickness lives down the street is relevant to them. If a physician who attends their child mentions other patients with the same disease who live in the neighborhood, the parents immediately become suspicious of the environment in the neighborhood.

"Any suspected hazardous agent found in the environment of that neighborhood could possibly be the cause of an illness and certainly should be investigated and recorded by public health agencies. However, logic says that such events should not panic a whole nation into illogical and irrational legislation. Zeus, you must recognize what I say to be true. Between 1977 and 1980, my influence as a muse turned good sense upside down.

"If the conduit of cancer causing substances to earthlings is through the liquids they drink or foods they eat, reason would call upon man to monitor and test these fluids and foods. Is it less expensive to test the chemistry of water and food than to implant chemical compounds into millions of rats and search for tumors?

"In the early 1990's, several studies sponsored by the federal

Government strongly questioned the laboratory methods and risk assessment done through the years to determine how substances were placed on the federal lists as carcinogens. If the funds used for these tests were directed to Farber, Kettering or other institutes pursuing cancer cures, more mortals would have been saved. Zeus, you have to decide whether I directed the lunacy that went into the Superfund legislation or mortals did it without me."

Now Zeus spoke, "I can understand why humans would vote to be on the side of safety. If there was any chance that an agent would cause cancer, it is better to eradicate that agent so it can do no harm.

"Rachel Carson wrote a book that she called *Silent Spring*. In the Second Chapter, she said, 'All this is not to say there is no insect problem and no need of control. I am saying, rather, that control must be geared to realities, not to mystical situations and that the methods employed must be such that they do not destroy us along with the insects.'

"I recognize that gods travel to earth to place their stamp on war and love. As a muse, you have the power to induce panic in the minds and hearts of mortals, but it does not follow that you influenced the legal profession to participate in the CERCLA legislation.

"However we should continue your testimony because Rachel Carson sensed that mortals could be destroyed along with the insects. At this point, I find Mr. Hutchins' story truly unbelievable whereas your claims to influencing the U.S. Congress are only bazaar."

Now the Muse reacted quickly, "Lord Zeus, soon you will see. Hutchins is only one of many examples of lives destroyed by Superfund. Let me show you how I helped lawyers frame that law to exploit the American citizen's desire for environmental remediation. Together we created a great hoax on the populace that redirected monies from remediation to litigation. When we are through with this tribunal, Zeus you will understand how much I accomplished in just a few years on earth.

59

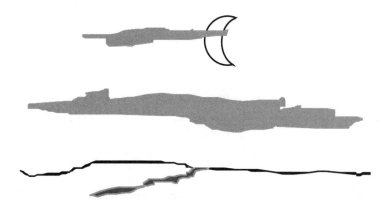

XI.   A Trojan Horse
Named Superfund

The Muse continued with her testimony, "Elated by the accepted translation of karkinos to carcinogen, I knew the time had come to proselytize America's craving for remediation. My work started to pay off when a lobbying effort from trial lawyers promoted tort concepts as a way to fund a Love Canal cleanup. This site had become the poster child for remediation because the ingredients were perfect: Pollution of unknown risk, confusion in spill occurrences, public displays of panic and neighborhood expectation of large damage settlements from corporations."

"As was said before, my Trojan horse was the title, Superfund. The impression we fostered was that Congress would vote massive amounts to clean up Love Canal as well as other polluted sites. After public funds had been expended for this effort, the big corporate culprits would be tracked down and made to replenish the public funds that had been spent.

"Plans for CERCLA passage were nearly scuttled when one junior senator questioned if the technology was available to successfully clean ground water. We knew that to remediate ground water was tedious, uneconomical and nearly impossible. Only two methods were available at that time: First, to remove the polluted soil and carry it to another site, second, to pump the groundwater from wells, filter the water and then pump the water back into the ground. Of course, then the filters had to be taken overland to solid waste sites. The expense for either method could be astronomical.

"Fortunately, for the legal profession very little funding was voted to fund technical advances for remediation. This was not a trip to the moon so hardware development was 'a hard sell' to the American people. Remediation science was not sexy enough to stimulate public investment.

"Who could complain? Under the plan we proposed there would be no loser. The law was called Superfund and Congress would vote moneys needed for remediation. Most congresspersons expected that the corporations would roll over and play dead and not dispute an environmental agency's claims for damages. However the exact opposite happened, with the cleanup costs extremely high and private lawsuits waiting in the wings, the only path open for those accused of polluting years earlier was to fight back and defend themselves in the courts."

The Jester broke in, "Hey, that's simple. That's a job for the environmental police. They could stop people from throwing beer cans out of their automobiles too. What kind of uniforms do those guys wear?"

The Muse broke back in to explain, "Superfund offenses are generally not criminal because we designed the legislation to invoke civil penalties. Think about it, now you can see how my scheme was working out beautifully.

"When all the parties to litigation are persons, disputes are settled under civil law. The mortals who devise, litigate, judge and interpret both federal and state civil laws are lawyers. Mortals who charge for environmental civil law services are lawyers."

Back came the Jester, "Big deal, how many legal questions could there be with the Love Canal? Obviously some large chemical companies spilled the stuff. Just send in a crew and clean it up and charge the chemical companies so the Superfund is replenished. Seems simple enough to me."

The Muse answered, "That's wonderful, now you're thinking the way we hoped that Americans would think. If an oil truck had an accident on a highway, a HAZMAT team would spring into action, clean up the highway, dispose of the waste oil and charge the oil-company for the service. Spills that occurred after the date of enactment of Superfund and the state remediation laws have led to very little litigation. There are very few disputes unless an oil truck is hit on the highway by another vehicle. There may be a question regarding who pays for cleaning up the spill if that type of accident occurs."

The Jester shot back, "Just like I say, simple. Why the hell do you expect to be queen for a day or the god of lawyers? You gave them nothing!"

Now, Zeus responded, "Muse move this thing faster. What's your point? You haven't shown me that this Superfund law, on which you put your stamp, enriched lawyers."

The muse rebounded with some facts, "Zeus as of 1997, billions of dollars have been spent for remediation in the United States. It is reported that less than 10% of those billions has gone to cleaning up sites. The major portion of the money has gone into the pockets of lawyers!"

"Bullshit, bullshit," screamed the Jester. "That's crazy. I bet it never happened. It's not possible."

The Muse broke back in to explain, "Offenses and wrongdoing under Superfund generally are not treated as criminal offenses. That is the genius behind what lulled Congress into creating CERCLA. Disputes under the Superfund law are treated as civil rather than criminal offenses.

"Let me give you an example. Generally under federal law, it is a criminal offense to kill a government employee working in an official capacity. A person accused of murder is investigated and brought to court for trial under a criminal justice format. The complaint reads the people of the United States versus the defendant. If found guilty, the murderer can be jailed or executed.

"The accused killer is protected under the criminal justice system and has rights granted to him under that system such as a right to a fair trial, right to a defense, right of bail, etc.

"Americans began to understand the system better by watching the O.J. Simpson trials. The first was a criminal trial. The criminal trial was comparatively simple in that the people of California attempted to prove that O.J. murdered his wife. If the jury had accepted the people's proofs and O.J. was convicted, he would have faced a long jail term or a death penalty. The jury did not find sufficient evidence of guilt, so O.J. was set free.

"Americans may not have agreed with the verdict but most people clearly understood the criminal trial procedures. Many Americans found the second trial, a civil trial, much more confusing.

"The crime was called, 'harmful death,' rather than murder and the rules of evidence were different, but the effort to prove guilt remained the same. The major difference in the trials was in the contestants. In the criminal trial it was the people versus Simpson. In the civil trial it was Simpson's dead wife's family as a person, the Plaintiff, versus O.J. Simpson as a person, the Defendant.

"During the criminal trial, the State of California paid for the prosecution and O.J. paid for his defense. In most criminal trials, because the criminal has no money to pay defense attorneys, the state pays for both the prosecution and defense.

"Civil litigation is quite different also regarding lawyer's fees. In practice, most civil litigation has at least one party using lawyers on a contingency fee. Under such an agreement, the lawyers receive a portion such as twenty, thirty, or forty percent of the settlement. Of course, the attorneys are betting that they will win because if their client loses, they receive nothing.

"Realistically, even this situation is rare because for most civil litigation in America today, neither party pays legal fees. The insurance industry underwrites the cost of the legal fees and pays the settlement costs on most major lawsuits. Therefore, personal injury lawyers practicing tort law today support many law offices. It is said that the automobile has played a larger and larger roll in promoting tort law. In some states over 40% of the appellate court workload involves automobile accidents."

The Jester jumped up and said, "I like that. I really like that scam. Do you mean that lawyers take their fees from the thousand to two thousand dollar auto insurance bills that the American drivers pay each year? They are like toll takers on a mortal's highway of life. The lawyers' toll booths are on both ends of life and at places in between, so if you get off early or late, they still collect."

The Muse went on with her statement, "Jester you are right and now you understand tort law. With what you have learned, you can see why I pushed to have Superfund be governed primarily by tort law, or more specifically by tort lawyers.

"In my quest to become the lawyer god, I influenced Congress to make CERCLA a tower of babble. Previous environmental laws successfully forced the elimination of DDT and other harmful insecticides to accomplish Rachel Carson's goals. They regulated waste being poured in waterways. These things were accomplished successfully using criminal type penalties for abusers. However, CERCLA's babble created the confusion, disputes and finger pointing I needed to exact monstrous opportunities and fees for lawyers.

"The Superfund law of 1980 and its offspring laws as duplicated in most of the fifty states have rejuvenated tort law as a specialty for lawyers all over America. I think it's time to have Mr. Hutchins tell us more of his story and recount some of his experiences with CERCLA. You can see that Hutchins is an insignificant mortal. He is one of the little guys who operate farms and small businesses in America. His story may also sound irrelevant until you understand that his life under the Superfund law is but a microcosm of a major disaster that is taking place all over America. His story is America's story."

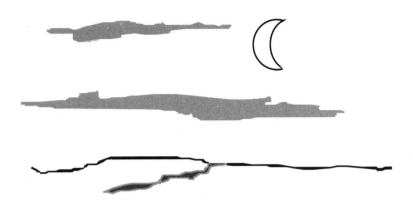

XII. A Civics Lesson
in Ex Post Facto

I'm not sure that I liked being called small or insignificant but I did agree that from eight years ago to the present, I learned about CERCLA in small, painful steps.

I resumed my testimony as I said, "Yes, my situation is exasperating in that it is not unique. Others who have been hurt are people that owned gasoline stations, trucking companies, farms, small manufacturers, etc. These are owners who reached retirement age with the expectation that a large part of their retirement funds would come from the moneys that they would receive from the sale of their business properties or farms.

"I have heard many stories where a sales agreement was written and an announcement made that the business had been sold. When there was no closing, the word would surface that the property had an environmental problem and the buyers could not get financing.

"Let me take you through the early years of my disaster to show

67

you how this law filters down to a common mortal like me. A few minutes ago, I told you that in October of 1990, Hutchins Tool received a questionnaire from the Massachusetts Department of Environmental Protection (DEP) which was my first indication of any problem at Panama Street. You should understand that we had leased this property seventeen years earlier, which is almost half a working lifetime of a mortal. I had not visited or thought about Panama Street for over eleven years. This was well past the time that the federal government requires a company to keep anything more than personnel and tax records. In other words, for an American company eleven years is history.

"After learning from Steve Peroulakis about the problem, I wrote nine pages of answers to the ten questions asked by the DEP. It was a very thorough set of answers that listed Hutchins Tool employees who had worked at the Panama Street location plus a description of our operation there. However, because we had left Panama Street at least 11 years earlier, I had no records of materials purchased for that facility. When I answered the DEP's questionnaire I thought that I was helping the DEP with their investigation and did so willingly. I didn't realize that this Agency's policy was to seek out any party that they could hold responsible who could pay for the cleanup.

"As I thought about the Panama Street site, two things surprised me: First, that a state agency was involved rather than the federal EPA. I learned later that while Superfund is federal law, Washington persuaded the states to copy the Superfund legislation with state laws and to organize departments in each state to administer these laws.

"This results in a layer of state laws, bureaucracy and litigation that superimposes itself over Superfund. In truth, it just adds fifty Balkanized armies of poorly trained troops to fight environmental wars. I believe that the deficiencies in environmental remediation originate from CERCLA, the 1980's federal legislation. The state laws and local environmental agencies are bureaucratic camouflage that disguises the failures of this federal law.

"My second surprise was that Hutchins Tool received a questionnaire on Panama Street from the DEP in October of 1990. The proposed sale of the Panama Street property to Precision EDM, which initiated the Chapter 21E investigation, was in February of 1989. Why did it take over eighteen months for Thompson, the owner of the property, to ask if we at Hutchins Tool had any knowledge of a spill?

"If you are establishing a time line in your mind, you may also ask why Hutchins Tool would be accused when we had leased the property at least fourteen years before Massachusetts General Law Chapter 21E was passed by the Massachusetts Legislature. Didn't we learn in school that the Constitution protected citizens against ex post facto laws, the laws enacted with retrospective effect?

"That's why the questionnaire from the DEP was of little concern to me. Hutchins Tool had always followed both federal and state environmental regulations religiously. We had maintained good documentation on all oils, lubricants or chemicals shipped into or out of our plants since the reporting rules were established in the early 1980's. Our plants were clean showcases admired by our customers and employees.

"Four months after returning the DEP's questionnaire, I was called to a meeting at the DEP offices to meet with the other tenants and former tenants of the Panama Street site to discuss the problem. To my surprise when I arrived I found only three parties represented along with some DEP staff. Those present were Thompson, the site owner, Steve Peroulakis representing Precision EDM, and myself. Where were the other 25 companies that had leased space in the building? Where were the other machine shops, furniture strippers and equipment distributors that were the current occupants of that building?

"Anna Symington, a DEP employee introduced herself and called the meeting to order. Then she got the meeting started by saying, 'Here we have Mr. Thompson an innocent property owner and two potentially responsible parties. Is there somebody here representing Hutchins Tool?' I nodded and said that I was Don

Hutchins from Hutchins Tool. I added that we had not done business at Panama Street in about twelve years so we could not be considered a responsible party. She answered, "Mr. Hutchins, when we hear all the facts of this case, you can defend your position, but my investigation and discussions with your former employees leads me to believe that your Company is responsible along with Mr. Peroulakis and Precision EDM."

"Now a DEP engineer described his visits to Panama Street and the reports from Contest, Inc., an environmental company that had done the environmental assessment for the property sale. Contest had drilled the first wells and lab tested the ground water for the property sale that was never consummated. The DEP engineer concluded that the proximity of the building to Pecousic Brook, which ran through the property, made Panama Street a priority site for remediation.

"Ms. Symington then said that she and her staff would leave the room for ten minutes and allow the three parties to discuss sharing the cost of remediation. At that point, she left.

"Before I could speak, Peroulakis said that he was not paying for something he did not do. Thompson, the owner, looked at me for answers and all I could do was say, 'You people have been discussing this for two years and you can't expect me to answer you after a five minute notice. I need to find out what is going on.'

"Upon Ms Symington's return to the room, she acted surprised that we couldn't agree on how to share a million-dollar remediation charge. In what appeared to be a fit of disgust, she closed the meeting and said that we would be hearing further from her office.

"I remember leaving the DEP meeting in a daze. What investigation did she conduct? She never made any inquiries with Hutchins Tool about current or former employees or about our operation on Panama Street. On what basis could she call Hutchins Tool a responsible party? Did she investigate the furniture strippers who used vats of chemicals in which they dipped wooden chairs and tables to remove paint, varnish and stains? Did she know the chemistry of the refrigerants used in Thompson's refrigeration business? I knew he stored both refrigerants and lubricants to be used for the large compressors that were part of the room size freezers he installed.

"Sometime later, my lawyer visited the DEP and photo copied the Panama Street file which was available as public information. I spent a day reading that file and learned what had been happening between Peroulakis, Thompson and the DEP staff between 1989 and 1991. It was like unraveling a bad paperback mystery.

"The first thing in the file that I spotted was my reply to the DEP's ten questions. It was the well documented nine pages that I have already talked about and with it were about fifteen replies from the other tenants. Most responders had replied with one page. A typical example came from J & S Machine. The answers were:

1. Jean A. Simonof, President
2. March 1988 – till present
3. No
4. No
5. No
6. None
7. No
8. No
9. No
10. No

"These answers would indicate that this machine shop never used or stored any lubricants or chemicals in their plant. Anyone who knows anything about machines knows that all shops have at least an oilcan to lubricate machines. To not have lubricants is akin to not using oil or gasoline in an automobile. Other renters had simply photo copied the questions and scribbled answers in the margins like (N/A) for not applicable plus many no's and question marks where they did not simply leave the answer blank."

At that point the Jester jumped to his feet and said, "Hutchins, mortals using liquids can not operate for 10 or 20 years without a spill. Certainly the current occupants who had seen the environmental drilling rigs on the site and had been questioned eight months earlier by engineers from Contest, must have reported spills in their sections of the building."

I replied, "Jester, no one saw or heard anything according to the reports accepted by the DEP. It seemed to me that everyone who might have been implicated had been informed that Hutchins Tool would 'take the fall.'

"Of great interest to me were Mr. Thompson's answers. To question number 9 he answered, 'The release or dumping of oil and hazardous material happened on different occasions between 1973 and 1979. The dumping was by employees of Hutchins Tool and Engineering. This dumping was witnessed by Steve Peroulakis who was an employee of Hutchins Tool and Engineering.'

"To that same question, Steve Peroulakis answered, 'There is a pipeline across the brook behind the site that leaked what looked like fuel oil a couple of times since the mid 1970's. When Hutchins Tool & Engineering occupied the site from approximately the early 1970's to approximately 1978, spent solvent called perch was poured down the floor drain, if the drain was clogged, it was sometimes poured in the ground behind the building. Employees of Hutchins Tool & Engineering witnessed this.'

"While to Anna Symington that was strong evidence of Hutchins Tool's guilt, to me it painted a totally different picture. I believe that after the 21E investigation revealed ground water contamination and Thompson and Peroulakis realized that Contest, Inc., the environmental consultant, would report the contamination to the DEP, they got together to find a scapegoat. Hutchins Tool was elected as the perfect scapegoat. First, it took Peroulakis off the hook. Second, Hutchins Tool was known to be a financially strong company with 'deep pockets.'

"Thompson never contacted me or anyone at Hutchins Tool to discuss the 21E investigation. If that had happened, it is possible that Hutchins Tool would have turned Thompson's claim over to our insurance company and they would have settled.

"Massachusetts General Law Chapter 21E encourages discussions and negotiation between all the parties involved as the preferred action before litigation. Attorney Moore knew that law well but made no attempt to bring the parties together, as is evidenced by the fact that he never contacted me or anyone at Hutchins Tool on the subject.

"Realizing that Thompson and Peroulakis had some discussions that could lead to making Hutchins Tool the scapegoat, I wondered how Anna Symington also named Precision EDM a responsible party. My answer was in the file with a letter signed by Michael C. Mackiewicz, an environmental investigator who investigated the Panama Street site and read the ground water lab reports.

"He reported that Peroulakis was using a solvent that contained approximately 30% perchloroethylene (PCE). The PCE was found in soil samples outside the back door where Peroulakis cleaned parts after machining. Mr. Mackiewicz concludes, 'In sum, the available data regarding the site is entirely consistent with Precision EDM, Inc. being a source of the hazardous materials contamination at the site.'

"I don't know what led Thompson to change his story. All I know is that Peroulakis was surprised to find that Anna Symington of the DEP named his Company a responsible party."

Now the muse stepped forward and said, "Zeus, I would like to point out that this is a perfect example of how my scheming in writing CERCLA has played out. If Superfund were administered under criminal rather than the civil code, the EPA or the Justice Department would have investigated Hutchins Tool. With sufficient evidence, Hutchins Tool would be fined. If this did not lead to cooperation, the officers would be held in contempt and the case could go before a grand jury. Later the officers would be taken before a federal court and judged guilty or innocent by a jury.

"If CERCLA had been written as criminal law, all of Mr. Hutchins' and Hutchins Tool's Constitutional rights would be protected. Hutchins would be considered innocent until proven guilty.

"You can see the American citizen's Constitutional rights such as ex post facto have no relevance under CERCLA. This law makes all parties including the DEP, a person under the law. Ms. Symington, working for the DEP, can accuse Hutchins Tool, another person, of wrongdoing using any evidence she elects to use. There is no accountability, she is not a detective and she has no legal experience. However, under Massachusetts Law, Chapter 21E, the bastard child of the federal Superfund law, Symington is anointed judge and jury. Earth hasn't seen something like that since the Spanish Inquisition."

Now the Jester spoke, "The Inquisition, is she claiming responsibility for the Inquisition? I thought that was Hades work. Besides, Ms Symington would have no more power than Hutchins Tool under the law. All Hutchins Tool has to do is defend itself against her allegations."

Zeus answered, "Hades, be damned. Go on Mr. Hutchins you've got the floor."

I continued, "What the Jester says seems to make sense until you realize that Anna Symington's has the power and unlimited finances of the State of Massachusetts behind her. For the small businessman this is totally unfair competition. We just can't handle the costs of fighting such a battle with a state agency like the DEP.

"Symington's conclusions after conversations with the four former Hutchins Tool's employees who had worked at the Panama Street site, bear this out. These employees say her investigation consisted of a few hours spent telephoning the names I had given the DEP when answering the questionnaire.

"John Bosini, who worked at Panama Street throughout the length of our lease, in his phone answer said that Peroulakis was not to be trusted. Bosini also said that he never saw any dumping or pouring into the drain which was located within ten feet of his machine. A second employee, Paul Benson said that Hutchins ran a real clean place and that he never saw any disposal inside or outside the building.

"Symington was not able to locate Courchesne for a phone interview. As a result, the only person who worked on Panama Street as a Hutchins' employee to accuse Hutchins Tool was Peroulakis. Of course, by accusing Hutchins Tool of responsibility, Peroulakis deflected responsibility away from himself and his Company, Precision EDM.

"Symington had all she needed to make up her mind with the statements of Thompson, who quoted Peroulakis. Of course, Peroulakis stated that, 'Employees of Hutchins Tool witnessed pouring of spent oil and solvent down a floor drain.' He didn't say that he poured or witnessed pouring. This is an unbelievable statement when we consider that during the term of that lease; Hutchins Tool averaged only 3 employees in a shop area the size of a three-car garage.

"In a criminal court, such hearsay would be thrown out. However, in Ms. Symington's personal courtroom you are guilty and must prove your innocence."

XIII.   The Complaint

My testimony continued, "In April of 1991, two months after that meeting in the DEP office, Thompson brought a civil action against Hutchins Tool and Precision EDM. After a 'Statement of Facts,' the Complaint cited M.G.L. Chapter 21E as well as negligence, trespass, waste, nuisance and strict liability for recovery of damages and other costs incurred and to be incurred with respect to hazardous materials contamination on and near Plaintiff's real estate property (Panama Street).

"You should note that neither the State of Massachusetts nor the DEP was suing Hutchins Tool. The owner of the building, Arden Thompson, was suing us for damages he could sustain if the DEP brought action against him and also to recover the costs of the environmental assessment investigations and his legal fees.

"Up to that time, he was not being sued by the DEP nor had the DEP forced him to pay any penalties. The lawsuit, as encouraged by Thompson's attorney, Mr. Moore, was designed as a first strike to allow litigation to begin. Moore was defending Thompson by taking the offensive and bringing us into the dispute. In this way,

Attorney Moore accomplished two things. First, it gave them the opportunity to call witnesses in the discovery phase that could implicate others and also it made the fee clock accelerate for Moore and the other attorneys involved.

"Served at the same time as the complaint was a 'Motion of Attachment.' The 'Motion and Attachment' was an attempt by Attorney Moore, as Thompson's lawyer, to attach the buildings and equipment of Hutchins Tool as security for the Complaint. In this motion, Moore speculated that the cost of the remediation of the Panama Street site could reach over one million dollars.

"Zeus, I've got to tell you, now this little environmental problem started getting my attention. It would be impossible for Hutchins Tool to function if its buildings and equipment were attached. Fortunately, while the Complaint stood, the Judge did not allow the 'Motion for Attachment.' However, the die was cast and Hutchins Tool's liability exposure was in excess of a million dollars.

"I was relieved that the pressure of the Attachment was off our backs. Unfortunately, a civil action even without attachments is no picnic because under standard accounting practice, litigation exposure to damage claims must be disclosed in a corporation's audited financial statements. As a direct result of Thompson's civil action, Hutchins Tool's statements have been footnoted since 1991 showing the exposure to these environmental claims to be well over one million dollars.

"These civil actions have eliminated our borrowing relationships with banks. When the Bank of New England went bankrupt, this footnoted litigation exposure was the stigma that forced our loans into the control of the Federal Deposit Insurance Corporation (FDIC).

"No financial institution wants to deal with companies with environmental exposure problems. The financial world knows that the costs of remediation are indefinable but potentially immense. What does it cost to find needles in haystacks? What does it cost to remove the needles? What does it cost to store the needles in a safe place once they have been found and removed?

"The first lesson learned by bank lending officers is to avoid financing property that has not been given a clean bill of health by environmental specialists. It may be easier to operate a company in bankruptcy than one that is environmentally at risk.

"I know that you gods live forever, so time and dates are not an important factor in your lives. However, we earthlings live and die by the clock and calendar.

"One of my first thoughts after receiving the Complaint was that Hutchins Tool was accused of breaking a law before the law was written. Under this scenario a citizen may be breaking a law today that may not be written for another ten years. I believe that this is unconstitutional. Even if the Supreme Court rules that ex post facto does not apply to CERCLA, the way the law is administered by state agencies does abuse a citizen's civil rights. The people of the United States have always abhorred kangaroo courts and unjust persecution by government agencies.

"The civil rights violations, which I ascribe to the Massachusetts DEP, are no different than that which Martin Luther King fought when he challenged government agencies that denied citizen's voting rights, equal employment access or equal education. The point is that a state agency should not be above the law no matter how lofty its goals. The goal of a cleaner environment should not allow DEP personnel to deny me my rights to due process granted by the State and federal constitutions."

"What's with this Martin Luther King thing, Hutchins?" said the Jester. "Do you believe that there were people in state agencies that thought they were doing the right thing by denying citizens voting rights before activists like King spoke out?"

"There is no question in my mind that the majority of the agency employees working in the southern states prior to the voter rights legislation, thought that it was their job to maintain the status quo. We know they did this by denying the disenfranchised their civil rights under the U.S. Constitution. In truth, many government agency employees have a history of thinking that they can use any tactic to gain an advantage over the average citizen with the current most publicized example being the IRS.

"I once had a math teacher who said that if you had a difficult math problem to simplify it by working it through with small numbers. I believe that this teacher's advice would work well for people trying to understand why CERCLA has been a failure. To get an answer to this big problem, think of the Panama Street remediation as a simple example.

"To put this in prospective, Hutchins Tool leased Panama Street from about 1972 to 1979 when I was between 37 and 44 years old. CERCLA was passed in 1980 when I was 45 years old and the Massachusetts General Law Chapter 21E was signed three years later in 1983. At the time the Complaint started litigation in 1991, I was 56 years old. When Mr. Thompson brought suit in 1991, it was 12 years since Hutchins Tool left the Panama Street site. During the time we leased the Panama Street site, Richard Nixon and Gerald Ford were Presidents of the United States, the Boston Celtics were champions of the NBA, the microprocessor was just being developed and there were no personal computers. Using Panama Street as a simple example, it is easy to see that the DEP administered justice was neither swift nor fair.

"If we were dealing with criminal law, a statue of limitations would have protected Hutchins Tool and we also would be considered innocent until proven guilty. However, because CERCLA was written as civil law, the accused may be forced to prove his or her innocence. This is very difficult when the issues span years and years. Truth gets cloudy as time passes.

"In April of 1991, the Massachusetts Department of Environmental Protection (DEP) sent Hutchins Tool, Precision EDM and Thompson an invoice for $244.11. Listed as a reason for the invoice was the fact that the DEP had cited Hutchins and the others as responsible parties. The invoice also stated that failure to pay would result in additional interest, legal action and liens on Hutchins' property. There was no allocation of costs among the parties, so in an effort to appease the DEP, Hutchins Tool paid the

$244.11. We also paid the next bill for over a thousand dollars hoping that with time sanity would prevail.

"These amounts that Hutchins Tool paid were never acknowledged by the DEP or credited to our account. They were shown only as a communal receipt from all the three parties billed. The DEP never differentiated, only accepted the money and continued by sending statements on a regular basis that now total close to $200,000."

The Jester piped in, "What did they charge you for? Did you get a list of the DEP's expenses or was it just a statement?"

When I answered, "Just statements," the Jester went ballistic and said, "I love it. I've got to get me a deal like that. Just bill citizens every few months for the costs applied to a given piece of property. I understand that government offices charge penalties and fees for some services such as fishing licenses, but how does the DEP get away with charging citizens the costs involved in investigating themselves? And who is to say that the right citizen is being charged for such costs? Even the IRS doesn't charge their investigation costs to the citizen being investigated. There may be penalty and interest payments due the IRS, but not charges for overseers to investigate a possible tax evader. I'd love to run the Massachusetts DEP and have my budget underwritten by the people I was investigating. That's even better than loan sharking."

Zeus calmed the Jester down with a glance. Because Zeus had zapped him earlier with a small lightning bolt and the Jester was in the embarrassing position of not being fully clothed; I could understand why he would not want to draw further attention to himself.

I continued by saying, "I found the DEP to be similar to a gathering of 'keystone cops' because they chased one another around from one event to another and accomplished very little. Their people gave the impression of being deeply concerned with the earth and environment. But, as time passed I realized that many of the DEP's employees were simple bureaucratic functionaries trying to hold on to their jobs.

"Because there was little education being offered for environmental professionals in the 1980's, most of the DEP officials with whom I have dealt had the good fortune to stumble into their positions. Now that there are environmental specialists graduating from college, those currently in the DEP live a dichotomy. They grumble about their low pay, lack of recognition and exposure to layoffs as state employees and at the same time they long to leave and collect the high fees of licensed professionals. For these reasons, they hang on to their jobs and as a reward they gain the simple pleasures of chastising citizens they see as polluters. Better still, they're allowed to play detective, judge and jury to confused constituents most of whom are responsible people who are caught up in something they don't understand. If this sounds like whining, it's because I'm one of those constituents."

Now Zeus spoke up, "I'll give this to you Muse, if you helped sculpt this CERCLA legislation, you certainly brought in massive amounts of confusion. Let me summarize to this point.

"First, even though most of Rachel Carson's goals in *Silent Spring* were being met, the U.S. Congress pressured by the Love Canal scare went off in a completely new direction and developed CERCLA. This law was designed to clean up waste sites that were the cause of great disease in America. Just like the plagues of the Middle Ages. I assume millions were dying each year poisoned by these hazardous wastes."

The Muse could not hold back a smile and said, "I'm sorry to interrupt so soon, but now you can see my genius. There were no deaths that could be directly related to this hazardous waste. It was the rumor and fear I provoked that made Americans believe that substances found in ground water would cause disastrous results. While there is pretty good proof that tobacco, tar and sunlight could stimulate cancers leading to death, forty years of research has produced no irrefutable evidence of deaths directly traceable to waste chemicals found in drinking water. Biological waste has proven to be a killer and such waste in drinking water has been listed as the cause of death. The truth is that <u>fear</u> is the foundation of CERCLA, not chemical waste."

Now Zeus just shook his head slowly back and forth in disbelief. He then said, "That's unbelievable, even the Roman senators had more sense. Let me continue.

"Second, I understand that the Federal Government legislated CERCLA and the states followed with copies of CERCLA. It sounds to me like the prohibition laws. A gang of people wanted to eliminate alcohol consumption in the U.S. so they petitioned and passed prohibition through the state legislatures and Constitutional amendments. There were criminal prosecutions for offenders like bootleggers, distillers, etc. Even though the laws were repealed, the laws gave citizens with strong beliefs against alcohol the opportunity to test prohibiting alcohol with, 'the great experiment.' Why would it hurt Americans to try another 'great experiment' to shape up those waste producing big businesses that lack concern for America's health and welfare?"

The Muse stood up again and said, "Zeus, you should understand that prior to CERCLA, there were many laws written to control the producers, distributors and users of chemicals considered dangerous. This was controlled with criminal law through fines and legal penalties. For example, DDT was taken from the marketplace.

"Our studies showed that these laws were workable and led to very little litigation. Before CERCLA, some lawyers had to chase ambulances to find victims of auto accidents or seek out product liability and malpractice clients. The boom to civil litigation in America came with CERCLA. Now, rather than chasing ambulances, lawyers could simply pick out companies they perceived as having deep pockets.

"The average American citizen is free to drive an automobile that produces exhaust and spills oil, gasoline, antifreeze, etc. He can also put medical waste, paint cans, solvents and cleaning agents on the curbside for collection. He beautifies his lawns and gardens with fertilizers that foul the drinking water of his neighbors. He can use septic tanks and leach fields that do not leach and are not septic.

"With the millions of Americans actively polluting the earth, why has the CERCLA legislation been directed at large and small businesses? The reason is simple. Lawyers do not see citizens as having "deep pockets." Most individual citizens can not pay the freight. It has been left up to governments to control citizens through criminal punishments such as fines and penalties.

"It was my genius as a Muse that deluded law makers into believing that polluters would be controlled with tort law. The largest percentage of funds earmarked for environmental problems has gone to lawyers. Very little has been used to clean up hazardous waste.

"Most Americans have knowledge of locations in their towns that can show a much greater probability for ground water problems than those on state and federal lists. Americans also know that the owners of these properties are not stupid and they would never allow exploratory wells to be dug that would expose them to the whims of agencies like the DEP. Why should they? It would only lead to bankrupting type financial problems.

"Americans also know that most drinking water supplies are tested especially if there is any question of health risks. For the most part, drinking water in the U.S. is considered safe.

"As the mover of CERCLA legislation, I, the Muse, convinced Americans that they were at great risk and should control the big businesses that were poisoning them. Zeus, we're not talking rational here, we are illustrating one of the best marketing campaigns to come out of the heavens."

At that moment, the Muse stopped speaking. Before she could resume her summation, I heard a clatter of hooves and the sound of a horse approaching.

In the next instant, a horse/man rode up to Zeus' pedestal. The Jester jumped back and Zeus raised his huge hand with his five-fingers spread skyward.

At that point, the man, or at least the torso on the horse's body, did the same. I couldn't believe it. Here was Zeus and this creature giving one another a "high five," one with five fingers and one with a raised hoof.

The Muse saw my amazement. I expect she knew that I needed an explanation so she came over and said in a loud whisper, "It's OK, he's one of Zeus' centaurs. He's captain of Zeus's team and wants Zeus's good wishes for the game tonight. They're playing Apollo's team for all the laurels."

In a flash, the centaur was gone and all was quiet again. When I heard Zeus begin again by summing up his third conclusion, all I could think about was this half horse and half man, playing ball. If he played soccer with four feet, he would be a very tough opponent or if he played basketball, he could really push Dennis Rodman away from the bucket. I could imagine Dennis tugging on his tail to upset him.

Of course, maybe they were playing football, sort of like the Budweiser Clydesdales or maybe polo, soccer, or golf. No, not golf, he'd mess up the greens.

Now I could hear Zeus again. He was saying, "I assume you brought Hutchins here to testify because he owns a business that is responsible for pollution. That being the case, it seems to me that if he made the mess, he should clean it up."

Then the Muse jumped with joy. "Zeus, that's the point. That is why I brought Hutchins to the heavens to stand before you. He is my proof. Hutchins is the evidence I needed to convince you that CERCLA could not come from human reason. It was legislation that I invented to make law my kingdom, the lawyers my handmaidens and me the lawyer god.

"Look at Hutchins, close to one half million dollars has been spent with the intent to remediate the Panama Street site and every penny so far has gone either to lawyers or environmental consultants. No moneys have been used to clean anything. Hutchins is a model, a microcosm of this CERCLA absurdity that is metastasizing like cancer cells through the body of America.

"When we speak of Hutchins as a microcosm, every element is there. First, the finding of pollution accomplished through a simple real estate transfer. Then a year of conspiracy to select a fall guy with deep pockets. Enter the state agency, the Massachusetts Department of Environmental Protection, with power but no public funding to do their job. This led to the confrontation between parties, all of whom needed to avoid the astronomically high cost of cleanups.

"At this point there was no choice but to call in the lawyers. The lawyers were accompanied by opportunistic environmental experts who were generally grand fathered into the profession because the environment is a new science. All these were followed by insurance companies dragged in claiming, 'no coverage.'

"As you listen, you will see that Hutchins' story is a long playing tragedy with no climax or resolution. The Greek chorus in the background keeps chanting the words, polluter, shame, liar, failure, bankruptcy and carcinogen. Eight years of uncertainty with no end in sight. Hutchins' story is important in that it is being played and will be played over and over again in America. Very little will be cleaned up and litigators will take the major share of moneys devoted to environmental remediations.

"Of course, that's OK with me and fine with the associations of trial lawyers. It shows that in America today, there is as much pain in law as in war, love and medicine. Zeus, this didn't happen by chance, lobbying or revolution. Legislators could not conceive of such a fiendish law. It must be obvious to you that my stamp as lawyer god is all over it."

This brought a quick response from Zeus, "Muse don't force me into a quick decision. I'll admit that Hutchins' story is bizarre. However, it was stated that tort law has been used successfully in America for years to resolve civil disputes involving automobiles, malpractice and property damage. What's the difference with environmental disputes?"

The Muse answered, "You should understand Zeus that the disputes to which you refer are usually between individuals. For example, one American citizen hits another citizen's automobile causing damage. Tort law is a method whereby the parties bring their arguments before the courts to determine the responsible party. With medical malpractice, it may be a client in dispute with a doctor. Most of the time, the damaged party is paid for damages or restitution.

"However, CERCLA was passed into law with the goal of preventing and cleaning up hazardous waste spills in America. The concept was that irreparable damage was and is being done to citizens. To most people, Superfund meant that the government would clean up hazardous waste sites. After the cleanup when the danger abated, the government would attempt to find those responsible and seek reimbursement for the government.

"When Congress failed to vote the huge sums needed to fund all the remediation; the cart was put before the horse. With no money for cleanups, the states and federal government started to use those parts of the law that forced citizens to do the cleanup. Worse still, it forced environmentalists to encourage the 'deep pockets' philosophy, which could only be exercised through tort law."

Now the Jester jumped in. "It seems simple enough to me. The guy that does the crime does the time. If the doctor screws up, he should make good. If two automobiles collide, it is best to let the courts decide who pays. Should the government pay for collision damage or if a surgeon screws up? I—don't—think—so!"

The Muse struck back, "Jester, there is something you don't know. The cost of most damage claims for both autos and malpractice is funded by groups of people who pool their money. In America, they use a system of payment called insurance. In America, over 90% of all damage claims are paid from insurance funds."

Now came the Jester, "Insurance, what is Hutchins crying about? He had insurance to pay the environmental damages."

At that point, Zeus held up his hand and said, "We'll adjourn for a while. I want to hear what Hutchins has to say about insurance. Muse, see me in my chambers. Jester, show Hutchins some heavenly hospitality."

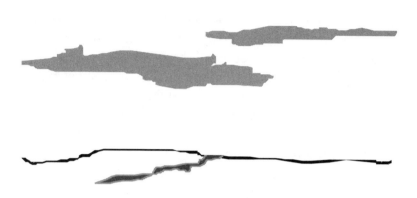

XIV.   The Jester

The Muse and Zeus were gone and I was left standing next to the Jester. While he looked like a pathetic little guy, I could see that he had a lot of spunk and spirit. I expected he would start sputtering about the way that Zeus had treated him, but I was surprised to hear him say, "That Zeus is great. He's doing pretty well considering what's been happening in the heavens."

Perhaps it was the Jester's sympathetic tone that made me ask, "What kind of problem could Zeus have, he's ruler of the gods? I don't know anything about you people, I mean you, whatever you are, but in school I read about Zeus and I remember the Greeks called him ruler of the gods. The Romans called him Jupiter, the ruler of the Roman divinities."

The Jester turned and retrieved some scattered pieces of the robe that Zeus had lightening bolted off his body. He patched his outfit together in an instant and then he turned back to me and said, "Let me show you what's happening."

In a flash, we were moving through space or maybe space was moving by us. Whatever the situation, I was looking down on things that looked like the Parthenon with water filled pools all around. At one point, we passed by what appeared to be the L.A. Coliseum. The Jester looked much better to me as we passed over the landscape. I suppose no one could look good standing beside a god like Zeus and statuesque Muse.

We stopped on a hill that resembled the third tee at the Mid Ocean Club in Bermuda. Next, he threw me a beer and snapped one open for himself. After a long swig, he said, "This is a hell of a lot better than our heavenly nectar. I started drinking beer on my first trip to Burbank. They set me up as a character actor in films and my best moments were drinking beer with the teamsters. I stopped here to give you some background before you see the junkyard."

At that point I said, "Thanks for the Bud. I really don't like those new house brews that are so expensive. I hate them even more when people get excited and ask me how I like them. I guess I'm just a blue collar type person or mortal or whatever you're calling me."

Now the Jester got serious. He said, "I'm happy that you know something about mythology and the Greek and Roman gods. You'll understand why Zeus is so agitated.

"What you called mythology is very real. Most of the time, Zeus doesn't care about mortals because they're clueless. They keep making the same mistakes over and over again. Generally, Zeus lets the other gods play with the minds of mortals. Your people are so much better suited to be guided by the lesser gods. Zeus is into order, truth, respect and responsibility. He leaves emotions like love, hate and jealousy to other gods. He lets Ares encourage wars on Earth. Aphrodite does her thing and Dionysus raises hell with the lives of mortals. But, about every 1500 earth years, Zeus gets involved.

"What Zeus likes to do is put his stamp on a civilization. He puts order into a society and caps it off with slight homage to himself and the other divinities. Can you guess the societies he has chosen in the last 4,500 years?"

The question surprised me. What did I know about Zeus and his deities? I responded to the Jester with some bitterness in my voice, as I said, "Jester, I'm a Christian, a Catholic, you know we don't believe all those myths. What can I tell you?"

At that point, the Jester leaned back and replied, "Hey man, you've got me wrong. I'm not knocking your God. I am on a different level of consciousness. I'm talking about the way you mortals look for understanding outside your faith in God. You must see it; it's all around you. Don't you have friends that go to palm readers, fortunetellers and astrologers? God is God, but earthlings need more vivid explanations. 900 telephone numbers that put people in touch with astrologers are big business in America. Americans are calling for spiritual readings all the time.

"It will take a while for you to understand, so just accept it for now. Humans need explanations for that which they don't understand and mythology fills that need."

For a moment the Jester sounded like a car salesman. Considering I had nothing to lose, I said, "Tell me about Zeus and how he gets involved with mortals every 1500 years. I'm sorry, I can't guess which civilizations were Zeus' realms."

The Jester frowned but soon resumed smiling and said, "The answer should be simple for you, Greece, Rome, and America. In each case, he found comparatively unscathed earthlings and gave them triumphant and noble civilizations. I'm sure that you studied ancient Greece and the Greek gods. Zeus even had his heroes fight for Greece in the Trojan War. About 1500 years later, Zeus selected some tribes on the Italian Peninsula and molded them into the Roman Empire. While you may laugh at the Romans, they did bring enlightenment to much of Europe and North Africa. While historians say that Romans followed the Greek tradition, we realize that Rome was a reincarnation of Greece established by Zeus. He did change the architecture a bit and renamed the lesser gods Venus, Mars, Saturn, Cupid and Neptune. At that point, he called himself Jupiter, but to us he was still Zeus.

"1500 years later, Zeus decided to become involved on earth

91

again and looked at the area around what is now Great Britain, but he found those tribes too arrogant and set in their ways. Finally, he settled on North America because it was sparsely populated with simple colonists brimming with expectations.

"Again, he established his senates and republican style governing bodies. Zeus encouraged most of the builders to utilize classic forms when building their civic temples. Things went well for a few hundred years and most muses felt at home when they came to earth and visited college campuses, city halls and the New York Stock Exchange. Scholars in America studied Latin and Greek. Speech in America can be traced to its Greek and Latin roots.

"I think Zeus found his greatest triumph when John Kennedy led America into the space age. Think of it, America was searching the heavens using equipment named Apollo, Mars, Mercury and Saturn. He gloated when NASA used his Roman name, Jupiter.

"Consider this, America is very similar to the ancient Greek and Roman civilizations. They all started with simple, uncultured people who were initially influenced more by their surroundings than by their ancestry. Each of these civilizations stood almost as isolated islands of compatible people who organized themselves in self-governing groups to survive. None of these civilizations championed individualism or invested kings, monarchs and emperors until they peaked and started to decline. These communal groups were called such names as tribes or parishes and were led by respected elders. Combinations of parishes organized themselves at a higher level with governing bodies named senates, councils, town meetings or assemblies. All three had an architecture that was basic, clean and majestic with a wide use of columns.

"Early in each of these Greek, Roman and American civilizations, there was respect for authority, strong family ties, and a special feeling for heroes or heroics. It was only in decline that the people of Greece and Rome became infatuated with the occult, scandal and massive entertainments, like the circuses.

"Hutchins, you may not recognize the hand on Zeus upon

America, but you can not deny the similarity to ancient Greece and Rome. You grew up learning of Washington and Lincoln as honest, strong and dedicated leaders. Sculptures and artists often posed Washington as a Roman senator.

"America used Greek divinities as models for comic book heroes. Superman is no more than an airbrushed-Mercury. Even American movies have been captured by Zeus' magic with such characters as Apollo Creed in the *Rocky* movies.

"I believe that Zeus became somewhat disillusioned with America when he saw it change. All of a sudden, there were no heroes in America. Defaming leaders, athletes and clerics became public sport. *Life* magazine with its brilliant photographs declined and the gossipy *People* magazine replaced it.

"Cities in America rushed to finance magnificent stadiums just as the Romans had done in their decline. Inane wrestlers became the modern gladiators acting to distract people from lives that had become meaningless. I was sure that Zeus saw America's decline in the same light as he had seen in that of Greece and Rome. I believed that Zeus was ready to throw in the towel and let America fall into the same sad state as ancient Greece and Rome.

"I was wrong. I was dead wrong! Actually, Zeus told me he is not ready to accept the idea that America is a civilization in decline. I didn't believe him until I followed him and saw the scrap heap. You'll have to see it to believe it. Come on, let's go."

The Jester flipped his beer can into the air and it evaporated from sight. He motioned to me and I flipped mine and it did the same. I thought this is a dream, these divinities never miss hitting a bucket with the empties. As I was in mid-thought, I found myself flying beside the Jester again. As we flew, the green grassy hills transitioned into a flat desert type plain. Keep-out signs started popping up. It was almost like seeing an abandoned airbase in Arizona or New Mexico.

Coming up on the horizon were objects that looked like silos except they were not all vertical. They stood at different angles and some appeared horizontal on the horizon. It was like seeing many hexapods huddled together.

Moments later, we were in the midst of this rubble or junkyard as the Jester called it. I recognized some of these massive objects as starships, missiles and unbelievably huge space stations. It was as if we had come upon a massive movie studio back lot where old sets and props were wasting away. While it was much less organized, it had the appearance of the desert in Arizona where they store old aircraft.

There was no sign of life. No humans, gods, divinities or any moving creature, just those massive, silent, metal monuments. Then the Jester broke the silence, "Hutchins, don't say anything. I know that when I saw this, I couldn't believe it. There was nothing I could do but look. When you're ready, I'll show you what bent Zeus out of shape."

Now we were moving again flying over miles of this space rubble. When the end was in sight, we swooped down to a small roofless building that looked like a computer lab. There were rows of terminals, screens, plotters and digitizers. A few were Digitals, and Suns, but most had a Silicon Graphics logo. Again, there were no gods or bodies present. It looked like someone had just shut down the power and walked out.

"Now you know," said the Jester. "I guess if I was Zeus, I would be upset too. I never met this Lucas, but he's sure giving Zeus a run for his money."

I couldn't help myself. I just blurted out, "What are you saying, I don't understand any of this."

"Sorry earthling," replied the Jester. "I forgot that mortals lack some of our godly reasoning. Let's head back because they'll be waiting for us. I'll fill you in on the way."

As we flew, the Jester said, "You remember that I was sent on an assignment to Burbank, California. My job was to check out the movie industry for Zeus. Zeus was aware that movies in America are like the stage in ancient Greece. For Greece, the drama was a window to the Greek soul. Zeus knew that to keep the classic tradition going, it was important to make a mark in the American movie industry.

"I started out as a character actor to be less conspicuous while I was on my mission for Zeus. Besides, I felt more myself having a human form that was short and a little plump. Even divinities can not change their voice so in some ways character parts fit my higher pitched voice. I played street types very well, which was good because it allowed me to take parts in all types of movies.

"The Marketing Department in the heavens wanted to push heroes in America as they had done in Greece and Rome. The Greeks and Romans developed a need to explain things that they, as earthlings, did not understand. Their mythology mixed mortal life with the divine to the point where the Greek gods as heroes participated in the Trojan War.

"Unfortunately, the type of movies I was able to infiltrate dealt with drugs, crime, violence and taxi cabs with nothing very heroic. When I reported this to Zeus, he accepted my explanation with disgust. That is when he decided to send the god, Mercury to earth to encourage the spirit of heroes, morality and glory that had fallen into decline in the American civilization.

"In a short time, Mercury was very successful guiding NASA to the heavens. John Glenn, Shepard and the other early astronauts caught his attention to the point where the gods joined the astronauts on their trips to the heavens. There was a renewal and worldly acceptance of the names Venus, Apollo, Mars, Saturn, Mercury and Neptune.

"With his success with the astronauts, Zeus turned his efforts to Hollywood. His goal was to make his mark on movies and television. His first effort was to create movie illusions involving space ships. That's when he gave the order to Hephaetus, the god of fire and metalworking, to build working models of space ships, rockets, flying saucers and space stations. He ordered Hephaetus to crash some of those into the American desert so that the U.S. Air Force could learn how to make inertial guidance systems. In fact some of the divinities came back with stories about the strange appearances of earthlings they had encountered. I mean weird; some of these mortals had rings on their fingers, ears, and noses, with tattoos on various body parts. Many had hair painted to make them look younger. These mortals were putting all sorts of smoke in their lungs and poisons in their veins. Hephaetus didn't find any mortal specimens that looked like the Greek and Roman heroes.

"While Zeus was disappointed, he continued to believe that he could influence Hollywood so that the ancient heroic legends would continue. Hephaetus impressed America with his space ships and flying saucers only on the fringes of society. Mortals that saw the saucers were ridiculed and except for a small group called Trekies, no Americans warmed to his spaceship designs. That's why Zeus closed down Hephaetus 'skunk works' and funded the computer graphics laboratory that we just visited."

When the Jester paused, I asked, "You mean all those graphic work stations, digitizers and editors we just saw?"

"That was it," said the Jester. "That was the real disaster for Zeus. That's where he bought the farm. He's still in a deep funk over that one."

I couldn't resist asking, "Why, what was the problem?"

"Lucas," said the Jester, "this mortal Lucas bested Zeus at his own game. He not only moved Americans away from the Greek tradition; he created a new set of deities for Americans to admire. Don't you agree?"

Just as I started to gather my thoughts to digest what he had said and answer his question, we descended back into the court. We were just in time because Zeus was mounting the podium. However, by now I could not help myself. Rather than take my seat, I walked by the Jester and in a low voice I whispered to the Jester, "What new set of deities?"

At this the Jester answered, "Luke Skywalker, Princess Leia, Obe Won Kanobe."

When I looked surprised, the Jester continued in a voice that may have carried to Zeus, "Yoda, Darth Vader, these are America's heroes today. Don't take it from me, ask Mattel, Milton Bradley and Hasbro who's selling? I'd sure like a piece of that action."

Now the Muse took her place. Zeus pounded his fist on the pedestal and signaled that my examination should continue. But before he started, Zeus looked up and bellowed, "Jester, I sense you showed Hutchins my relics. Just to set the record straight, I don't feel that this Yoda or Darth Vader will last. Great civilizations need great heroes. It's a sad thing that we even have to talk about Yoda, Darth Vader and lawyers. We lost a small battle to this mortal Lucas. However, I doubt that Americans are so blind as to worship two-dimensional graphic depictions like these figures that Lucas deified. It's a fad.

"Now we shall try to answer the question of whether lawyers are responsible for loss of respect and reason in America. Evidently, the Muse thinks that Mr. Hutchins will show us that lawyers are now contributing to this decline. I'm willing to weigh the facts. Go on Mr. Hutchins, please tell us about environmental insurance."

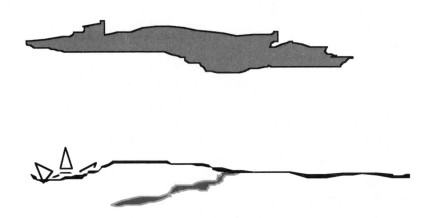

XV. Insurance

Things had moved so quickly, I had difficulty focusing. My mind was still jumping with the trip to the dump and the Jester naming the Yoda and Darth Vader America's new gods. To collect my thoughts, I decided to read sentences from the DEP's Notice of Responsibility that I thought were relevant. I started to repeat the sentences out loud as I continued my testimony, "Hutchins Tool engaged in activities that may have caused or contributed to the contamination of the Site...Notice of Responsibility says liability is strict, meaning it is not based on fault. It is also joint and several, meaning that you may be liable for all response action costs, even if there are other parties who are also liable. Also, Hutchins may be liable for up to three (3) times all the Department's response action costs."

"Zeus, while I know that these words came as a form letter out of a word processor, my experience told me this was serious business. As I would do with any threat of liability, I contacted Hutchins Tool's attorney and also our insurance agent.

"Hutchins Tool had done business with our insurance broker, Chase, Clarke & Stewart for forty years through three generations. The younger generation of Clarkes and Stewarts currently manage the Agency and I'm happy to say that in forty years, Hutchins Tool had made no major insurance claims.

"When I called Bob Stewart, Sr., who had taken over Hutchins Tool's accounts from Arthur Clarke, he told me that policies had changed with regard to environmental liability between the 1960's and 1990's. The more current policies have exclusions limiting coverage on environmental damage while the older policies had few, if any, such exclusions.

"Policies had changed gradually so that there was a good chance that we would be covered on policies written during the 1970's. Stewart said that his office didn't archive old policies and the insurance companies do not admit to maintaining outdated records, my best bet was to find copies of the old policies.

"That's when I learned that even though my mother was dead, she was still watching over her son and the books of Hutchins Tool. Fortunately, I found policies for the 1972 through 1979 time period in a safe deposit box where she had placed them for safekeeping. Better still, they had no coverage limitations for damage caused by chemicals, toxic substances, etc.

"When Bob Stewart, Sr. reviewed the policies, he agreed with my interpretation and filed a claim with the carrier, New Hampshire Insurance. A conglomerate, AIG, had purchased New Hampshire Insurance some years earlier but the Company was still active and the claims were acknowledged.

"I received a letter from the AIG claims department registering the Panama Street claim and agreeing to provide a defense. Unfortunately, the response continued by saying that New Hampshire Insurance was defending 'With reservation of rights.' When questioned on the meaning of this reservation, the insurance claims department responded by saying that all environmental claims are defended with such reservation of rights. Essentially, it means that they will underwrite the cost of defending but pay for damages only under specific conditions depending on the wording of the policy.

"Crazy? I think so. Would an insurance company put up the best defense if it felt it would not have to pay if the insured lost the case? I had never heard of an insurance company defending with reservation of rights. The first information that lawyers seek in automobile cases is the coverage of the responsible party. If most Americans knew that their automobile insurance carriers could defend with reservation of rights, they would go ballistic.

"When these policies were written in the 1970's, Hutchins Tool was flush with cash. For each year there were two policies each of which recognized that we were leasing space on Panama Street. The first policy was a basic corporate blanket that covered fire, property damage, liability, etc. The second policy was rather unique in that it was an umbrella policy protecting the officers and Corporation from liability above and beyond the basic package. Arthur Clarke, who sold me the policy, said during his sales presentation, 'You never know, maybe your company car hits a vehicle carrying four beautiful young girls. What would a jury award to restore their beauty? It could be well above your auto limits and Hutchins Tool would have to pay the excess over the limits. Or maybe you, as an officer of the Company, slander somebody. You should be aware that it might take lots of money to settle that kind of case.'

"As I have said, Hutchins Tool was doing well in the 1970's so we could afford the best insurance coverage. This policy was sold for umbrella protection against almost any damage we could do to another person or business. That's the way Arthur Clarke understood the policy and as he understands it today. He may be over 80 years old, but he and Bob Stewart, Sr. have stated that their understanding as sales representatives for New Hampshire Insurance is that we are covered for any damages due to negligence on Panama Street.

"It is easy to see why insurance companies want to limit their exposure to remediation claims. They do not want to pay the cost of cleaning up pollution all over America. By everyone's measure, these costs will be unbelievably high and well beyond the insurance industry's capacity. Quite simply, a rush of settlements would quickly bankrupt the major long time players in the industry.

"It's obvious that pollution damage did not enter the underwriters' equations when they set insurance rates prior to the CERCLA legislation. Underwriting data was available for fire, product liability, malpractice and auto accident damage, but nothing on environmental liability. Is it fair to force insurance companies to pay claims for incidents that were never considered by either the insurance companies or their clients? My reaction is that under normal policies, the answer is no, but under umbrella type policies, the answer must be yes.

"Zeus, you can see that Hutchins Tool is an example of the irrational sections of CERCLA. We are asking an insurance company to pay claims that could reach millions of dollars to clean up ground water that is probably of no risk to anyone. No technology is available to make this cleanup affordable and there is also no method to determine the cost. Therefore, we are asking an insurance company to give us a blank check to pay for remediation plus legal fees together with the thousands of dollars of uncontrolled and loosely audited expenses of the Massachusetts DEP.

"While I do not know how other insurance companies are handling pollution claims, I feel that the claims department of AIG is not on top of our claims. At the beginning, when Bill Hadley, Hutchins Tool's attorney, asked who would represent New Hampshire Insurance, their claims department said that because he was familiar with the case, he could handle it for them. This means that Hadley is serving two masters, Hutchins Tool and New Hampshire Insurance.

"I have seen little or no evidence that the AIG claims office maintains a staff familiar with its environmental case load. I expect that it would be in their best interest to understand CERCLA and the various state environmental laws. Should companies like

Hutchins start losing in the courts, this will open a floodgate for others to hold insurance companies liable for coverage all over the country. Because the environmental laws have not been severely tested, there is only a limited amount of case law. During the past seven years, this Panama Street case has been on the cutting edge. Legally, everything is gray and untested. If I were AIG, I would have the best lawyers in Massachusetts contribute to Hutchins Tool's defense effort. Unfortunately, AIG does not understand their vulnerable position as a defender for Hutchins Tool. A large number of environmental judgments going against AIG could send them on the road to insolvency.

"Zeus, I'm sorry to belabor these insurance issues, suffice to say that I was flabbergasted to hear that most environmental claims are defended by insurance companies while reserving their rights to pay claims. Actually, it has worked for AIG because they have paid Attorney Hadley fees of over $200,000 for our defense while they have not paid any claims. I am sure it is cheaper for them to keep defending rather than to settle.

"As long as the AIG is in the defense mode, their assets are collecting interest and dividends. For example, if they had paid a damage claim of $200,000 in 1991, those assets would be gone. By not paying claims early and allowing litigation to continue, they pay legal defense fees continually, but retain the earning power of their assets. They may have paid Hadley $200,000 over the past eight years, but they were paying those fees out of investment earnings and continue to retain the $200,000. Also, chances are good that by denying coverage or reaching a small settlement, they may never lose most of their $200,000 original asset that they continued to hold in the claim reserve account.

"The frightening part is that Attorney Hadley is making a good living with environmental litigation fees as have the other lawyers. As long as insurance companies keep the defense going, lawyers are happy to be receiving their fees monthly."

The Muse jumped up and shouted, "That's my point, Zeus. When it comes to insurance company involvement, the remediation sections of CERCLA are imponderable. They make no sense. To become lawyer god, I, the Muse, convinced various trial lawyer associations to lobby for those sections of the law that would cause the most litigation. As Hutchins has said, the insurance company has paid his own lawyer, Attorney Hadley, massive fees. While Hadley may agree with Hutchins in private conversation that such things as strict liability and joint and several are unfair, he has been enriched by the system. It's a lot better than making a few dollars with automobile tort cases where insurance companies have years of experience and generally settle quickly."

Zeus pounded the podium. "OK Muse, we recognized that you may have played a part in pushing the CERCLA legislation. It is also evident that Hutchins' attorney has found a good thing, but please let Mr. Hutchins continue."

An explanation entered my head that might explain the high legal fees for environmental law. I turned toward Zeus and said, "I read once what an automobile would cost if a buyer went to an auto parts supplier and purchased all the parts separately and then had a mechanic assemble them into a complete unit. When you add the individual part prices like $2.00 screws, $400.00 transmission, $5.00 windshield wipers, etc. together, one automobile could cost a million dollars to build.

"Litigation is much the same. A lawyer can price body parts such as eyes, arms, legs, etc. in settlements so high that an assembled human body could cost millions of dollars. As another example, couples could have a dysfunctional marriage, but in the hands of a 'good lawyer,' consortium between the two could be worth two million dollars if it were lost. Juries can be convinced by lawyers that a mortal's life and love has unlimited value."

Now the Jester broke in, "I know those things happen in America. When I was assigned to Burbank, California, I had this palimony lawsuit. Had to pay some lawyer a bundle to get a settlement. Hey Muse, you want to claim responsibility for those California palimony laws?"

The Muse shot back, "No, but Aphrodite is the goddess of love and she may make the claim. She's recognized as a goddess. Why shouldn't I be the lawyer god?"

The Jester smiled and said in a mischievous voice that sounded like locker room bragging, "Sweet Muse, I am afraid the goddess of love didn't visit California when I was there. I sat at the feet of that Roman god, Bacchus. Not to bust your cookies Muse, but the Romans had no lawyer gods either. Most of those legal types were fed to the lions in the Coliseum. They certainly weren't looked upon as heroes."

This brought a smile to Zeus' face. I think he enjoyed the Jester. Then he looked at me and said, "Mr. Hutchins, you have brought us up to 1991 when Hutchins Tool was served a legal Complaint from the owner, Thompson. Certainly, even in America earthlings have to accept responsibility for poisoning others. A society can not function without rules. How could Hutchins Tool expect to use cancer causing solvents and cancer causing oils in an unsafe manner and not pay the consequences? Can you answer that question, Mr. Hutchins?"

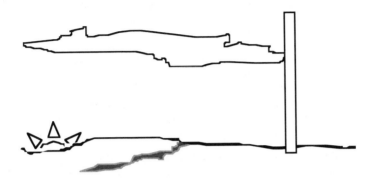

XVI.   Carcinogens

With Zeus' accusation that I had poisoned people, that same sick, empty and frustrated feeling came over me that had visited so many times since Ms. Symington of the DEP referred to Hutchins Tool as a responsible party. The loathing in her voice continues to haunt me.

I could hear my voice crack as I replied to Zeus, "Your honor, I mean Zeus, my conscience is clear, I poisoned no one. I'm sure throughout history mortals died of cancer. However, it is only in the last 50 years that the word cancer has gained the reputation of being a massive killer of mankind. I'm a simple citizen and am not knowledgeable about the causes of cancer. I can't recall if I've read that any historical figures like Jefferson, Washington or Napoleon died of cancer. Perhaps Madame Curie had a cancer caused by using radioactive substances like radium.

"In this generation cancer is the big "C" in America. It not only kills, but much pain and suffering can come before death. Cancer has no respect for age in that many young Americans and babies have died from such cancers as leukemia. There are also many different cancers that can affect almost any part of the body, from skin to the prostate. There are cancer cures and remissions, but cancers can attack again with little warning.

"I am totally sympathetic to those that suffer from cancer. I understand the damage this sickness can do to families and to the lives of those that have the disease. But, except for donating to cancer research and following rules of prevention and detection prescribed by medical authorities, there is very little I can do to fight the disease. I have to look upon cancer as another of life's trials in the same way that I look at auto accidents and heart disease.

"Given this view, you can imagine my disdain at those humans who would either knowingly or through ignorance, brand me a killer. Cancer has been called the silent killer, but those writers and politicians who have put a scarlet letter on my chest are responsible for causing me irreparable harm with their voices of suspicion.

"There are very few things that can scare mortals more than cancer. It is not surprising that Americans have great fear of anything that is suspected of causing cancer. Unlike heart disease, automobile accidents, war and other causes of death, cancer is not obvious. Mortals can understand that an overweight person could expect a heart problem or that a drunk driver could die from an auto accident, but whom do you blame for cancer? There are few indications of how or when the disease starts or how long it has lain dormant in the body.

"Cancer is scary and scary things cause mortals to panic. While we usually think of panic as fast moving, loud and explosive, it can also be quiet and gnawing. Cancer causes this nervous, gnawing panic. The fear of cancer is always there."

Now the Muse jumped up. "You see Zeus, the fear of cancer was the foundation for my campaign. I used this panic described by Hutchins as a tool in my scheme to multiply litigation opportunities for American lawyers."

Zeus pounded his fist on the podium. "Muse, sit down, we want to hear Hutchins deny that he has spread cancer causing substances through the bowels of the earth."

I was surprised at Zeus' dramatics and upset that he continued to accuse me. However, I decided to be calm and attempt to explain the ambiguousness in that word carcinogen, so I said, "When Hutchins Tool was first named by the Massachusetts Department of Environmental Protection as a responsible party, I started to feel like a guilty person. It was similar to my first days in the Air Force boot camp. The system gets to you very quickly so that within hours you lose much of your identity and you become a changed person.

"With regard to this environmental problem, I was filled with immense defensiveness. I had never dumped any solvents. I had never ordered or seen any solvents dumped.

"I'm the type of fastidious person who hangs up clothes and picks up paper thrown on the sidewalk. I don't throw things out the car window or leave empty popcorn boxes on the floor of a movie theater.

"Of course, the doubts would creep in. Could any of my workers have poured solvent behind the Panama Street plant? Where did it come from? The truth is that I will never be totally certain of the answers to these questions. However, I came to realize that if the primary goal of the environmental movement is to remove the danger; that is where emphasis should be placed by both the public and private sectors. The overemphasis on assigning blame has diverted the environmental movement from its goal of providing a safe environment for citizens.

"For example, I saw no remediation effort coming from the DEP at the Panama Street site as evidenced by the fact that in the first two years no clean up had been started. The reality was that an outside force was dominating all the actions taking place at the site and that dominant force was environmental law.

"Think about it. If a fire is burning, the first reaction by humans should be to pull people to safety and extinguish the fire. The DEP was not keeping people away from the polluted brook or cleaning the pollution from the brook. Public safety had taken a back seat to the machinations of a cast of actors playing out some sort of legal ritual. In the years that have passed since that time, it has been my mission to discover just what was behind this drama unfolding before me.

"I realized that the experts at the local DEP office and the lawyers knew almost immediately that there was no imminent danger at Panama Street. Under such circumstances, why was I being persecuted? Was this charade being played for me and repeating itself all over America to delude people into believing that government was providing an effective anti-pollution effort?

"I have found that many people who may be considered experts, have only a superficial knowledge concerning things where they are presumed to have expertise. Scratch the surface and you'll find that you are dealing with paper tigers. While people place politicians and lawyers high on the list of paper tigers, it also exists in the industries of software and manufacturing where I spend most of my working hours.

"Zeus, at first, I believed what I was told. If experts at the DEP said that toxic substances were in the ground water on Panama Street and they posed an imminent danger to human life and health, they must be right. They should know because they were the experts.

"Actually, I have learned since that time that the DEP is staffed with mortals who act as marionettes. For the most part they follow lists and guidelines as faithful serfs. Just as I had found in other industries, much of the environmental industry is a massive paper tiger that uses a framework of half-truths to force an illusion on America.

"After Hutchins Tool was accused by the DEP, I began to investigate carcinogens. What are they? Who did the scientific investigation? How many carcinogens had been discovered? What is the methodology used to determine an agent to be a carcinogen?"

Now the Jester broke in, "That's easy, when I was on assignment in Burbank, California, I knew that the U.S. Government had a list of carcinogens. What more is needed? The federal government must know. They have test labs. What's your answer to that, Mr. Hutchins?"

"Jester, you are correct," I said. "I learned that the Occupational Safety and Health Administration (OSHA) regulates a number of carcinogens through scientific standards, but they do not have their own scientific labs studying carcinogenic agents. They rely on data from the Internal Agency for Research of Cancer (IARC) and/or the National Toxicological Program (NTP)."

Back came the Jester, "Mr. Hutchins, you're just splitting words. So OSHA and the EPA have no labs. I'm sure that IARC and NTP can produce accurate lists of carcinogens."

Now it was my turn to take the offensive, "Jester, it depends on how you define the word carcinogen. In this case, both IARC and NTP did what you accuse me of doing. They split the word into categories:

The IARC categories are:

Group 1: **The agent is carcinogenic to humans.**

Group 2A: **The agent is probably carcinogenic to humans.**

Group 2B: **The agent is possibly carcinogenic to humans.**

The NTP categories are:

Group 1: **Substances or groups of substances that are known to be carcinogenic**

Group 2: **Substances or groups of substances and medical treatments that may reasonably be anticipated to be carcinogenic**

111

"So you see Jester, I learned that there are very few agents which bear tenable scientific proof of being carcinogens. Most agents on the federal lists are only anticipated to be cancer causing in humans. Those are not my words, but the words of the test labs that do the testing."

Again the Jester, "Hey Hutchins, proof, no proof, what's the difference? Would you want to be exposed to anything that may cause cancer? Why take the chance?"

"Jester, I agree with that part of your thinking," I said. "I do not want to ingest or be exposed to anything that places my health or life at risk; but we mortals are not like you gods. We get sick, we get injured, we die and we understand these things to be a part of life. For mortals risk is a part of life.

"We have fairly strong proof that sunlight, asbestos fibers and tobacco smoke cause different types of cancer. Humans continually weigh the risk/reward factors in dealing with these substances. We continually weigh risks and make life style choices. Do you suggest that humans should never leave their homes during the day to avoid sunlight? Most of us would prefer death to a life deprived of being outdoors during the daytime.

"The important thing I learned was that on the federal level, distinction is made as to the risk level of materials called carcinogenic. To use the word in the context of an "absolute" is a disservice to the environmental effort and has caused billions of American dollars to be misdirected. Wars to protect the environment under CERCLA have been fought in the wrong places, at the wrong times and by the wrong troops.

"Lawyers are currently the troops fighting for a cleaner environment. Unfortunately, lawyers do not have the skills, equipment or knowledge to wage the cleanup wars. Moneys that have been spent on lawyers should have gone to persons and equipment that can actually clean up the environment."

When I looked over, the Muse was beaming. I thought that she would jump up and say something, but she didn't. By mentioning the flow of dollars to lawyers, I realize that I had unintentionally helped plead her case.

Zeus looked down with great interest. When he spoke, it was not with a bellow. In a reserved voice, he said, "Mr. Hutchins, do you believe the EPA has been deceptive?"

I thought for a moment and said, "No, they were required by CERCLA to publish a list of hazardous agents, so the categorized lists from IARC and NTP filled that requirement. For that, they can not be faulted. The truth was there for anyone who wanted to understand it. The published lists are not in themselves deceptive, but they were and continue to be very exploitable and political."

"By political I mean that the EPA has always been staffed by people who had a certain attitude about pollution, polluters and the environment. As a result, the EPA allowed the lists to be misinterpreted by the press, legal profession and state agencies without attempting to clarify those errors of understanding."

Now the Muse could not stand it. She jumped up and said, "That's it, political. Now do you see it? I set those policies in action. As Hutchins goes on, you'll see that I got into America's head. I gave Americans just what they wanted. I scared the hell out of them and sent them on a witch hunt to find a culprit, whether it was a cancer causing agent, medical procedure, life style or another citizen, that could be blamed."

When the Muse ended, I started speaking again, "When I realized that *carcinogenic* was a misnomer for a whole litany of possibilities, I questioned how the State of Massachusetts handled those categories from IARC and the NTP. I found that the pressure from Massachusetts' citizens and also the federal government forced the state legislature to conform to many of the federal guidelines contained in CERCLA. With very few dissents, Massachusetts passed MGL Chapter 21E and bedeviled it with the same fallacies and ambiguities as CERCLA.

Now the Muse spoke, "Not bedeviled, Hutchins, beMused; I'm responsible."

I didn't react to the Muse's little pun because I wanted to say more about the understanding of the word carcinogen in Massachusetts. Therefore, I said, "Because MGL 21E was written in haste, the legislators and Governor delegated most of the decision making power to the Department of Environmental Protection (DEP). The 21E legislation bundles carcinogens into a massive category called 'hazardous material.' This allowed the DEP to pick and chose from about any substance on earth.

"Now the DEP in its wisdom went to work. In an effort, which might be characterized as sloppy, they collected data for a few years and finally by 1989 had a list of 565 items, many of which were footnoted by the category, "c" for carcinogen. I suppose the decision-makers said, 'What the hell, why make it hard on ourselves? Let's just combine any list we can get our hands on. We have no lab to verify the accuracy of the lists one way or the other. Let's go for it.'

"Massachusetts included agents suggested by nine different sources: IARC, OSHA, NTP, ACGIN, NFPA49, NFPA325N, CAG, EPA, and NCI. With one sweep of the pen, or in this case a word processor, Massachusetts anointed a minimum of 565 items with the name hazardous. The DEP has given Massachusetts' attorneys, bankers, DEP employees and Licensed Environmental Professionals a list of 565 items that Massachusetts' citizens call carcinogens with no defining categories. At the same time, OSHA has a list of 27, that they consider proven carcinogens.

"All a Massachusetts lawyer has to do is refer to any of those 565 items to designate a person to be a polluter. Did the accused polluter buy it, store it or transport it? These are the only questions that need asking. A Massachusetts company that stores one of the 565 is just as responsible for damages as a company that admits to spilling all of the 565. This empowerment of DEP officials and Massachusetts' litigators in my estimation is unconscionable. I'd happily tar and feather any of the DEP officials that did not have the guts to do the right thing and create a more definable list. Many Massachusetts citizens have suffered because of the

DEP's negligence in not producing a list based on scientific evidence."

Zeus banged his fist on the podium and said, "Mr. Hutchins, I understand your frustration. You must avoid these outbursts. I am sure the DEP officials were simply trying to touch all the bases. Certainly, they did not want to place the people of Massachusetts at risk. Is it so wrong to list every possibility even if many of the agents on the list are not scientifically proven carcinogens? Public officials must be responsible."

"I came back swinging and said, "Let me tell you just how concerned and responsible those boys were. Among items listed by IARC as carcinogens were tobacco smoke, marine diesel fuel, fuel oil and gasoline. You must remember that IARC was one of two agencies that actually ran lab tests for the federal government. They also furnished their list to Massachusetts. It is interesting to note that tobacco smoke, marine diesel fuel, fuel oil and gasoline did not make the Massachusetts' list of 565 hazardous substances."

"While you do not live in Massachusetts, you should be aware that political influence is part of the Massachusetts' lifestyle. There is no question that strong lobbies kept these four items off the Massachusetts' list."

Now I could see that Zeus had settled back and started to slowly shake his head and rub his eyes with his great hand. He looked up and said, "Mr. Hutchins, I can understand why you are angry. Placed in the same position, I would also vent my feelings."

Zeus' words calmed me down. This was good in that I was about to talk about perchloroethylene, one of the agents found in the groundwater at Panama Street and one of the agents that was bringing Hutchins Tool down. Then I replied to Zeus, "Zeus, I'm sorry, it's just that nobody understands. When I get someone to listen, I get a little carried away.

"I can recall that after I studied the federal and state lists of carcinogens and found those discrepancies, I expected Bill Hadley, our attorney, would be happy to hear. I thought it would give him strong arguments to be used in our defense. What could be better than saying in court that the Massachusetts DEP was jostling with windmills? That the DEP's concerns of agents dangerous to the public's health and safety in the Panama Street groundwater may have no basis in scientific fact.

"I brought the subject up with Hadley at lunch in Boston after he deposed a representative of Safety Kleen, Inc. a solvent recycler. To my amazement, Attorney Hadley's reaction was simple and direct. He said that as an attorney in Massachusetts, he had to litigate under MGL Chapter 21E. If a state agency had a list calling the agents found on Panama Street hazardous, that classified them as hazardous waste under the eyes of the law. If the State said they are carcinogens, he would be unsuccessful arguing against that list in court.

"It was at that point that I started to question how my lawyer was representing me and Hutchins Tool. It was then that I realized that he was not a creative thinker. He was a journeyman who worked at the law, as other workers would man a machine. Turn it on, follow the rules, make the parts and turn it off. Hadley's a nice guy, very honest and hard working. As I see it, while he is doing his best for us, most of his creative juices in the Panama Street case have been spent on trying to collect fees from New Hampshire Insurance. Our file folder shows a 5 to 1 ratio of copies of collection letters to the insurance claims office compared to other letters from Hadley related to Panama Street.

"Sometime after this lunch with Attorney Hadley, I studied the federal and state lists to see how perchloroethylene, the commercial name for one of the pollutants found on Panama Street, was categorized. The State of Massachusetts made it easy for me because perchloroethylene carried a "c" standing for carcinogen.

"On the federal list ARC places perchloroethylene as 2B, "The agent is possibly carcinogenic to humans." This is the least critical of the three categories. This hit me like a brick. The DEP was calling for cleanup of perchloroethylene found in groundwater in one well with a maximum of 6,000 parts per billion and with other wells drilled on the property showing little or nothing. The readings for the water in the brook, which placed the Site on the highest Massachusetts' priority list, showed few, if any signs of the chemical.

"A half million dollars in remediation fees have gone to attorneys and consultants and nothing has been cleaned up on the Panama Street site. This money could have gone to cancer research where every reasonable American would agree it would do more good.

"For years people in Massachusetts have been ingesting gasoline fumes and tobacco smoke which IARC considers a greater hazard. Why would such effort and attention be placed on Panama Street? The answer is that unenlightened bureaucrats compound a mild risk factor established in Washington into a major danger by the time it hits the provinces. Like a lie being told enough times to be understood as a truth.

"If CERCLA was litigated under criminal statutes, fines would be the punitive instruments used to carry out public policy. Under tort law, any lawyer can use the peoples' ignorance as to the true danger of pollutants as a club or wedge to gain a competitive advantage. When used by Massachusetts' lawyers, the word hazardous agent can be used interchangeably to denote the most dangerous form of poison such as mustard gas or for oil used as a lubricant in automobiles."

I think Zeus had started to feel my pain because he looked down at me and said, "Mr. Hutchins, I realize that life on earth is not simple. Perhaps some day, the causes of cancer will be known and all this will pass. I'm sorry to see your business die. It is also painful to see the earth's wealth being diverted to lawyers rather than being spent to eradicate health problems. It's easy for me to understand that every dollar spent for lawyers has no benefit for other mortals. Did your studies on environmental issues reveal any other unusual situations?"

I paused for a moment and then pulled a folded newspaper clipping from my wallet. It was from the December 5, 1994 issue of *The Washington Times* Newspaper. Tony Snow, a Washington based editorial page columnist for the Detroit News had written an article titled, *"Caught Crying Wolf About Carcinogens."* It reads:

>   *"The federal government has finally admitted that a huge proportion of recent environmental regulation is hooey. The confession appears in a document prepared for the Energy Department's Sandia National Laboratories.*
>
>   *"Choices in Risk Assessment: The Role of Science Policy in the Environmental Risk Process" argues that federal offices routinely rig environmental studies to protect some products and ruin others. The secret is to manipulate "science policy", which the report defines as the strategy for filling in "the gaps and uncertainties in scientific knowledge and data."*
>
>   *If regulators want to go easy on an industry, they just think positive. Uncle Sam adopted this approach in refusing to purge drinking water of fluoride, which has a far higher correlation with cancer than many banned chemicals. The reasons for the inaction are obvious: Too many people like fluoridated water, and the scientific justification for its prohibition is shamefully weak.*
>
>   *Similarly, the Environmental Protection Agency decided not to declare motor oil a toxic substance because the designation would have to set loose laws requiring motorists to obey rules designed for the disposal of things like plutonium and radioactive river sludge.*
>
>   *Unfortunately, federal agencies don't often commit this kind of common sense. Bureaucrats reverted to form last week when the Environmental Protection Agency published its latest Toxic Release Inventory -*

compilation of substances deemed so dangerous that businesses must disclose their presence in any workplace.

The roster includes nearly twice as many compounds as last year's. Many of the products on the sheet pose no measurable threat to human health - including the drug thenytoin, which has received Food and Drug Administration approval for the treatment of epilepsy.

Steven Milloy of the Regulatory Impact Analysis Project, which drafted the Energy Department report, complains that the thenytoin listing exposes the "moral and intellectual corruption in the system". The pharmaceutical has no business on the roster because it's difficult to think of a scenario in which it would harm the community at large - unless, perhaps, a user had the misfortune of detonating in a lower atmosphere and thus contaminating innocent life forms below.

But environmentalists may have ulterior motives. "This decision", Mr. Milloy explains, "lays the groundwork for placing pharmaceuticals on the toxic release inventory" - and thus giving the EPA a role in controlling which drugs get to market.

The government invites that kind of bureaucratic imperialism. Under guidelines now in effect, researchers can label virtually anything a carcinogen.

Here are a few of the more dubious assumptions, crudely paraphrased:

- *If a substance causes cancer in an animal, it will cause cancer in humans. In other words, a mouse equals a pig equals a boy.*
- *If cancers develop differently in test animals than in humans, ignore the difference.*
- *When deciding which animal specifics to use as the best predictor of cancer in*

> *humans, pick the one most prone to the disease.*
> * *When developing an estimate of cancer risk, reply on worst-case-scenarios in all available studies.*
> * *If any study shows a possible link between a compound and cancer, scientists should disregard contrary investigations. Avoid all silver linings.*
> * *The effects observed when investigators administer megadoses of a substance to an animal should be considered typical of normal human exposure.*

Using this theory, the government banned Alar because it found cancers in mice that ingested the equivalent of 80,000 bottles of apple juice a day for a lifetime.

Mr. Milloy complains: "They're chasing risks that are completely hypothetical and formalizing a process that is the equivalent of the Salem witch trials. If you tie a brick to a witch and she sinks, she's a witch. If you tie human risks to animal risks, it's a foregone conclusion that you'll predict cancer".

This approach produces bizarre policies. The Energy Department has been mulling over a plan to clean up a nuclear-bomb test site in Nevada. Authorities would use special vacuum devices to scoop up the top 4 inches of sand for hundreds of square miles around the detonation area. Then they would decontaminate the sand and spread it out again. Since the original removal would kill off the local flora, the feds would build huge greenhouses and cultivate new plants to replace the old. Yet, the sand poses no health hazard, and what little radioactivity it may contain actually could prolong life.

*Republicans plan to review risk-assessment proce-
dures soon after they take over Congress next month, so
the public can rest assured that when researchers
declare something a cancer risk they're not just crying
wolf.*

"I was so excited with the potential of this article changing public thinking and EPA policy that I sent for a copy of *Choices in
Risk Assessment* and I did gain some vital information reading
this book.   One of the eight case studies involves
tricholoroethylene, the second agent found in the ground water at
Panama Street.   When I read the study, I learned that
tricholoroethylene should be deleted from everyone's list because
scientific evidence showed it was not carcinogenic.

"Armed with this information, I approached Attorney Hadley
again and he said, 'Send me the information.' After I sent this
information, we never spoke of any of these things again. Hadley
followed the journeyman course he usually followed and pressed
the insurance company to settle with the DEP. This became more
difficult as the DEP's expenses passed the $240,000 mark, which
was the cost of departmental work on Panama Street incurred by
the DEP.

"Soon I realized that neither scientific data, common sense nor
rational thought would prevail over the DEP or Attorney Hadley's
institutionalized thinking. Americans were comfortable thinking
that the Superfund laws would provide remediation for all those
sites that polluters had created. Better still, American businesses
would pay the cleanup costs.

"I expect I was one of only a few Americans to read, *Choices in
Risk Assessment.* I felt sick when I realized that the non-scientifi-
cally grounded default assumptions in cancer risk assessment would
lead to hundreds of needless business failures in America. These
non-scientific risk assessments would become truths in courtrooms
because they have been given validity by a federal agency.

"To me, it was no different than the government's assessment of the Bay of Tonkin incident that led America further into the Vietnam War. Each was an interpretation with a purpose and the purpose was not necessarily in the best interest of American citizens."

Now the Muse stood up and stepped forward toward the podium and said, "Let's sum up what Mr. Hutchins has said about carcinogens. First, there is no scientific evidence to show that agents found in the ground water on Panama Street are carcinogenic. Even if they were carcinogenic, it would take massive amounts, far in excess of the levels found, to cause cancer in humans. Also, the bottom line is that there are no drinking water supplies for miles around the property. However, because those substances remain on the Massachusetts list of 565 items called hazardous, litigators recognize them as such. A judge will look at the list and pay no heed to risk assessment. The law is what matters and fear is what prevails.

"I raised that fear and marketed my plan to bring wealth to lawyers in America. In the case of Panama Street, it is simply a reflection of what is happening all over America. I am sure that with this evidence, I will become the lawyer god. Haven't I given Hutchins years of misery surpassing the length of most wars? Certainly, that time has been longer than most love relationships. I have caused misery that reaches the levels achieved by Aphrodite, the goddess of love, and Ares, the god of war."

Now Zeus interjected, "Muse, I agree that Hutchins has suffered from irrational legislation and that his own lawyer lacks creative juices, but you have not shown that other lawyers have benefited from CERCLA. We shall recess for a few minutes and later ask Hutchins to tell us of the other lawyers involved in the Panama Street controversy. I assume there are many lawyers involved, so we shall have insight from Hutchins on how a number of different lawyers approach these environmental laws."

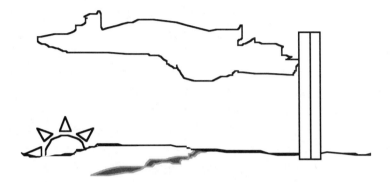

XVII.   Attorney Moore

When the Muse asked me to testify, I was uneasy. I didn't know the lawyers in the case personally. I expected they were all honest citizens, loved by their families, who went to work every day trying to do their best.

To pass the bar exam, lawyers are intelligent and above average students. To make a living, they must have the skill to create documents quickly as part of their service. Lawyers must also accept tasks that most humans would find tedious, boring and totally non-creative. Oh there may be some exceptions, but for the most part, lawyers can sleep walk through their day.

I assume lawyers must be needed in America because there are so many of them. I suppose it follows that they are not needed as much in Japan, because in Japan there are comparatively few.

Seconds later, Zeus moved off the podium and the Muse was at my side. She said, "Don't worry, you do not have to say anything personal about the lawyers on the Panama Street case, just tell Zeus how they acted in terms of the litigation. We know that you can not rate a lawyer's professional competency because you are not versed on the industry standards. Of course, you can report how they appeared to you as a layman. You don't have to slam them. Tell it like it is and if it is warranted, they'll slam themselves."

I am not comfortable talking about the failings of others. My shortcomings and weaknesses are abundant, so my style is to accept people the way they are. I suppose that I, as many Americans, have found fault with the way lawyers operate because their actions are at odds with how I expect they should act. Most lawyers, with whom I have worked, have a poor grasp of technology and lack creativity. I'm sure some of my distaste could be a jealous response to their professional stature. However, if this is the case, I question why I have no negative feelings about doctors, dentists and accountants?

Whatever my feelings, I was happy that the Muse wanted me to talk about the lawyers only as they related to the Panama Street litigation and explain how, in my eyes, they performed. With renewed confidence, I returned to my testimony by saying, "The Complaint listed Arden T. Thompson, the owner to the Panama Street property, as Plaintiff and Hutchins Tool and Precision EDM, Inc. as Defendants. Thompson was represented by Louis S. Moore, Esq., Precision EDM by Edward B. Fogarty, Esq. and Hutchins Tool by William Hadley, Esq. of Doherty, Wallace, Pillsbury and Murphy.

"I discussed Bill Hadley's involvement as our attorney a few moments ago. I have very little knowledge of Fogarty because he was on the case for a very short time. I have had a history of eight years with Moore and while I know nothing of the man personally, I can report on my observations as I followed his actions in the Panama Street litigation.

"I might as well say it up front so you know how I feel, Attorney Moore has been my worst nightmare. Personally, I know very little about him. Associates at a law firm where he previously practiced called him a Boy Scout. I think that they were referring to his eagerness to achieve merit badge type accolades from environmental advocates. Suffice to say that he appears to me to carry an excessive zealousness toward punishing polluters not shared by most attorneys. The vast majority of lawyers recognize that CERCLA type laws are designed to find funding for remediation from a deep pockets source. Eliminating pollution does not enter their equation any more than does punishing one of the partners in a divorce settlement.

"I fault Moore for not following what I believe is the spirit of MGL Chapter 21E when he did not encourage the parties to sort out the Panama Street problem prior to instituting litigation. You will recall that Moore was negotiating with Thompson, the DEP and Precision EDM for at least a year before Hutchins Tool was apprised of the pollution problem. Chapter 21E calls for the parties to exhaust all the opportunities of settlement prior to instigating litigation. It may seem unfair for me to hold Attorney Moore responsible, but, as Mr. Thompson's counsel, he was familiar with the law and well informed on the parties that he would later oppose. Perhaps if Moore had brought all the parties together early, discussed tort law as it applied to Chapter 21E, instructed the parties on legal terms such as strict liability, joint and several, and triple damages, it would have forced all the parties to press the insurance companies to pay for the cleanup.

"In 1990 remediation at the Panama Street site may have cost the insurance companies $200,000, which could have been divided between them. This is a small amount when compared to the half million dollars already paid to lawyers for litigation with the cleanup yet undone. Moore should have known that the small companies involved in Panama Street could not accept responsibility and pay for a potential million-dollar cleanup. It appears to me that Moore took aim on Hutchins Tool almost immediately. It is my opinion that he viewed Hutchins as the one company of the approximately twenty-five former tenants that had 'deep pockets.'

Now the Jester jumped up and said, "What's this 'deep pockets?' I kept hearing the phrase when people talked about movie production. They would say, 'We have no angel with deep pockets.' They showed me a photograph of an angel and she had no pockets, white wings, but no pockets."

I laughed at the Jester. I understood how this could be confusing, so I said, "By deep pockets, Americans mean an earthling who has a lot of money. Deep pockets would indicate that the person could dig deeper and deeper into his pockets and keep coming up with a continuing supply of money.

"The term angel is much more difficult to explain, so I'll tell you later. However, I think that the movie industry is similar to the financial thinking of many lawyers. Generally, most businesspersons understand finance and are capable of reading a balance sheet. However, it is not unusual for many lawyers to know very little about finance. Certainly, I can attest to a few times when I have seen lawyers having difficulty reading financial reports. This surprised me the first time it happened, but it doesn't now. I doubt the average law student has the opportunity to take a college level accounting course.

"Think of the difference between the listing for lawyers and doctors in the yellow pages of the telephone directory in most cities. Under the heading lawyers, you'll see the names of individual lawyers and law firms. Under the heading physicians, there is a notice directing readers to specialties like surgery, geriatrics, hematology, neurology, etc.

"It is difficult to pin lawyers down as to their expertise. They migrate to where opportunity leads them. They change like the chameleon to blend with the needs of the moment."

Now, Zeus raised his head high and said, "You should understand that physicians are sponsored by Apollo, the god of medicine, and Asclepius, the god of healing. Lawyers have no god. The same yellow pages will show lawyers in garish ads selling themselves like used car salesmen. The doctors follow the classic tradition and are recognized under Greek and Roman names for their specialties. Jester, do you want to speak?"

I could see the Jester fidgeting and his mouth quivering as if he had something to say. I guess this is why Zeus gave him the opportunity to speak that he accepted by saying, "Lawyers are democratic and they have a spirit that says that you are what you are. Lawyers shouldn't be confined to the same kind of tradition as doctors. Let them freelance. Let them do their thing. America is a democracy."

Now Zeus came back. "Hold on Jester, I believe that you are not thinking clearly. You spent too much time in California. Let me tell you the truth. First, the United States is a republic modeled on the Greek and Roman classic tradition.

"Most societies are established by the god, Chaos. Even Webster's Dictionary gives tribute to him by reporting that chaos is the confused state of primordial matter before the creation of orderly forms. Early Greece was chaotic. To survive and flourish, the early Greeks needed orderly forms and we gods gave that to them. Most of their neighbors did not invest in order and tradition so they died as civilizations. Orderly forms gave Greece and Rome hundreds of years of stability and allowed them to thrive. When the classic gods moved on, Chaos returned to fill the vacuum and those civilizations died.

"Democracy is an opiate for the American people which gives them a surrealistic view of their world. Ask 100 different mortals and you'll get 100 different explanations of what the word democracy means. For some mortals, it means they are all equals, which to us gods is patently ridiculous. For mortals to believe they are all created equals is one of the myths that is spread by politicians to keep Americans in chaotic servitude. Reason, which is the realm of the gods, encourages orderly forms to insure a society's survival. Order is what I brought to America. It must be supported by respect and noble deeds and enhanced with heroes for the American civilization to prosper. Americans must learn that the reputations of its heroes must be jealously guarded. We understand in the heavens that moral weaknesses should not discredit the great achievements of our deities."

With that, Zeus sat back satisfied. It didn't appear to me that the Jester understood what Zeus had said. To be honest, I didn't understand all of it myself, but when I thought of the Watts' riots, the homeless and the nightly shootings in America's cities, I realized that order was an under used and unappreciated word in twentieth century America.

I tried to get back on track with my testimony. I hoped that they now understood that, except for patent law, American lawyers do not represent themselves to the public as specialists. Generally, a client is tied to one lawyer or one law firm. Many times, this leads to the client's interest being poorly represented. Rarely does a law firm refer clients to another attorney even if they know the client will be given better representation by a competitor. The bottom line is that lawyers generally protect what they have above the opportunity to give service. In my opinion, there is more malpractice in the legal field than in medicine, but what lawyer will take a case against an associate?

As I see it, Attorney Moore did a disservice to all the parties involved in Panama Street for not encouraging discussion prior to litigation. In that spirit, I continued my testimony by saying, "After serving both Hutchins Tool and Precision EDM with a summons initiating the lawsuits, Moore returned to the courthouse with a motion to attach Hutchins Tool's buildings and assets in the amount of $600,000.

"Attachments are very strong documents in the American court system. By registering an attachment at the Registry of Deeds, the attachment essentially ties up any sale of real estate and equipment. It severely limits a company's ability to borrow money and constricts credit when lines of credit come up each year for renewal. Essentially, an attachment is comparable to those darts that banderilleros sink into the base of the neck of a fighting bull. They lower the bull's head and prepare the bull for slaughter.

"As evidence to prove our guilt, Moore copied the claims made by Anna Symington of the DEP. In that way, what started as one DEP clerk's afternoon attempt at playing detective now had the stature of a legal document. These claims were similar to a rumor that circulates sufficiently to become a fact. To make matters worse, Attorney Moore handpicked and illuminated only the most damaging portion of Ms. Symington's accusations.

"As I felt the noose tighten, our attorney, Bill Hadley went to the judge and challenged Attorney Moore's petition on the grounds that our insurance should cover an exposure of $600,000. Fortunately, the judge accepted Hadley's argument and denied Moore's petition.

"I have always felt better taking an active interest in my affairs. I expect I suffer from that syndrome that says that to get a job done right, it's best to do it yourself. Intimidated by Attorney Moore's aggressive tactics, I began to study environmental issues while I deluded myself into believing that I could learn to understand environmental law. This delusion blinded me into thinking that I could prove that Hutchins Tool was not responsible for the problems on Panama Street. Now I know that neither responsibility nor guilt was ever a relevant factor.

"I searched and copied the Panama Street file at the Springfield DEP office. One of the documents in the file showed the locations where the pollution was found both in the exploratory wells and the soil borings. I was overjoyed to see that the most damaging evidence was from a well and soil samples taken near a rear door that was blocked when we occupied the site. I later learned that this was the location where Precision EDM had cleaned parts and blew solvent off the parts allowing the misty vapors to condense on the ground.

"Our defense became even more secure when we hired a licensed environmental specialist to do a study of the data gathered by the DEP. By using computer models that involved information like soil content, depth of agents, rate of underground water flow, chemical breakdown, plus other factors, the experts were able to show that thousands of gallons of perchloroethylene would have had to be poured into the soil prior to 1979 for a residue to remain that equaled that which was found.

"Perchloroethylene as a chemical compound breaks down into

other products with time in much the same way as radioactivity dissipates. The half-life degeneration is accurate to the point where an expert could testify on Hutchins Tool's behalf that the polluting occurred after we left the property.

"Buoyed by these proofs of innocence, I suggested to Attorney Hadley that we press for a quick trial. Hutchins Tool would emerge vindicated and we could reestablish ourselves as a business.

"Unfortunately, Hadley sat me down and showed me a court tracking order which listed all the dated steps through litigation. I was appalled to find that it could be up to eighteen months before the scheduled trial.

"My bubble really burst when Hadley said that his office had researched some case law on MGL Chapter 21E. One of their findings that was being upheld by case law was the passage which said that a party could be considered responsible if it could be shown that they stored the abusing substance on the property. In other words, if it could be shown that we stored even a small container of a cleaner with perchloroethylene as an ingredient, we could be declared a responsible party. Essentially, MGL Chapter 21E, which is patterned after CERCLA, requires no evidence from the DEP showing a party is responsible for a spill; all that is needed is information showing the party may have stored the agent on the property.

"Considering the DEP has over 500 hazardous agents on its list, this leaves very few citizens free from concern if test wells are drilled near their homes or workplaces. On Panama Street alone, thousands of automobiles have parked in the parking lot over the years. There are over ten agents like antifreeze, catalytic converters, lubricants, etc. found in automobiles that could be hazardous. Should that make hundreds of workers, visitors and truckers potentially responsible? This is to say nothing of the many companies that had leased various parts of the Panama Street building through the years.

"My frustration with CERCLA and MGL Chapter 21E mounted with this news. I was incensed to learn that under the CERCLA statutes, named responsible parties would need to prove their innocence. The plaintiff did not have to prove anything except that a hazardous substance may have been brought to the site. I felt and continue to feel that the law encouraged an atmosphere of guilt by association. If criminal laws were administered in this same manner, Ryder Truck Rental would be held responsible for the Oklahoma bombing and the New York subway system would be held responsible along with Bernhard Goetz.

"Just because a lawyer can create a connection, does not make this concept morally right. I believe that it is morally wrong for the U.S. Congress to create a law that looks for scapegoats simply because Congress did not have the fortitude to vote the necessary remediation funds. M.G.L. Chapter 21E forces Hutchins Tool to pay to clean up pollution where guilt can not be proven by the evidence. More importantly, it just is not fair to bankrupt companies like Hutchins Tool, small farmers and manufacturers to underwrite the costs of cleanups to protect Americans against the boogieman."

At this point, the Jester said, "What's the boogieman?"

I replied, "Jester, the boogieman is the scary creature that rustles curtains and moves shadows before children fall asleep. The soothing words of mothers tell us that the boogieman is not real and will not hurt us. Sometimes soothing words are not enough and parents have to install 'nightlights' to allay children's fears.

"While I have never read about it, I assume that it is possible that children could die from ingesting pollution. If congresspersons agree that this threat of pollution is valid, Congress should be the 'nightlight' and not force a company like Hutchins Tool into insolvency to allay the unwarranted fears of millions of citizens. Life is a series of risks and people should be responsible only for pollution created in the present. Private citizens should not be held responsible to pay the cost of eliminating ancient environmental problems that are as elusive as the boogieman.

"It is obvious that the Massachusetts Legislature and the U.S. Congress could not find a source of funds to remediate sites that were polluted before the CERCLA legislation. However, witch-hunts to find companies with deep pockets are not the answer. I can guarantee that no one has the kinds of money needed to clean up all of America's groundwater to drinking water standards.

"Even when the Native American Indians walked the continent, all groundwater could not meet such a test. Nature itself is a polluter that constantly dissolves all sorts of animal waste and volcanic ash as part of life's cycle. Man has never been able to drink the salted ocean waters and even prior to the industrial revolution wine was a staple because most water was not of sufficient purity to drink.

"Have we read about any deaths directly attributed to humans drinking water that contained perchloroethylene? Personally, I haven't, but I have read about waterborne illness such as typhoid, cholera, amebic dysentery and hepatitis that emanate from the Ganges River, which are responsible for the deaths of over a million Indian children each year.

"Think what even a small percentage of the moneys diverted to lawyers by CERCLA would do to finance algae producing pond systems along the Ganges to eliminate the dreadful bacteria that cause these deaths. It is time for Americans to get their priorities in order and realize that sections of CERCLA are totally self indulgent and play to our politician's attempts to curry favor by being on the popular side of issues."

"What do you mean by that?" Asked the Jester. "How can you blame politicians, they are only carrying out the will of the people."

"That's the point," I responded. "Many politicians have their eye on future elections rather than reasoned legislation. The opinion of citizens at times is based on emotion rather than thoughtful consideration. Legislators must understand that it is their responsibility to understand issues and vote for legislation that may often go against popular sentiment."

"Many politicians and lawyers also do not understand finance. When lawyers see high fees and huge damage awards, they are actually seeing the accumulated funds of millions of insurance policy holders. A little from you and a little from me add up to form a fund to pay insurance claims.

"Politicians use tax moneys accumulated from ordinary citizens so they can spend big. The public sees massive corporations that are owned through small investments by stockholders, pension funds, etc. and feel that corporations have slush funds available for payments to any cause. The truth is that every dollar in large corporations is budgeted or allocated. There is no 'mad money' available from corporations to throw at remediation in America.

"When the American public called for remediation to protect against the perceived risks from hazardous waste, Congress thought it found a funding source with the CERCLA legislation. However, that part of the law has been a failure. A 20-year history of CERCLA proves that it is a funding source primarily for the legal profession.

"With the moneys already spent on Panama Street, the State of Massachusetts could hire ten new policemen each year to patrol the toughest neighborhoods and protect against family abuse. This funding could have saved two or three lives in Springfield alone this past year. Americans must weigh the risk of death from waste contamination to the risk of lead poisoning from bullets in the streets. The CERCLA legislation has turned priorities for safety in America upside down."

Now the Muse stepped in, "Mr. Hutchins, it sounds like you are preaching. I've told you that I introduced this madness into Congress and kept it there through my lawyers. You are wasting your time preaching. Any fool can see that reason is on your side. Fortunately as a Muse, I can overpower the small amount of reason that mortals possess. It would be better if you just go on with your story about the litigation and Attorney Moore. That story will weigh more heavily here."

She was right, I do get carried away hoping that someone will listen. She has already convinced me that she used her cunning ways to encourage lawyers to support CERCLA.

At that point I heard myself saying, "I'm sorry Muse, where

was I with the litigation? Oh yes, I guess I had just said that I learned that proof was not an issue under M.G.L. Chapter 21E. All that Attorney Moore had to show was that Hutchins Tool had stored perchloroethylene on the Panama Street site any time between 1972 and 1979. Of course, storage is a relative term, so any lawyer intent on proving responsibility could show that a one-gallon sample kept overnight awaiting a demonstration could be considered storage. I'm sure the drafters of the legislation intended that storage refer to a warehousing type operation. In the hands of a persistent lawyer, storage is equivalent to extensive use of the agent on the property even if the hazardous portion is 2% of the contents of a small sample container.

"My first face to face dealings with Attorney Moore were at the depositions that I was allowed to observe. At these events he appeared as a dower person and the only emotion I encountered was the negative attitude he showed toward the oil, solvents or grease commonly found in manufacturing companies. To me, these are the necessary components of industry just as gas, charcoal and garbage are to the finest restaurants.

"I once saw an auto bumper sticker that said, 'shit happens' and realized that it does happen as simply a by-product of eating. It is the way that waste is treated that is important and not the fact that it is waste. For a manufacturer the use of lubricants and solvents is a necessity and the selective use of the least hazardous is the main priority. Control and disposal of hazardous products should be the important issuc. It appears to me that some environmental attorneys treat agents that could be hazardous to human health as evil in themselves, much as the average person would think of heroin.

"I believe that Attorney Moore did a great disservice to Arden Thompson, his client, by not evaluating the financial condition of Hutchins Tool and Precision EDM early and realizing that neither company could underwrite a million dollar cleanup. A simple D & B or credit report, which is used by most law firms, would have borne this out.

"When Moore was shown that Hutchins Tool could not afford to pay for this cleanup, he brought Bob Hutchins, my brother, and Steve Peroulakis into the litigation by suing them individually as former managers at the site. Again he moved under MGL Chapter 21E using wording that could hold individual managers responsible for pollution.

"With this action, Attorney Moore raised the stakes considerably. It added to the cost of litigation for all the parties while not enhancing the potential for collecting more money for remediation. Suing my brother removed any feelings of conciliation that I may have harbored and made me suspect that Attorney Moore was not taking prisoners. People form business corporations to limit this kind of liability. It is evident that no one involved in the management of most businesses is immune from charges made under CERCLA type laws."

Now the Jester jumped up and said, "That's crazy, it can't be right. Why would Moore go after your brother? No one had ever accused your brother of dumping any hazardous waste."

At that point, all I could say was, "Jester, under MGL Chapter 21E, priority goes toward remediation. As a small part of his duties, my brother managed the Panama Street plant for Hutchins Tool and under the law is responsible for anything that happened at that facility. As a Massachusetts residence he is open to litigation.

Back came the Jester, "But in the long run, wouldn't most companies bail a manager out?"

I thought about this and said, "Probably the large corporations would. Unfortunately, we have found that environmental litigation moves very slowly and tort law is insensitive to the parties involved. The law does not differentiate between the size of companies, the actions of the manager or the time when a spill might have occurred. Today, tomorrow, or 40 years ago are all the same under the law.

"A manager could lose all his assets to a damage suit if there were no other party to pay remediation costs. The damage could occur today as a malicious act with a manager ordering that a known carcinogen be dumped in a city reservoir or 40 years ago with farm manager unknowingly creating a spill when refueling tractors. It's all the same under the law. The only difference is which of the managers has money to share in the remediation if the company involved can not pay the damages in full. I am sure that the possibility of a company not paying all the damages seems remote, but how many small companies can come up with the millions of dollars in cash that may be required for an average size remediation effort? You should remember that most corporate insurance policies now carry exclusion clauses for environmental damage.

"As proof to what I'm saying, you must realize that the DEP has come close to settling with Hutchins Tool. Even as negotiations with the DEP have continued, Attorney Moore continued pressing for legal action against Hutchins Tool and my brother, Bob. After eight years, Attorney Moore's relentless push continues.

"Arden Thompson, Attorney Moore's client, appeared to be in good health at times when I would see him in the courtroom or at depositions. Therefore, I was amazed to read in early 1997 that Arden had died. At the same time, I learned that the Panama Street property had been left to his wife and grown children as part of his estate. I was told that because of a trust arrangement, the Panama Street property stood alone and could be sacrificed without exposing any other moncys in the estate.

"At that point, the State of Massachusetts moved for a summary judgment against the Thompson estate based on the strict liability nature of 21E. It was assumed that the DEP would seize the Panama Street property, remediate the site and sell the remediated property to pay for a portion of the cleanup. We expected that in time Hutchins Tool would also reach an agreement to settle with the DEP and Attorney Moore's fees for this case would cease.

"Unfortunately for all the parties involved, Attorney Moore

continued to defend for the executors of Mr. Thompson's estate against the Commonwealth. This has resulted in no settlement and continued litigation and therefore continued legal expenses."

Now the Muse broke in, "Thank you for telling us how Attorney Moore handled the litigation. I suppose we could all agree that early on, he should have gotten the parties together. But, to give the man his due, it should be evident that without the threat of litigation, nothing would have been resolved. You can see, Zeus, that I directed the Congress to write CERCLA in such a way that litigation between parties is the rule and not the exception. Oh, they did not realize the witch's brew they were cooking up when they voted for passage, but I knew. This monstrous bill was not fashioned on reason. You can see in the Panama Street case, that CERCLA and MGL Chapter 21E have furnished a nice income for Attorney Moore. By writing the CERCLA legislation, I put a lot of money in the hands of lawyers. You will see that in recent times many law offices have departments of lawyers that deal only with environmental problems."

Now Zeus grew impatient, "Muse, I'm not ready to accept your arguments just because Mr. Hutchins complains about the endless opposition of one attorney. Oh, he has said that these environmental fees are enriching even his own attorney, but I believe that most environmental lawyers are just doing their job and the money is of secondary importance. I don't think that most lawyers enjoy defending murderers and rapists, but they do it as their sworn duty."

At that point, I stood up and said, "Zeus, I believe that what you say is true. Moore and the other attorneys are not unfair, unjust or unreasonable; it is just their job.

"What has to be changed are those parts of CERCLA that put lawyers in a position to be unjust. As part of World War II, it was necessary to bring down the Nazi Government and the laws against Jews to stop those mortals that ran the gas chambers."

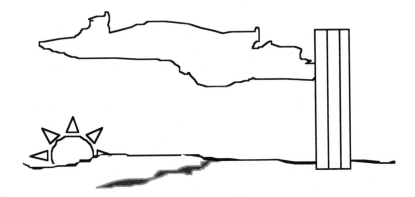

XVIII.   Attorney Doherty

I looked at Zeus and started to think about his statement. I agreed with him because I was sure I knew lawyers who would give environmental remediation priority over their own fees. Of course I was at a disadvantage because most of my dealings with lawyers in the past few years involved the Panama Street litigation. I started grasping at straws because most of the names that came into my head did not fit his view. I finally blurted out, "Chuck Hieken, I mean Charles Hieken, my patent attorney."

The Jester laughed out loud and said, "Come on Hutchins, you can do better than that. Everyone knows that patent lawyers do not handle environmental issues."

I knew he was right and I laughed too. At that point, I could see Zeus starting to get agitated so I said, "Paul Doherty, Attorney Doherty of the law firm, Doherty, Wallace, Pillsbury & Murphy. I'm sure that as clients we come before his fees. I'm surprised I didn't think of Paul immediately. We've known him from our days in high school and he has done most of our law work through the years.

"Attorney Doherty is a brilliant lawyer who has always written good contracts. He was responsible for getting Hutchins Tool one of the first Industrial Revenue Bonds in Massachusetts.

"Paul is one of the best athletes I've ever known and has a wonderful family. He has been active in the area of community service and served on the boards of banks and different large corporations. Paul is very sensitive to the needs of others and has supported liberal causes throughout his life. I remember he was a strong supporter of Governor Dukakis when he ran for President of the United States.

"I believe that Paul is not surrounded at his law firm with associates of his same superior caliber because I have found many of his associates rather weak when they have done work for Hutchins Tool. To both his credit and detriment, Paul has always supported these associates and stuck with them when he would have served our needs better by assigning a different lawyer to our work. When I have complained, Paul has listened and convinced me that everything was OK.

"I expect that the weaknesses that I see today at large law offices can be traced to the fast growth of legal services during the 70's and 80's and, as a result, the quality of lawyer applicant has not kept up with the old standards. The word processor and legal databases have made lawyers more productive, but this technology has also allowed lawyers the opportunity to produce documents in areas outside their expertise. Hit a button, fill in the squares and print a will or an industrial revenue bond.

"Doherty was active in creating the wording for our Industrial Revenue Bond which was one of the first of its kind written in Massachusetts. I remember feeling complimented when other attorneys in Springfield asked to borrow a copy of our IRB. A few years later, I learned that some of the attorneys that borrowed it, also copied it, placed it on word processors and used it as a model for IRB's they wrote for other companies.

"Before I talk further about Doherty, I should say that in the years that followed the filing of the Thompson lawsuit, Hutchins

Tool's fortunes became increasingly worse. In the late 80's and early 90's, banks began to fail in Texas, California and Oklahoma primarily due to bad real estate deals. These failures led to a financial crisis that threatened many banks insured by the FDIC.

"For years, Hutchins Tool had been considered an excellent client for any bank. Even as New England banks started to tighten credit, we carried the highest-ranking possible for a company of our size with the Bank of New England. At the same time, the Bank of New England, having suffered major losses in the real estate lending market, was tightening its requirements on all loans. These bank credit restrictions came at a very bad time for Hutchins Tool because it was also at that time that we were forced to foot-note our financial statements with a cautionary statement that said that Hutchins Tool faced environmental claims that could be well over a million dollars.

"I'll never forget a meeting at the Bank when our line of credit was reviewed and I was asked to answer questions about the Panama Street lawsuit. Unfortunately, I had no answers except that the Insurance Company was defending us. This news was reassuring to the loan officers until I was forced to admit that, should we lose the lawsuit all our non-encumbered assets would be exposed and could be lost to damage claims.

"The bank officers were both understanding and cordial to me and that year they renewed the line. However, in the months that followed, the loan officers suggested that my brother and I should co-sign the 'line of credit' notes that up until then had never been collateralized. Feeling that co-signing would lead to further peril, I did a dance for another year to avoid that situation.

"On the next anniversary, things had changed considerably at the Bank of New England. It seemed as if there was a bank examiner hiding in every file drawer. Loan officers were laid off and everyone was in a nervous state. When we again refused to co-sign notes, our loan officer forced the only alternative; he tied all the Company assets to the Company loans. A few months later, the Bank of New England filed for bankruptcy and our notes were purchased by Fleet Bank in a FDIC bailout.

"Hutchins Tool's defense contracting business was in a decline as a result of the end to the cold war. However, our medical parts business continued to increase, so there were opportunities if we reorganized production and invested in new equipment.

"At that point I realized the value of a good working relationship with a bank. Unfortunately, the failure of the Bank of New England altered that good relationship. Now we had to deal with loan officers who did not know our business or us. To make matters worse, the environmental footnote on our financial statements struck fear into the hearts of the new loan officers.

"Within six months loans to companies with problems, like our environmental problems, were moved from Springfield to the Fleet Bank offices in Boston. The department handling these loans was essentially a workout unit. We continued being current with the payment schedules and I met every few months with the loan officer. He was likable, young and easy to work with, although he continually asked how we were coming with the environmental litigation. On that subject, I had very few answers.

"I once asked him if we could finance some new equipment to be used for medical parts manufacture. He was reluctant to do anything while we had the environmental exposure. Soon, it was obvious that even though our loans were current, we were in a straight jacket and had to depend solely on cash flow.

"Things got even worse when the young loan officer made a trip from the Fleet offices in Boston to Springfield to tell me that our loans were being transferred to RECOLL. He was embarrassed to say that under the contract Fleet signed with the FDIC, Fleet had the option to return any Bank of New England loans to the FDIC within one year. We were among a large group of customers transferred to the FDIC as the one-year time frame ended. Our loans were turned over to RECOLL, a unit of Fleet that serviced FDIC loans. While all this was happening, we continued to pay off the loans on schedule.

"As I previously stated, I always considered Paul Doherty to be a person extremely sympathetic to the needs of others. Therefore, in November of 1994, feeling mauled by this environmental litigation over which I had no control and embittered by seeing Hutchins Tool continue on a downward spiral, I sent this letter to Doherty:

November 1, 1994

Paul Doherty, Esquire
Doherty, Wallace, Pillsbury & Murphy
One Monarch Place
Springfield, MA 01103

Dear Paul:

Bill Hadley is very pessimistic about our East Longmeadow litigation. Even if we are only found to have had hazardous substances on the premises sometime in the 1970's before the Massachusetts environmental laws were passed, we are still considered a guilty party.

Because other parties involved can afford to pay very little, we are exposed to what could be a million-dollar settlement that could take years to resolve. At the same time our insurance company is defending with reservation of their rights to pay the losses.

As Fleet Bank came to the end of their grace period for turning loans over to the FDIC, they placed Hutchins Tool's loans with RECOLL because of concerns of the exposure emanating from our environmental litigation. Also, as part of the Fenn Manufacturing lease of a portion of our building, the City promised a $60,000 loan to repair our roof. After a letter of commitment from the S.B.D.F., Attorney Ellen Freyman held up the closing on this small loan three weeks ago for further review of this litigation disclosure.

Our Constitution rights are being bulldozed by the DEP

under the c21E laws of Massachusetts. I am not speaking in terms of theory. We are suffering in real time. Our losses are real, our apprehensions are real, our costs are real, and our future is dim. We are not polluters; we are victims. There is an accumulation of four years of graphic evidence to prove this point.

While I can agree with the policy of a clean environment, the masses should not impose their will at the sacrifice of individual rights guaranteed by the Constitution. Paul, I implore you to attempt to understand our position and defend our rights. It could be the most significant law work your firm has ever undertaken for us. If parts of c21E are unconstitutional and our rights are being abused, is there any better defense than to right these wrongs? You know the law. We look to you to determine a way to make this happen.

Since February 19, 1991 when Stephen F. Joyce, Regional Engineer, Bureau of Waste Site Cleanup, contacted the Officers at Hutchins Tool naming them and Hutchins Tool a Potentially Responsible Party, we have suffered extreme damage and harm. The civil rights of our Officers have been violated and continue to be violated through the DEP's use, supervision, and interpretation of M.G.L. c21E, section 5 as cited by Mr. Joyce in this Notice Of Responsibility of February 19th. I further believe that an investigation of M.G.L. c21E as it pertains to the Officers of Hutchins Tool will show that certain parts of this law characterized in its administration by the Massachusetts DEP are Unconstitutional under the U.S. Constitution and its Bill of Rights. While not limited to the Amendments and the violations I shall cite, I believe that there is more than sufficient reason to test these civil rights violation under the Federal Judicial System.

The following in laymen's terms are the specific Amendments that the Massachusetts law and the DEP has violated and continues to violate:

144

FOURTH AMENDMENT: (Right of privacy, right against reasonable searches and seizures, right to confront adverse witnesses.)

The DEP was furnished testimony stating that Hutchins Tool was the sole responsible party by the property owner sometime after March 24, 1989. Prior to the DEP Declaration of February 19, 1991 naming us a PRP, we were given no information regarding witnesses against us nor were we given the right to confront adverse witnesses.

FIFTH AMENDMENT: (Right to trial by jury, right to due process of law, [life, liberty, property], right against self-incrimination, freedom from double jeopardy.)

The notice of Responsibility cites both 21E laws and other laws under which we could be prosecuted under criminal statues of the Commonwealth. While the intent may be to scare us into paying remediation expenses, the threat of criminal prosecution is both implied and real as demonstrated by the conviction and jail sentence of a Massachusetts corporate officer "polluter" within the past year. As a result, we are forced by the DEP to pay remediation costs without the right of due process of law.

Having lived with this thing for over four years, I have great respect for what the German people suffered after 1934 when the National Socialist Party gained control and bureaucracies exceeded their authority and became both judge and juries.

The DEP also presses a PRP for self-incrimination and for what is called "Bounty Hunting" litigation under Proposition 65 in California. One could believe that many of the DEP's methods were refined during the Inquisition or the Salem witches trials.

After four years, nothing has been resolved with regard to the extent of the damage or the cost of cleanup for the Panama

Street site. It's just a matter of time before the litigants include the town of East Longmeadow and other Western Mass residents who can find the right lawyer. We should also expect to see the defendant list increased to Don Hutchins, other officers and to suppliers during the 1972-79 period such as F.L. Roberts. It is my belief that this jeopardizes our <u>freedom from double jeopardy</u>. How many actions can we defend?

<u>SIXTH AMENDMENT</u>: (Speedy and public trial, right to representation by counsel, right to confront witnesses, right to subpoena witnesses.)

We are threatened with jail terms, strict liability, three (3) times the DEP's costs, interest, plus liens on our property, bank accounts, homes, estates, with a potential exposure to cleanup costs of millions of dollars with no Sixth Amendment protection.

Essentially none of the Sixth Amendment's rights are available to the PRP until years after the DEP forces the PRP to capitulate or expose themselves to triple damages. Most parties want to cooperate with State agencies to avoid expensive litigation and fines. Environmental terminology and technology is complicated to the point where the individual and small business owner can be financially devastated by simply trying to understand the Agencies' procedures and regulations and to pay for expert help.

<u>SEVENTH AMENDMENT</u>: (Right to trial in civil cases.)

I can produce countless instances under which the Massachusetts DEP exceeded Federal guidelines and misinterpreted Chemical data from Federal lists. Substances that may be equal to coffee, gasoline and heating oil on Federal lists are published in the same category as coal tar, cigarette smoke, and asbestos on the Massachusetts lists. The DEP lists were

*established in haste with little concern to damaging the rights
of Massachusetts' citizens.*

*Are triple damages punitive? Are we cleaning up the envi-
ronment or punishing those who polluted? Constantly, the
words, "deep pockets," "bounty hunter" and "strict liability"
are bantered about by attorneys while the question is asked,
"Well, who is going to pay for the cleanup if not big business?" Unfortunately, no exception has been made for individuals, small business, farmers, etc. There is no limited liability protection for stockowners. The statue of limitations does
not apply and ex post facto is a phrase not considered with this
litigation. (The c21. E laws were passed in the 1980's and we
are being accused of polluting in the 1970's.)*

*If the State or Federal Government funded environmental
cleanup through taxes on fuel oil, gasoline, automobiles, etc.
just as they have for defense, much more progress would have
been made in cleaning up old sites. To date, most environmental funding has gone to litigation and not to cleanup. However
worthy the result of cleanup can be, it should not be at the
expense of the Massachusetts citizens who's rights are violated
in the process.*

*No one can afford the litigation we are going through. We
would be better off in criminal courts with public defenders. If
Massachusetts can put us in jail as a polluter; they had better
offer a criminal defense and the <u>right to a trial in civil cases,</u>
which includes the cost of our defense.*

*<u>EIGHTH AMENDMENT</u>: (Right to reasonable bail, ban on
cruel and unusual punishment.)*

*If you commit the crime, you've got to pay the time. Well, we
didn't commit any crime unless leasing manufacturing space in
the 1970's was a crime. I believe there can be no more unusual
punishment than for respected business people to live with the
DEP's judgment that a company and its people are potentially*

responsible parties.

*After four years, the DEP has not finished the Phase I evalu-
ation and no one can predict the price of cleanup. There are
monthly litigation bills. Legal costs for all participants have
exceeded $150,000 and no cleanup has been started.*

*To us, the loss of reputation, homes, assets, etc. is totally
cruel and unusual punishment. To think that it is all based on
the false testimony of a former employee and current competitor is particularly vexing. To know now that he gave this
testimony to diffuse his own guilt is terrifying and it should be
terrifying to any Massachusetts citizen who owns or rents
property.*

*It should be terrifying to anyone who respects the law and
Constitution. While I am sure that many defenseless people
have been victimized by c21E, we may be the first to bring this
travesty to the people of Massachusetts.*

*If we can not right this law, the Inquisition will continue and
the DEP will run roughshod over the rights of many farmers,
individuals, and small business owners. It will only stop when
the sale of residences incurs the same 21E investigations.
Then many people will be exposed to the unfairness of the
DEP.*

*FOURTEENTH AMENDMENT: (prohibits the states from
denying their citizens due process of law and equal protection
of the law.)*

*A reading of the DEP's Notice of Responsibility to Hutchins
Tool includes threats, interpretations, time limitations, accusations, sufficient for most people to understand how our civil
rights are being trampled by the DEP. There is nothing subtle
about this notice. We are guilty until we prove ourselves
innocent.*

*When we tell people of our plight in East Longmeadow, very
few can believe that renters in the 1970's could find themselves*

with these costly legal problems. No one can believe that the officers are not protected under the Corporation's limited liability.

The average person does not understand that if we were the only PRP that can afford to pay that we would have to underwrite the total cost. People can't understand that the word of a former employee who is now a competitor could weigh very highly with the DEP.

How about the "Super Fund" they ask? There is no "Super Fund" money available to us, is the answer. The problem is not with Steve Peroulakis, Thompson, or the attorneys involved, because they are all doing what they have to do. The problem is with the Massachusetts law and its administration by the DEP. We may go down, but we would feel better going down while doing what we can to alter an unconstitutional law.

The legislator can theorize all they want about c21. E; we have proof that it violates our rights guaranteed as U.S. citizens.

Sincerely yours,

Donald C. Hutchins

"Just writing the letter was a catharsis. Finally I was able to confess to someone my fears of closing Hutchins Tool and placing my employees on unemployment. Some had been with us so long, I knew that they would have difficulty adjusting to other employment. Everything about this environmental litigation was so frustrating that I recalled a movie where the leading actor threw open a window and screamed to New York City words that I remember as, I've had it and I'm not going to take it any more."

Now the Jester spoke up, "You must have been crazy. You make it sound like you were being oppressed like women or minorities in America. It looks to me like you were living pretty well. Why should anyone feel sorry for you? When the Bank of New England failed, lots of people lost their businesses."

"Jester, you're right," I said. "I did have mixed emotions. But I had learned in school that no citizen should have his rights violated by the police or an agency of state or federal government. I had become very sympathetic to the plight of blacks in America. I knew that if anyone would, Paul Doherty would understand my position. He would accept the challenge to face up to the DEP who were trampling on my rights as a U.S. citizen. I expected he would amaze me with a creative approach to bring these issues all the way to the Supreme Court of the United States."

Again the Jester laughed. "You are crazy," he said. "There are well over two hundred million people in America. Why should you be the one to challenge the administration of laws that have been unchallenged for years?"

I replied, "Because I knew we were on the leading edge. Not many environmental cases have gone this far and lasted so long. Most Americans that have suffered are people that decided to sell property and retire. People who owned small businesses like gas stations or machine shops. When environmental problems were encountered, the deals would fall through or the owners would sell below market value, pay for a cleanup or abandon the property. There are thousands of sites standing idle in America because of environmental problems.

"Few are able to fight back and for that reason, very little litigation has gone to court. Most who have suffered are not mentally prepared to take up the challenge and defend themselves. I was prepared with the help of Paul Doherty to fight these wrongs with every bit of energy I could muster."

Now it was the Muse's turn, "I understand, Mr. Hutchins, that Attorney Doherty didn't respond as you expected."

"I'm sad to say he did not," I said. "He did call a meeting that included Attorneys Hadley, Brown and himself so that I was strongly outnumbered by lawyers. After giving me about five minutes to go over my opinions in the letter, Paul said that they had discussed the letter and felt that his law firm was supplying the best defense possible. He said that Bill Hadley's approach, which was an attempt to use the insurance company's funds to settle, was superior to my approach. He saw MGL Chapter 21E as difficult to challenge either at the state or federal level.

"I was deflated. My hopes destroyed by Doherty's reaction to the letter. To this day I have not heard a sound argument against my stands in that letter. Even if CERCLA is found to be constitutionally acceptable, there are reasons to suspect that the way it has been administered by agencies, like the Massachusetts DEP, creates civil rights violations against American citizens. If I found any attorney willing to help fight this battle, I would join him or her and offer every bit of help possible to right these wrongs."

As I ended, the Muse took the stand, "Paul Doherty's law firm would nominate me for lawyer god if they knew what I have done for them. In fact, all major full service law firms throughout America would do the same. The facts are simple, before CERCLA there were no lawyers who considered themselves environmental specialists. Today, Doherty's office alone has at least three lawyers that advertise environmental law as one of their specialties. It should be evident to everyone here that something was needed to fill the void and complete the firm as a full service law office. The Panama Street litigation has averaged fees of $25,000 per year to be split among the partners including Attorney Doherty. American law is under my spell and lawyers will not back off from environmental litigation while it is so profitable. What would replace that income?

"Mr. Hutchins, I think that you were unrealistic to think that even a person so liberal as Paul Doherty would champion your cause. There is no glory in fighting for the rights of a polluter."

I bowed my head and quietly agreed. I truly felt the fool to discuss this further in front of Zeus. I didn't want to continue. I had bled enough for the Muse. I didn't cry, but I felt my throat tightening and my eyes starting to water.

Then Zeus stepped in and said, "Muse, I would not gloat yet. I sympathize with Hutchins. It's difficult for a mortal to be up against divine forces that can overcome the small amount of reason that mortals possess. We shall recess for a short time. I expect Mercury to drop by to give me a report on his visit to Earth."

At that point, Zeus came down and stood beside the podium. He was standing at my level but was still an imposing figure. I remembered that Mercury was a Roman god. He was always portrayed in sculpture as a messenger with winged feet.

The Muse moved up beside Zeus acting like a groupie awed by a celebrity. Seeing that I was alone, the Jester walked over to me with that mischievous look that was always on his face. As he approached, he said to me, "Hang in there, kid. I know this must be tough for you to talk about. That Muse is some bitch. You know that she's just using you to show Zeus how well she has marketed lawyers in America. Her goal is to become the lawyer god. Personally, I don't think that Zeus is buying it. He just doesn't like sleaziness."

Before I could reply, there was a whoosh sound like a 4th of July rocket being fired in the air. In a flash, Mercury swooped down and landed in front of Zeus. He was as magnificent as the sculptures had shown him to be with a sleek body and long, firm muscles.

I realized that the sculptures had been wrong, or possibly it was my perception. I suppose because sculptors had used light colored stone, I had thought of Mercury as Caucasian just as I had always been mistaken by thinking of Christ as Anglo-Saxon.

But Mercury was black and his features were African. Seeing my surprise, the Jester said, "Did the new shoes surprise you?"

All I could say was "No, I, well yes, the shoes." Then for the first time, I saw the shoes. They were flashy basketball sneakers with a logo. Because I had pictured Mercury with winged feet, the shoes surprised me, although they looked real good. I bet they would retail for at least $190.00.

At that point, Zeus saluted Mercury with one hand raised with the fingers pointing up. Mercury responded by slapping Zeus' hand with his. It was a high five. Who would believe that the divinities greet one another with a high five?

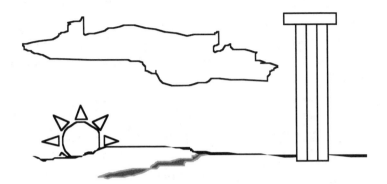

XIX.   Dismissal Without Prejudice

I did not hear the conversation between Zeus and Mercury. I could see that they were happy to see one another. When Mercury flew off, I saw Zeus rap him on the butt like a coach sending a man into the game.

Now a happier Zeus ascended the podium and banged his fist saying, "I know this is tough for you to talk about seeing your business slipping away, but I'd like to hear more of this story. Please go on, Mr. Hutchins."

I stood up and started back into my story saying, "Zeus, things were getting tougher and tougher. For a business to live off cash flow without the ability to borrow is debilitating. There is a continual series of crises: What workers do you lay off? What bills do you pay? Can we meet the payroll this week?"

"Big deal, where's the problem?" said the Jester. "I understand that most Americans live like that. In California my friends called it living hand to mouth."

"Jester, it's different with a business," I replied. "A business may have to survive for long periods before a contract is complete or a series of jobs are ready to invoice. In the meantime, as the owner you have to pay your employees and for supplies and services. Commercial banks furnish cash with line of credit loans that make up for the peaks and valleys of receivables. With these easily accessible line of credit funds, the desperation of trying to find cash disappears. Unfortunately, when the environmental litigation started, the banks cancelled our lines of credit.

"You should also realize that much of American business is based on faith. Employees have faith that they will receive a paycheck and that their health insurance is being paid. Suppliers ship supplies based on a faith built up through years of prompt payments. Such faith is tough to build, but is easily lost with the slightest interruption. I am sure that most of the staff members of state environmental agencies have no idea how their actions can affect a small business, but let me tell you that from my experience, the effects are very real.

"In the end, payroll had priority one. The minute you stop paying your employees, you're dead. Of course, the same thing is true when it comes to group health insurance. I could run through a whole litany of problems that occurred when we became delinquent paying Company bills, but I should get back to my story.

"The Panama Street litigation was moving forward with the attorneys for all parties deposing potential witnesses. I attended most of the depositions as an observer because I felt I could help our attorney with his questions.

"A large percentage of the witnesses were employees or former employees of Hutchins Tool. They included Steve Peroulakis and many of his people because most had been trained in our plant. Much of this discovery pointed to the fact that Precision EDM had used solvents containing perchloroethylene and trichloroethylene. To prevent his employees from slipping on the floor of Precision EDM during the 1980's, Peroulakis laid 4-ft. by 8-ft. fiberboard to soak up the spills. When these boards became saturated with solvent and oil, they were stacked outside and replaced with new boards.

"The attorneys spent a great deal of time with each of Precision EDM's employees discussing the practice of blowing solvent off the parts and out the back door. There was also talk about times when dirty solvent was poured down the floor drains.

"I was not surprised when Peroulakis testified that years before he had seen co-workers at Hutchins Tool disposing of solvent both outdoors and down the drains. Considering that such testimony deflected suspicion from him and that he could not name the actual Hutchins' employees who had poured the solvent, his testimony was not seen as damaging to us.

"In his deposition Thompson changed his testimony from the earlier story he had told Ms. Symington of the DEP to include Peroulakis and Precision EDM as villains. He stated that, although he was at the property on almost a daily basis, he had never seen any employee of Hutchins Tool dispose of solvents. He did acknowledge that the drains, which he designed and constructed when he built the building, were sound and led to the municipal sewer system.

"With the exception of Peroulakis and Thompson, there was very little testimony during the depositions that would link Hutchins Tool to the pollution. I hoped that in court a jury would see that Peroulakis and Thompson were determined to place blame on Hutchins Tool, because compared to all the other former tenants we were looked upon as having the deepest pockets.

"Steve Peroulakis once told Thompson that a company called F.L. Roberts distributed perchloroethylene and so they were deposed by Thompson's attorney. F.L. Roberts was also a client of Doherty, Wallace, Pillsbury, & Murphy, so Attorney Hadley asked them if they had knowledge of ever supplying this material to Hutchins at the Panama Street address. Bill Hadley told me that the President, Steve Roberts had no record of shipments to Hutchins Tool and would so testify. There was no reason for me to attend the deposition.

"For some reason, Steve Roberts couldn't attend, so he sent his brother, Seth. I was later told that one attorney asked Seth for records of deliveries during the 1970's. Seth replied that they sold that part of the business many years earlier, and had no records.

"Seth followed this by volunteering that he did remember when on one occasion he, himself carried a small container of perch to Hutchins in East Longmeadow. He did not recall the time or date; nor did he remember anything about the building; to whom he delivered the container; or the street address.

"While Hadley tried to rebut or diffuse Mr. Robert's recollection, Hadley acknowledged that he thought that some damage had been done to our case. I point this out to show that vague recollections from 12 years earlier, which would not even be considered in a criminal case, could become relevant in a tort action. This insignificant deposition enlightened me as to how vicious MGL Chapter 21E could be. Again, I was reminded that in these cases, there is no assumption of innocence. Our innocence is something we would be forced to prove."

At this point, the Jester jumped in with a smile on his face. "Hey, Muse, I suppose you got to Roberts too. Are you going to tell us that you were sitting on his shoulder at the deposition?"

"Jester, I didn't have to," the Muse answered. "I'm much subtler than you think. Can't you see that the way laws like CERCLA were written, there is no statute of limitations or ex post facto? For that reason, lawyers can go back past the 1980's to before the laws were written and use anything they can get their hands on. Under civil law, all that the lawyers have to prove is a preponderance of evidence, rather than reasonable doubt. The opportunity to reach back years and years for testimony causes confusion, impeachable testimony and most importantly, it keeps the fee meter running. Sort of like taking a taxi from New York City to Chicago."

Zeus spoke up with that resonant voice saying, "Did you run into any more problems, Hutchins?"

I answered, "Surprisingly, we got through the depositions with only the Roberts' blip on the record. The only other testimony negative toward us was from a former Thompson employee who said that he saw an employee of Hutchins Tool pour liquid from a container onto the ground while he was eating lunch during the 1970's. He testified that he saw this pouring only one time and that he had no idea what was in the container. Was this retiree simply trying to be loyal to his old employer with this ancient recollection that he had originally given to Ms. Symington of the DEP? To me it was just another of the imponderables in this litigation.

"To sum this up, if we went to trial, I believed that the testimony against us would be considered either prejudicial coming from Thompson and Peroulakis or inconsequential. I expected that a jury could see that both the DEP and Thompson were looking for a source to fund the cleanup. Knowing that we were not guilty of polluting and hoping that the judicial system would treat us fairly, I was ready to go to trial.

"My greatest wish was to have all this finished. Win, lose, or draw, it was in the best interest of Hutchins Tool that the litigation ended. By now our financial condition was very poor, so we had nothing to lose. The only damages we could pay would have to come from our insurance carrier. To be honest, we were broke."

Then the Jester spoke up, "If Hutchins Tool was broke and there was no chance for the DEP or Thompson to get money from you, why would they continue that effort without hope of a payoff."

"Jester, we show the symbol of justice as blindfolded," I said. "It is my belief that those that administer law in the United States, such as the courts, lawyers and government agencies are not blind because we know they can read the law, but they are dumb in that they can not speak an interpretation of the laws that they read. As a divinity you may not have had the opportunity to reason with an agency clerk from the local assessors office, or IRS, or to an assistant attorney general, but most Americans will tell you that it is a fruitless task.

"Lawmakers realize that they do not have all the answers when they pass a law. They expect that an administrative person down the line will provide interpretations for situations that the lawmakers never had the opportunity to deliberate. Unfortunately, job security for lower level administrators depends on their not rocking the boat. The administrator's best friend is to say there is nothing I can do, that's the law. For an administrator to be creative and interpret the law for a given situation is a short road to losing a job. In the case of the Panama Street site, the law does not mention a responsible party's ability to pay, so why should the lawyers or DEP clerks concern themselves with that fact?"

"Slow down Hutchins, you're going too fast for my head to follow," said the Jester. "I know that the courts in America were established to interpret the law. Why would you need administrators to do that? You're asking for a lot to expect earthlings, whose job it is to administer laws, to interpret them fairly. Leave it to the courts."

At that I replied, "OK Jester I'll see if I can simplify it. First of all, you are correct in thinking that the judicial branches of government were established to interpret laws passed by the various legislative bodies. But something not taught in schools is that in practice the judicial procedure is so slow and time consuming that it is generally only effective for major, long-term decisions. In everyday life people like the police, school officials, lawyers and everyday citizens must interpret the laws as part of their jobs.

"Let me give you a simple example. I once served on my town's school committee. At one point during my tenure, the administration became concerned with the school system's policy on suspending students. The primary concern was one section that said that students who were truant from school for more than 5 days would be suspended from school for 3 days as punishment."

"I love it," said the Jester. "A student skips over 5 days, so for punishment they put him out for 3 more days. The truant kids must have loved that policy. I can see why the school system wanted to change it."

"That was the idea, Jester," I said. "But in voting to change that policy we changed a number of other sections of the policy statement without much discussion. One section that was changed said that if two students fought one another in school, that both would be suspended from school for 3 days.

"While at the time this policy did not get my attention, it did six years later when my son Ryan was attacked at school by another boy and he defended himself. When the school principal called me, he told me that Ryan was being suspended for 3 days even though he was not responsible for the fight. When I questioned the principal's punishment for Ryan, he said that he had no choice, that the school committee's policy was a 3-day suspension for both students. When I said that I helped write the policy and that his reading was not the intent of the policy, his answer was that there was nothing he could do.

"If he had any guts, the principal could have acted differently. The lesson to be learned is that thousands of humans are being screwed every day by poorly written laws and regulations. Without intervention from reasonable administrators, all these humans can do is grin and bear it. It is no different with the Panama Street litigation. If the DEP's personnel were clear thinking, reasonable administrators, there would be no litigation. Early on, the DEP could have cleaned up the site and received what reimbursement they could from the various insurance companies. That is a far better deal than the DEP or the various parties can expect as this thing goes on to Infiniti.

"To get back to my story, the trial was ready to begin in March of 1996 on a Monday. On the previous Friday, I told Hadley that I wanted to go to trial. I knew we had a strong case and hoped a jury would see how the DEP and Attorney Moore had bullied us. The Panama Street pollution was discovered in 1989 and now it was seven years later. Nothing had been done to clean up the pollution and thousands of dollars had been spent on legal fees for litigation. Certainly, it was time to throw the cards on the table face up.

"Hadley said he thought that he could get a settlement without a trial. He felt that all the insurance companies would come to an agreement with the DEP because it would be very expensive for the insurance companies to try the case. When I continued to say I wanted to go to trial, he asked for a meeting at our offices. As a gesture of respect, I agreed. Attorney Hadley arrived at our offices with Attorney Doherty and joined my brother and me for the meeting.

"After the four of us sat down, Hadley started by saying that he was very close to a settlement and that Thompson's and Peroulakis' attorneys were in agreement that they could settle without the trial. I continued to say to Hadley that I wanted to end this thing and that Hutchins Tool could not survive much longer because the Panama Street litigation was holding us in a straight jacket. We could not refinance or sell the business because of the environmental litigation. Our cash flow was intermittent and at times I had to personally loan the company money to make the payroll.

"Now Hadley said that if we went to trial and lost, the damages could be heavy. I replied that I would then seek bankruptcy protection for Hutchins Tool to gain time to work things out while we reclaimed our customer base. If this was the worst result, it was far better than the slow death the Company was suffering.

"Attorney Doherty was looking at me as if I was a petulant child. He finally spoke as the voice of reason, or should I say the voice of legal reason. He pointed out that a lot of effort had gone into getting the other parties to settle; that a trial would be costly and its outcome would hurt everyone."

Zeus became involved by saying, "Mr. Hutchins, reason is reason. There is no difference between legal reason and reason."

I felt that there is a difference, so I replied, "Zeus, lawyers deal with pages of written rules of conduct. The businessperson deals in the real world that involves the lives of customers, employees and suppliers. A settlement could cause Hutchins Tool to lose such things as hope, vitality and the ability to prosper. A settlement may satisfy a lawyer, but the businessperson knows that the protection of bankruptcy may be a better option because it can give a business a second chance and the vitality needed for the future.

"I continued to resist until Hadley reminded us of the litigation against my brother. Essentially, the cases against Bob and Hutchins Tool had been tied together by a court ruling, so they would go to trial together and damages could be divided between him and Hutchins Tool. Unfortunately, he as an individual would not have bankruptcy protection. Now Bob asked how much they could get out of him personally. Doherty told him that if his assets could not cover the damage claim, they could garnish his pay for the rest of his life and leave him very little to live on.

"That took the wind out of my sails. While I could take the heat, I could not be the one who caused Bob to lose everything. I then acknowledged to Hadley, that I could not take responsibility for ruining my brother. At that point I quietly backed down and told Hadley to work out the settlement. Therefore, in March of 1996, we did not go to trial. The action was dismissed by the courts, without prejudice, which means that Thompson could re-instate litigation at a later date if he elected to do so."

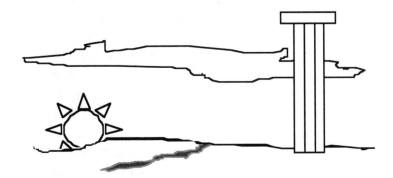

XX.   An Attempt at Reason

"As Attorney Hadley and Doherty were leaving the meeting, I asked Bill Hadley what kind of settlement the insurance companies had accepted. At that point, he said, "Well, nothing has been resolved, but I met with the other attorneys yesterday and we're fairly sure that we can all get together."

"Having just been told that a settlement was imminent, I asked, "Do you mean that no amounts have been discussed with the insurance companies?" He answered in a frustrated manner just as a father would answer a child. 'Don, you must realize that the DEP does not know the cost of cleanup. We can't tell the insurance companies the amount of damages because there is no hard cost data for remediation.'

"As Hadley left, I realized he had accomplished what he came for. I had backed down and there would be no trial. I was blown away. I knew that there would be no ending. It was fated to go on and on. All the lawyers could sleep at night because they had done their job. They were prepared to settle."

"That was it, no trial," said the Jester. "What kind of crap is that? I'll wager that up until that time the insurance companies involved had paid the lawyers about 2 or 3 hundred thousand to get everyone ready for a trial. I may not be one of the smartest guys in the heavens, but even I know that that doesn't make any sense."

"Its worse than you think," I replied. "This same thing is happening with environmental litigation all over America every day. Think of the millions of dollars that have gone to lawyers rather than to remediation. This is the tragedy of CERCLA. I realize that Hutchins is nothing; we are bush league and our story is not even worth telling in the grand scheme of things. But, if you multiply our story by the thousands that are happening today in the United States, you can understand why most of the large law offices in our nation have established departments that do nothing but litigate environmental confrontations. Few cases ever get to court, but millions of dollars are spent on legal research, court actions, depositions, etc. There should be no reasonable environmentalist in the U.S. that could condone this mockery."

"I'm starting to believe what you have told me, Muse," said Zeus. "As incredible as it sounds, I can see now that all these small environmental lawsuits could add up to the billions that have been spent in America.

"At least now Mr. Hutchins the lawyers had gotten together to iron out a settlement. It appears that the beginning of the end was near. Go on with your story."

"Thank you Zeus," I replied. "To put these things in motion, the lawyers scheduled a joint meeting with the DEP to determine cleanup costs. I did not sleep that night. I just lay in bed wondering if I could hold everything together at Hutchins Tool for a little longer.

"As the months passed after the dismissal, Hutchins Tool barely kept its head above water. About every third week, I wrote a personal check to Hutchins Tool to cover the payroll. During that same period of time, my office manager said that Hutchins

Tool had missed some tax withholding payments because of the low cash flow. He hoped to make up the deficiency by the end of the quarter.

"As part of the discussions on settlement, the three attorneys involved agreed to do the site evaluation demanded by the DEP. The lawyers and the environmental experts that each retained believed that a study would show that the DEP's plans were overkill and that a less expensive remediation could be accomplished.

"I was not included in these meetings where the experts and lawyers worked out requirements for this site evaluation. When they finished, they presented a plan for a site evaluation that would cost $50,000. It would involve drilling more wells around the floor drains plus collecting additional soil and water samples from the brook. Hadley took the lead and pushed the plan through the DEP office.

"When the DEP accepted the plan, Hadley went back to the two other attorneys seeking their share of the $50,000. At that point, the other attorneys said that they would not participate so Hadley was forced to get all the money from our insurance company. It was a struggle, but he finally received the commitment of $50,000 and hired an environmental consultant to direct the site evaluation.

"Within a short time, Attorney Moore demanded that the environmental consultant carry two million dollars of insurance to cover potential damages incurred while drilling at the Panama Street site. When the consultant would not comply with the coverage request and didn't like the truculent attitude of Attorney Moore, she refused the job and Hadley had to find another licensed site professional."

"Wait a minute, let me get this clear," said the Jester. "First, you told us that Attorney Moore would not pay for his share of the evaluation to which he had already agreed. Now he was holding things up further by demanding two million dollars of insurance coverage to be carried by the consultant. What was his problem? It looks to me like he had really lost it."

"I can't begin to explain why he did these things," I said. "All the parties had agreed to satisfy the DEP by doing this site evaluation and Hutchins Tool was paying for it. Now Attorney Moore was preventing the team from accomplishing the site evaluation study. Moore held up the study for three months and to this day I do not understand why. Some would say that he was just being a lawyer protecting his client's property. However, time would show that this delay served no purpose other than to frustrate the DEP.

"At long last the DEP called for all the parties to get together at their Western Massachusetts office in Springfield. As I remember, there were twelve people present, including three from the DEP and a new face, Attorney Michelle O'Brien, an Assistant Attorney General for the State of Massachusetts.

"You can call it anything you want, but it was not a discussion. Attorney O'Brien took the floor, announced that the DEP had run up over $150,000 in Department costs for the Panama Street site, demanded payment of these costs and instructed the parties get together and divide the costs of cleanup using the pump and treat methods recommended by the DEP.

"All those attending were rather rattled by Attorney O'Brien's aggressive approach and the lawyers made only muted replies to her demands. Because no one else appeared ready to take a stand against O'Brien, I said that I understood the pump and treat extraction method to be slow and costly. I asked that she wait until the results of the $50,000 study were ready because it could lead to alternative methods rather than pump and treat. Perhaps all O'Brien was looking for was a reaction from one of the parties. Whatever I said seemed to turn her around and she agreed to hold her decision on the remediation technology pending results of the $50,000 study.

"It seemed that finally everything was coming together. All the parties including the DEP were around a table. Attorney O'Brien was forcing everyone to compromise on a settlement and she would consider an alternative plan for remediation.

"Further good news came to us with the $50,000 site investigation report. With around 200 pages of test data summarized, the report said that the pollution was confined to certain areas at the site and the well tests showed rapid lowering of the agents present. Most importantly, a section completed by Dr. Jerome J. Cura, a highly regarded independent consultant, concluded that, 'No imminent hazard exists in regards to the presence of VOC's in the water of the brook.'

"The brook contamination had given the Panama Street site a high priority for cleanup with the DEP. If the brook showed no imminent hazard, this would change things drastically."

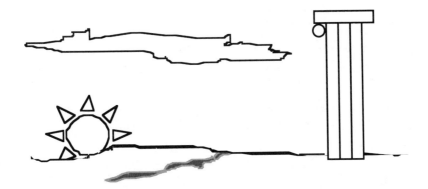

XXI.   Preliminary Injunction

"I should have known that good times don't last very long under the CERCLA laws. Evidently, Attorney O'Brien, the Assistant Attorney General, had less patience with her fellow lawyer's delaying tactics than was expected. Within three weeks of the meeting, O'Brien sent a short letter to the attorneys representing Hutchins, Thompson, and Peroulakis demanding a commitment to perform a Response Action on the Panama Street property."

"While I expected that the letter was simply her method of keeping things moving after the meeting, it was not. Reality set in when the letter was followed shortly by a Preliminary Injunction by the Commonwealth against all three parties. The Injunction requested that the Court order the parties to do an Immediate Response Action or be subject to fines of up to $25,000 per day.

"Attorney O'Brien followed up with this wording, 'Although the statue authorizes the Commonwealth to conduct cleanups using money from especially designated funds and seeking cost recovery from liable parties later, the funds available for cleanups is limited.' As a conclusion, O'Brien said that ordering responsible parties to perform the remediation is a more efficient use of the Commonwealth's resources."

"$25,000 per day," screamed the Jester, "that's roughly 9 million per year. Were they crazy?"

"Jester," I said, "you must realize that Massachusetts is an equal opportunity state that shows no prejudice to the financial condition of its subjects. The size and wealth of the victim has no bearing in the eyes of M.G.L Chapter 21E.

"While I may laugh at O'Brien's letter and Injunction, it was no laughing matter. Sad but true, that letter exemplified one of the basic problems with CERCLA and the state laws patterned after CERCLA. The truth is that the State of Massachusetts had no moneys at the time to do a cleanup. When government agencies have no money, anyone can be chosen to pay the cost of remediation. In the case of Panama Street, Hutchins Tool was chosen and Attorney O'Brien was the State of Massachusetts' enforcer."

The Muse broke in with a comment, "Just as I've told you Zeus. You can see that the lawyers talked settlement, but never settled. They probably saw that there was still a little meat left on those bones and raised the ante by forcing the State to bring a preliminary injunction against all of the parties."

"Tell us more, Mr. Hutchins," said the Muse.

"I think the Muse is wrong in her evaluation of the situation," I said. "Actually I believe it was the legal jousting that made Attorney O'Brien decide to push on with the Injunction. She had certainly given all the lawyers involved enough warning.

"By this time, I was sure that no one was in control of this Panama Street environmental problem. For example: The DEP gave this Site their highest priority listing and then let things slip with no cleanup for seven years, the lawyers thought they had a settlement and did not go to trial, the Attorney General's office was taking the DEP's case by filing a Preliminary Injunction.

"The risk to human health from what was called carcinogenic agents in the brook had abated to the point where the most prominent independent expert in Massachusetts called it no imminent hazard. As crazy as it sounds, I decided that I could do something. To do something was better than doing nothing and meekly accepting what I had been going through.

"Sensing that I could get the Judge's attention and relief for Hutchins Tool, I sat down and wrote a Counterclaim to the Preliminary Injunction. It took me until two o'clock in the morning to finish the Counterclaim and I drove 90 miles to Suffolk Superior Court in Boston to present it before Judge Ireland. As a preface before Claim One, I stated that I was not an attorney but said that I realized that I, as an officer of Hutchins Tool, could be named personally as a responsible party. Recognizing the potential personal exposure, I was defending myself, not Hutchins Tool. Attorney Hadley would submit Hutchins Tool's Counterclaim to the Court.

"I arrived in Boston early because I was unsure of the location of the courtroom. I was fortunate to find the courtroom quickly and it was empty except for a guard. When the court clerk came from the judge's chambers and sat at his desk, I walked up to the desk and told him that I was unfamiliar with presenting the Counterclaim. He casually said, 'No problem.' He then date-stamped a copy of the Counterclaim and brought it back to the Judge. I was elated. I would have my Counterclaim read along with those of the named parties. Here is a copy of my Counterclaim if it is of any interest to you, Zeus."

Zeus looked down from the podium and said, "Hold it up." He then said, "OK, I've got it."

I have heard of quick reads, but I still found Zeus' method unbelievable. Expecting that the Jester lacked these reading skills, I gave him this copy:

July 29, 1996

Michael Joseph Donovan
Clerk for Civil Business
Suffolk Superior Court
Old Courthouse, Room 117
Boston, MA 02108
ATTENTION: Session Clerk

RE: COMMONWEALTH OF MASSACHUSETTS
VS HUTCHINS TOOL & ENGINEERING CO., INC.

My name is Donald C. Hutchins and I am an officer and an owner of the Hutchins Tool & Engineering Co., Inc. I am not an attorney and am not familiar with the prescribed format for answering the Commonwealth's Complaint No. 965036587-G. However, I understand that liability under Massachusetts G.L. 21E is not restricted by a corporation's limited liability status. Therefore because I am an officer of Hutchins Tool, liability, penalties, and punishment could extend beyond the boundaries of the Corporation and expose my home and assets to seizure. As a consequence, I could be exposed to all the penalties of this injunction. For this reason, please accept my answer to this summons as my Counterclaim against the Commonwealth of Massachusetts and the Massachusetts Department of Environmental Protection. If the DEP can attach my estate, I feel it is only just that I defend myself against the DEP's transgressions.

1. As a counterclaim, I claim:

The Massachusetts DEP and certain persons employed by the DEP have violated my civil rights under the United States Constitution through their actions and threats over the past five

174

*years. Using hearsay and unsubstantiated testimony gathered
and submitted by the property owner's Attorney and neglecting
opposing views she gathered from former Hutchins Tool employees who worked at that site, Ms. Symington, a DEP employee with no credentials in the field of law or ground water
chemistry, named Hutchins Tool a potentially responsible
party. The alleged incidents, for which she judged Hutchins
Tool guilty, she claimed took place in the 1970's many years
before the environmental laws were legislated. On the recom-
mendation of the property owner, Ms. Symington passed over
investigating over 20 other former occupants from a list, which
included a furniture stripping company, machine shops, an oil
distributor and a refrigeration dealer.*

*Initial environmental legislation created the DEP to educate
the public and do priority cleanups. The laws were known as
"Super-fund" laws because these Superfund moneys would be
used by the Massachusetts DEP and their federal counterparts
to do the cleanups. The intent was that after the DEP did the
cleanup, they would seek out any responsible party and seek
reimbursement. Unfortunately, the drafters of the environmental legislation were unaware of two vital factors. First, the
technology for economical cleanups was not developed. Second, when the limited funds voted for cleanups were depleted,
the public would give little support for increasing taxes to
provide additional funds. It is no secret that the DEP has no
funds and therefore the DEP must get cleanup funding from
any source available. The sources they must attach in their
hope of raising funds must come from what the DEP and legal
profession has called "deep pockets." Unfortunately, Hutchins
Tool was named because of the presumption that Hutchins Tool
and the owners had "deep pockets." This assumption was
made without any investigation of our financial status at the
encouragement of Attorney Moore who represents the owner of
the building.*

Attorney Moore's proactive stance to involve Hutchins Tool included gathering statements from Mr. Peroulakis which Mr. Peroulakis later rescinded. With Attorney Moore's encouragement, the DEP has nurtured this idea that Hutchins Tool has "deep pockets." Once put in this category, it is easy for DEP personnel to paint us as obstructers to their plans of having us fund their $148,000 in Departmental expenses, a potentially million dollar cleanup, triple damages and any further fees they might need to fulfill their mission. The public will not vote the DEP tax moneys, so the DEP taxes Hutchins Tool with their unique collection system.

These actions by the DEP have destroyed Hutchins Tool as a viable business. Because we disclosed this DEP liability on our financial statements, our mortgage and bank debt was turned over to the FDIC when the Bank of New England failed. Also, we can not sell the business because no buyer can accept the DEP liability.

The Court can understand that a small business like Hutchins is the sole income and support for the owner's life and family. By destroying Hutchins Tool, the DEP destroys my livelihood. I claim that I have a right to work and to support my family. I also claim that the DEP and DEP personnel have preempted my constitutional rights to a fair trial, judgment by my peers and speedy justice. The DEP's ongoing penalties and threats of triple damages have been cruel and abusive. The fines, assessments and remediable funding demanded by the DEP are in reality disguised taxes which will be used by the DEP to pay their Departmental expenses. Therefore, I claim that I am a citizen being taxed by the State unfairly. This violates my rights granted by the Constitution of the United States.

Because the DEP has no funds to carry out its assigned task of cleaning up polluted sites and the press demands an accounting, the DEP has turned to their own devices to raise this money. Rather than work with companies and persons involved in these sites as they are chartered to do, the atmosphere of the DEP is immediately adversarial. The first correspondence we *received from the DEP was a letter naming us a potentially responsible party and telling about the massive penalties and triple damages we faced for not paying the DEP Departmental costs. Also, with every letter citing laws and penalties, it became impossible for us to talk to the DEP without expensive legal counsel. To date, we have spent over $100,000 for legal fees, which in itself is an unjust penalty. Even worse, it is money that could have been spent on cleanup.*

I welcome this opportunity to air our story to the Court. Attorney O'Brien has commented to us through our Attorney that this injunction is simply to tidy up the case. As a Massachusetts citizen, I don't understand this logic. We'll have legal fees and there will be court costs for an injunction that has no hope of fulfillment. We have no money to pay and as a result, we could be considered in contempt of court. I, as an owner of Hutchins Tool could be included in a contempt charge. As Attorney O'Brien tidies up, we are forced deeper and deeper into trouble. At $25,000 per day, we'll be down three million dollars by Christmas.

I expect that very few environmental cases have reached this point of litigation. This may be one of the first times that a party has come forth to tell the judicial branch how the executive branch in the form of the DEP is administering these environmental laws. Most people know that in Massachusetts, probably 90% of environmental spending has gone to litigation and little for cleanup. Those parts of the law dealing with cleanup have failed. What people do not know is that the DEP in a desperate effort for some success has decimated the civil rights of owners of property and small companies. DEP personnel act as evidence gatherers, judge and jury not unlike the Spanish inquisitors or the Salem witch hunters. I solicit, beg and petition the Court to investigate my claim that the DEP and DEP personnel have violated my civil rights. If this challenge by the Court allows me to present evidence of these violations, we can bring the balance of power held by the *judiciary branch to right these wrongs. It will send a message to the DEP that they can better succeed in their mission by working with people rather than to litigate their destruction. I pray that no one will have to go through what I have gone through for the past five years. Five years after Ms. Symington's "judgment," the lawyers are $200,000 richer and Attorney Moore is now considered a leading environmental attorney.*

The time has come for the Court to say no to the DEP. They can not trash the rights of citizens even if it will help them meet their goals. How awful it is to think that they have destroyed my business while not one dollar has been spent to clean up the Panama Street site.

2. As a counterclaim, I claim:

Massachusetts DEP personnel have withheld information from the Court which would show that the conditions of Pecousic Brook do not pose an imminent hazard to human health or the environment. Because Attorney O'Brien has cited such imminent hazard as the primary reason for the Injunction, withholding this information will obviously encourage the Court to allow the Injunction against Hutchins Tool.

I have included a report from Menzie, Cura, & Associates, Inc. entitled, "Imminent Hazard Evaluation of Pecousic Brook." Menzie, Cura, and Associates of Chelmsford, MA are considered the preeminent hazardous water experts in the State and were invited to investigate the brook in response to a DEP letter dated June 8, 1994.

As the Court will understand, this report, done at the request and following the mandates of the DEP, should have been included with Attorney O'Brien's Pleadings as part of her Attachment J. After the Court reads this report, the Court may draw its own conclusions as to why it was omitted by the DEP.

I believe the Court will realize that the major premise that made Panama Street a high priority/primary site is without substance. The Menzie Report states that there is no imminent danger to health through the brook. Therefore, there is no reason for a Fast Track Injunction against Hutchins Tool. As a mater of fact, there is every reason for the Court to force a downgrading of this priority rating to allow the DEP to focus on sites that do pose a threat to health. It is senseless and uneconomical to waste the time of the Court and the resources of the DEP dueling with windmills.

3. As a counterclaim, I claim:

DEP personnel have conspired through Attorney Moore over the past six years to extract moneys from Hutchins Tool and its Officers on the mistaken notion that we had "Deep Pockets." Specific examples of the collusion can be found with two digested versions of depositions from Mr. Peroulakis and Mr. Vallerie found in Attorney O'Brien's Pleadings. (The Court should understand that the hazardous materials were discovered through a MGL 21 E drilling test being conducted so that Mr. Peroulakis and Mr. Vallerie could finance the purchase of the building from Mr. Thompson. There are depositions available that testify to the fact that Mr. Vallerie supervised the use of the hazardous material listed in these complaints at the time of the 21E drilling and for the previous 10 years.) We continue to challenge the truth of these depositions on grounds that both Mr. Peroulakis and Mr. Vallerie conspired to name Hutchins Tool to deflect the real blame from themselves.

Attorney Moore selected only small portions of these two depositions to pass on to the DEP from the thousands of words said in our defense. Hutchins Tool would be pleased to furnish the Court with about twenty other depositions and statements, which refute the two that Attorney O'Brien, elected to use. For the DEP to use these prejudiced statements without allowing me to face and challenge my accusers violates many of my civil rights. As such, they should not be used as evidence in this civil action.

4. As a counterclaim, I claim:

With this request for an injunction against Hutchins Tool, the DEP has changed our status from "Potentially Responsible" to "Responsible Party" without due process. Who changed Hutchins Tool's status? Who made that decision? Again, the DEP has exceeded its authority and acted as judge and jury. Hutchins Tool is not a responsible party and I challenge the DEP's right to change our status without a hearing before an impartial body empowered to make that decision.

5. As a counterclaim, I claim:

Attorney O'Brien's claim that Hutchins Tool is responsible for the NAPL as listed in paragraph 32, page 7 of her "Description of the Action" is without merit as it applies to Hutchins Tool. Attorney O'Brien does not show any evidence that Hutchins Tool stored or used NAPL at the site within the meaning of C. 21E.

The Court's inquiries will show that an oil distribution company occupied that section of the building within the past two years and that Brookdale Associates, Inc. is the current occupant. Both of these companies used or are using NAPL at the site within ten feet of the floor drain where this well was drilled.

———————————— *CONCLUSION* ————————————

Attorney O'Brien's request for a "Fast" Injunction against Hutchins Tool on this complaint is totally without merit. Now that the Court knows that the Menzie Report states that the Pecousic Brook poses no imminent danger to health or the environment, the need for a Fast Track Injunction would be counterproductive and continue to be overly punitive to Hutchins Tool. Attorney O'Brien should be refused an Injunction against Hutchins Tool and with the refusal should be a warning to the DEP that they are violating the civil rights of those citizens that they should be serving. Here is an opportunity for the Court to balance the power of the executive branch with reason. In the long run, education and cooperation from the DEP will get more remediation than bullying. The only losers will be the lawyers who think of environmental legislation as their endowment fund.

Donald C. Hutchins
1047 Longmeadow Street
Longmeadow, MA 01106

Now Zeus stood up so that his imposing figure loomed high over the podium. In a louder voice than usual, he said, "Excellent Hutchins, your claims make sense. You finally cut to the truth. Judge Ireland must have appreciated what you were telling him."

Zeus startled me with his enthusiastic response and as he sat down again, I said, "Thank you, thank you for saying that about my Counterclaim. Unfortunately, it didn't happen that way. The truth is that I waited for Hadley and the other attorneys to arrive before the Judge came from his chambers. I gave each of the attorneys a copy of my Counterclaim as we exchanged greetings. Hadley gave me a copy of the Counterclaim he had prepared for Hutchins Tool.

"I leafed through Hadley's Counterclaim as we waited quietly for the Judge. When the Judge called for the attorneys to come forward to sit at the tables, I walked forward and sat down with them. The Judge called for the representatives to introduce themselves. At my turn, I stood up and told the Judge my name and

said I was an Officer of Hutchins Tool, but I was there to represent myself personally. After the lawyers introduced themselves
and we all sat down, the judge asked me to come to his bench.
When I got there, he said, 'I can't allow your Counterclaim to be
included because you are not a practicing attorney in Massachusetts. Please pick it up from the clerk and return to the spectator
seats. I can't even allow you to sit up front at the lawyers' tables."

At this point, the Jester started shaking his head and he said,
"You don't know when to give up, do you? You've got nerve, I'll
give you credit for that."

Now Zeus said, "They didn't let you speak. The citizens in
Greece and Rome had the right to petition. What's happening in
America? Americans talk about democracy, but I see no signs
they practice it. The government has been holding your business
in bondage for seven years and you can't speak up in a Massachusetts' courtroom! Everyone else in the courtroom was earning a
big fee or held a nice civil service job. You were defending yourself from the State that was about to take away your business and
assets. You couldn't speak up to defend yourself? You can have
your democracy; I'll take the Greek's republican form of government where citizens had a voice in their legislative bodies. Greece
had no Bill of Rights, but the citizens had rights. It's time for
America to add a 'Bill of Responsibilities' that applies to both
citizens and elected officials."

When Zeus finished, I was happy with what he said. I was also
happy when Attorney Mark Bluver, who represented Precision
EDM at the courthouse, told me after the session that he thought
I had some good arguments in my Counterclaim. I never did get
a reaction from Attorney Hadley. I assume all he wondered was
what is this fool Hutchins going to do next?

I continued by telling Zeus, "Six weeks after the court session,
Judge Ireland gave his Opinion on the Preliminary Injunction for
an Immediate Response Action. In his Opinion, he denied the
Injunction on grounds that the State had not proved that an immediate response was required. You should realize that this re-

fusal applied only to the Injunction for an Immediate Response Action and that the litigation of the Commonwealth vs. the three parties continued on a regular court-tracking schedule.

"Things at Hutchins Tool continued their downward spiral as this Panama Street problem dragged on. My office manager was unable to make up the withholding taxes he had missed paying. He showed me a notice from the IRS that noted that we were behind although we were not being pressed for payment. Our business had recovered to the point where I did not have to personally supplement the payroll. Unfortunately, our cash flow was not good enough to pay the back taxes owed. I should also add that I had been drawing no salary from Hutchins Tool for about 20 months.

"When we attempted to sell assets, such as one of our buildings, we could not get approval from RECOLL, the FDIC administrator that was holding our loans. Each time we had buyers, the RECOLL loan officer managing our file was changed before he or she could bring it to committee. RECOLL was then moved from East Hartford to Boston, which totally complicated any transaction we could make.

"The financial advisors at RECOLL told me that the solution was to have a commercial bank refinance our loans. RECOLL would even discount the loans by 30% to get it done.

"Hearing this, I visited banks in the area that had been soliciting our business for years. In every case, the banks were excited to do the refinancing until they read the environmental litigation disclosure on our statements. At that point, they all had to back off. They could not loan money to companies where damage settlements could wipe out the majority of all assets. The best the banks could say was please return with a loan request when the environmental litigation is resolved."

XXII.　　　The IRS

I continued to testify by saying, "I'm sure that even the heavens have heard about the United States Internal Revenue Service. Just that name raises fear in the hearts of taxpayers. Americans are concerned with audits and worry about such things as writing off too much for childcare and deducting expenses for a business office in their home.

"Because Hutchins Tool had breezed through IRS audits with no problem, I nurtured no neurotic concerns for the IRS. To me, they were just another government agency doing their job.

"This complacency was shattered one day when my office manager came to me and said that the balances of Hutchins Tool's checking accounts were screwed up. Because cash flow had become critical to our operation, he had the habit of checking Hutchins Tool's account balances every morning. On this particular day, he was frantic as he told me that all the balances came back as zero.

"After working through a maze of bank officials at different offices, we finally found one person who could tell us what had happened. She said that the IRS had seized the accounts. She couldn't tell us if our checking accounts would continue to be drawn down by the IRS or if future deposits would remain in the accounts. She did say that it was her experience that they hit once and not again for thirty days.

"All this was particularly disturbing to me because six weeks earlier I had met with Attorney Penkethman, who specialized in credit problems, and presented him with the notices we had gotten from the IRS. Penkethman treated it as a common problem that he dealt with frequently and contacted the IRS office to set up some kind of payment schedule for Hutchins Tool.

"When our checking accounts were seized, I called Penkethman and he was in disbelief. He said it had never happened to any client before. When I asked if we should deposit cash to cover outstanding checks, he was confused as to just what we should do. It was then that I became a good telephone friend of the bank official. She seemed to be the only one with any answers and encouraged me that I probably had a grace period of thirty days before the IRS drained the accounts again."

"What about the payroll checks and the checks that would be cashed the next day?" Asked the Jester. "You must have gone wacko. All you would need is to have a payroll check bounce and your employees would walk!"

I replied, "You've got that one right Jester. I'm sure my office manager hasn't gotten over that scare to this day. Fortunately, I was able to cover the accounts with a personal deposit and, true to the bank officer's prediction, the IRS didn't hit the accounts again.

"When Attorney Penkethman finally talked to the right people at the IRS, they said that the seized funds could not be retrieved and that our future dealings would be with Revenue Officer Fred Lyons at the Springfield Field Office.

"Some weeks later, I met with Attorney Penkethman and we walked a few blocks to the IRS office. I should have been suspicious when Penkethman appeared confused as to the location of the office. I didn't find it unusual that he did not know Mr. Lyons because I assumed that the IRS staff changed frequently.

"We met Fred Lyons and he led us to a very small room that contained one table, three chairs and one calendar on the wall that showed three months at a time. Lyons was carrying a slim file folder, which he placed on the desk. He started by asking Penkethman for some forms that he had sent Penkethman the week before.

"Attorney Penkethman's reaction startled me. He acted like a schoolboy who had not done his homework. He stumbled over his words as he tried to explain why he did not have the forms with him. I point this out not to fault Penkethman, but only to show my stress in a legal forum where I had no control.

"I think that it was at that point that Lyons and I formed a small bond. He left the room and returned with some blank forms. From that point on, he acted as though Attorney Penkethman was not present. He told me to fill out the blank forms and return them to him in two weeks. He glanced up at the calendar and called out an appointment date and time.

"As we stood up to leave, Lyons continued to ignore Attorney Penkethman. As he shook my hand, he said to me in a very loud voice, 'Mr. Hutchins, I think we can work this out together. I'll see you in two weeks.' That was the last time I ever saw Attorney Penkethman although I did call him when I received a bill from his firm for $1,700.00 for services. The time billed on the day of that visit was for two and one half-hours. I can only assume that the remainder was for his phone calls to the bank and IRS offices plus a one-page letter of engagement. Considering his actions in the IRS office, I did not assume that he had spent much time on research.

"You may imagine that paying monthly installments for these back taxes was touch and go. For a long time, I had an IRS payment calendar in my mind. This was superimposed by a mental biorhythm chart that reflected my mood swings a month at a time. I would scratch funds together and see Fred Lyons and hand him the payment. That would place my IRS mood clock at a high point. Then he would search the calendar to select a date for the next appointment, which to me was the next payment. Holiday months were great because I could pick up an extra week. Each time I left the IRS office, the high would end and I would start moving things around in my head to find money for the next payment. At times when Hutchins Tool had no funds, I would have to write a personal check.

I know that Lyons had heard every excuse and every story so I never bullshitted him. The district manager rated revenue officers on collections and seizures and I knew that Lyons needed reasons for not seizing our assets. I think we were both relieved when I could show him offers from buyers for our buildings or equipment that could furnish the cash to pay off this IRS debt.

"Federal agencies change staff assignments frequently. I shouldn't have been surprised when my secretary came to me one day to say that a Fred Lyons was in the waiting room. After she brought him to my office, I could see him looking around at the carpeting, stuffed chairs and watercolors on the walls.

"He started by telling me that he had been transferred to another office and needed to clear up his case load. He then suggested that he could wave some penalties and interest on what we owed if I could pay off the balance owed immediately.

"He showed disbelief when I said that that would not be possible. I'm sure that when he saw our valuable property, he expected that I would simply get a bank loan and pay off the IRS. It would save me the huge penalties and the IRS's usury type interest that was accumulating rapidly. I thought I should tell him about the Panama Street litigation and the impossibility of refinancing, however, before I could get into that, he stood up and started to leave. As I walked him to the door, he said, "I had hoped we could close this out because I've heard that the IRS District Office is looking for more seizures. Good luck."

"Within a month after Fred Lyons left, one of our buildings was seized and advertised in the local newspapers. The large block type advertisement announced the seizure and called for a sealed bid sale to take place at the IRS office.

"That Lyons is the man," said the Jester. "He was really trying to help. The IRS gets a lot of bad raps, so they should have more agents like him."

"You're right on," I replied. "There is no doubt in my mind that Fred Lyons knew what would happen after he was off the account and I'm sure he had visited my office in an attempt to help us out. I had lived in the community all my life, so you would expect I would have been extremely embarrassed by the seizure notice in the paper. Actually, starting at the time of the real estate seizure my mood became one of defiance toward bureaucracy. I know that there are intelligent, hard working and decent people like Fred Lyons everywhere, but bureaucratic systems just eat them up and make them conform to unreasonable codes of behavior.

"I was concerned when the sealed bid was advertised as to the reaction of the Hutchins Tool employees. It was only natural for them to anguish over their jobs and future. I also felt badly for my wife and children because I knew that they had to answer questions and had no answers to give. I'm sure it was not pleasant for them to have me advertised as a deadbeat.

"Prior to the sale, a few bottom fishermen visited the plant at different times to inspect the building. Before you ask, Jester, we call investors looking for assets they can steal at a low price, bottom fishermen. Fortunately, my office was not in that building so that I did not have to deal with them.

"At the appointed time and day, I sat with a revenue officer at the IRS office and waited, but no bidders came. When it was over and the IRS Officer declared no sale, he said to me, 'I didn't think anyone would bid.' When I asked why the government would spend the time and money to seize and advertise if they expected no sale, he simply said, 'That's just part of the collection process. We have to show Boston that we're doing the job.'

"I wanted to scream, 'You created all this humiliation and bad press for Hutchins Tool, so you jerks can show that you're doing the job! Fred Lyons was doing the job. He was collecting back taxes, penalties and interest every month. Why does the Boston office have to rate revenue officers by the number of seizures they achieve?'

"I held back my anger to ask what would happen next. He answered that he could now put us on a regular schedule of payments, which would clear things up in two years. That happened and we recently finished paying on that schedule. As a result, the IRS has gotten back every tax dollar we owed plus tremendous penalties and interest. I'm sure that the IRS assumes that their collection system did its job. Actually, I give all the credit to Fred Lyons."

I was surprised how quiet things had become in that celestial courtroom. I sensed that Zeus, the Jester and the Muse were fascinated by my story. I realized that what I told them must have sounded like a soap opera. I wondered if the gods did have 'soaps' for their afternoon entertainment.

Zeus interrupted my thoughts by saying, "Mr. Hutchins, I can see that the Panama Street litigation was affecting every part of your business. I didn't realize that businesses in America are so fragile. It appears that the ongoing litigation makes it impossible for Hutchins Tool to borrow, sell assets, downsize, reorganize production capacity, etc. It all stems from a DEP manager doing a limited investigation and declaring Hutchins a responsible party. Using that declaration as evidence, the attorney for the property owner sued Hutchins Tool to pay the cost of a cleanup at a potential cost of over one million dollars.

"Mr. Hutchins, when will this end?"

"Zeus, I can't answer that question," I said. "Every few months, Attorney Hadley tells me that settlement will come soon, but it never happens. We have a saying in America. It is that you can't see the forest for the trees."

The Jester jumped up with a smile on his face and said, "The forest, the trees; is this one of these environmental expressions?"

"No," I said, "it means that people deal with individual things like the trees and do not see the overall picture, like the whole forest. What I am trying to say is that people working in both public and private bureaucracies are so intent on doing the tasks assigned to them, they lose direction, they lose sight of the goals they are organized to meet.

"While much of this is harmless and gives the staffs of government agencies gainful employment, it also creates an atmosphere in which citizens can be badly harmed. That is what has happened under CERCLA. Since this law was enacted in 1980 and the states copied this law in the early 1980's, a government clerk can accuse any person, a city or any business of being a responsible party. Once accused, the person can carry that burden for years with little hope of changing that summary judgement."

Now Zeus spoke, "I can't believe that would happen in America. That's not in the classic tradition of Greece and Rome. To survive, America needs to follow the classic model that I introduced when America was a young nation. A great nation can not allow office clerks to be both the judge and jury of their peers. Of course Hutchins, you may be wrong. I'm sure the DEP would try to work with Hutchins Tool if you gave them the opportunity. Certainly their mission is to clean up sites like Panama Street."

I replied, "That was my hope. However, the reality is that in the DEP there are many that see the trees and not the forest. As an example, let me tell you about Clean Harbors, Inc."

XXIII.   Clean Harbors

I continued my testimony by telling Zeus about my attempt at working with the DEP to complete the remediation of Panama Street. "Zeus, in the summer of 1996, I was encouraged to take action myself after reading Dr. Jerome Cura's expert opinion that, 'No imminent danger exists in regards to the presence of VOC's in Pecousic Brook.'

"As you know this brook runs through the back of the Panama Street property and was cited by a DEP engineer originally as the reason for their priority classification. Now that Dr. Cura's report indicated that the Brook showed little if any presence of VOC's, purging the pollutants from the soil at the site could result in a Response Action Outcome (RAO) statement or in laymen's terms, a clean bill of health.

"I carried all the information available to me for Panama Street to Jim Gagnon, a Licensed Site Professional (LSP). Under current Massachusetts's regulations, an LSP is licensed to test water and soil samples and to evaluate the condition of hazardous waste sites. Most importantly to me, an LSP has the authority to write an RAO.

"After studying the data, Jim Gagnon told me that the pollution was localized around the floor drains and in one area of the ground behind the building. Therefore it would be possible to excavate these areas and ship the soil and water collected to a reclaiming facility or a registered waste site.

"I turned next to Clean Harbors Environmental Services, Inc., an environmental company experienced at doing remediation. On August 8, 1996, I met with Nick Nicotra, a technologist at Clean Harbors. He too studied the Panama Street reports and concluded that Clean Harbors could clean up the Site by removing the polluted soil and water. Essentially, Clean Harbors' giant trucks would haul it away.

"Energized by this information and believing that the insurance carriers would pay Clean Harbors for this work, I decided to discuss these ideas with Debra Kelley-Dominick, who was responsible for the Panama Street project for the DEP. Therefore, I sent the following letter to her attention at the DEP."

August 6, 1996

Ms. Debra Kelley-Dominick
Massachusetts Department of Environmental Protection
436 Dwight Street
Springfield, MA 01103

Dear Ms. Kelley-Dominick:

After the Injunction Hearing in Boston, I was encouraged by Attorney Paul Doherty, an associate of Attorney Hadley, to attempt to personally intervene to find a business solution rather than a legal solution to the Panama Street environmental problem. With this in mind, I consulted with a local Licensed Site Professional who has worked with your office but has not been involved with the Panama Street site. I furnished him with copies of the reports available on the site including the latest report done last December by ECS

This LSP feels there is sufficient data to do remediation and furnish a Response Action Outcome (RAO) statement to the DEP. He has told me that the current procedures for remediation, assessment, and resolution were designed by the DEP to cover such sites as Panama Street in the most economical and effective way. The route through litigation is endless, enriches only lawyers and has not shown positive results. With our experience over the past six years, I expect both you and I could agree with him.

The LSP's study of the Panama Street site-documents indicates to him the source of the pollution. The reports show the migration, the extent and the decrease in measured levels, which indicate the source has not continued to produce pollutants, and probably has been removed. Most importantly, ECS's investigation, which was performed by methods prescribed by your office, shows no evidence of DNAPL within the deeper soils.

The LSP finds the problems are localized around the two drains and one area behind the building. His suggested remediation is removal of contaminated soils from the site to a licensed disposal area offsite. At that point, the remaining soil and water can be tested to guarantee that what remains meets the current guidelines.

The beauty of this plan is that it can be completed under the guidance of the DEP and LSP. It is effective in that if the pollution is removed, the potential for harm is removed. However, most importantly, the cost for cleanup can be reasonably estimated because the cost for removal and off site disposal is specific as compared to such methods as pump and treat which go on indefinitely.

To confirm the LSP's concept, I have talked with "Clean Harbors, Inc." a well-known environmental-services-company.

Having reviewed the same Panama Street reports that I showed the LSP, the people at "Clean Harbors" agree with his conclusions. They see a plan to remove contaminated soils and liquids from areas around the drains and in back of the plant as doable. They are able to quote me hard costs on doing the work and disposing of the soil and liquid waste in a controlled, environmentally safe manner. They can test on site and extend the removal to that point when the current DEP standards are met. They caution me that this work will be costly but that the costs will be known and the results obtainable within a specific time period. With pump and treat, vapor extraction and other methods one never knows the eventual cost or the extent of time required achieving the result. The open-ended unknown costs and the indefinite completion term are totally unacceptable to the insurance companies and are the basic reasons why this conflict has dragged on.

Please advise me if the approach I am taking could gain acceptance by your office. From what I have learned, this Panama Street site could be handled under the DEP's RAO procedures. Please call me at 781-6280 to discuss this matter.

I would be happy to visit your office to discuss this with you and your associates. I would prefer to discuss this privately in your office so that I can learn your approach and attitude before we involve the other parties, attorneys, etc. I prefer discussion rather than any formal, written reply from you. I think discussions, directly between us, can get us further than we have gotten through all the legal intervention.

My hope is to get all the parties, including the DEP, through this as quickly and efficiently as possible.

Sincerely yours,

Donald C. Hutchins

196

"I assumed that there would be an immediate response and that all the parties involved could have a productive meeting to arrange this Clean Harbors' solution.

"The key was the fact that Clean Harbors could give an accurate estimate for the cleanup costs. To judge the cost of hauling soil to a waste site is much more accurate than estimating the time, manpower, equipment and energy needed to pump groundwater out of the ground and put it through a filter. This pump and treat method could take years.

"This Clean Harbors' plan eliminated the need for the insurance companies to write a blank check which had been a big stumbling block. If all agreed, we could start almost immediately.

"I had no response from Kelley-Dominick and do not know what type of DEP constraints kept her from discussing the Clean Harbors' plan with me. I was surprised to receive this very formal, legally phrased letter from Michelle O'Brien, the Assistant Attorney General of Massachusetts, who led the DEP litigation team."

August 22, 1996

Donald C. Hutchins
Hutchins Tool & Engineering Company
60 Brookdale Drive
Springfield, MA 01104

Re: One Panama Street, East Longmeadow

Dear Mr. Hutchins:

I am writing in response to your letter dated August 6, 1996 to Debra Kelley-Dominick of the Department of Environmental Protection (DEP). We appreciate your interest in trying to achieve a solution to the environmental contamination problems at the Panama Street site.

As you know, DEP spent many months working with the parties, attorneys, and consultants involved in this matter in an attempt to achieve a resolution that would ensure successful remediation of the site. In addition, I initiated meetings and other discussions among the parties to try to reach a negotiated settlement of this matter. For various reasons, however, our discussions were fruitless and the matter is now in litigation.

The Commonwealth remains willing to discuss settlement of this matter and, as a necessary part of that, the remediation alternatives for the site. Our goal continues to be to have one or more of the parties commit to performing the necessary response actions at the site, with particular emphasis on the actions necessary to prevent the further migration of hazardous materials in groundwater. The commitment must be in the form of a judicially enforceable agreement, however. We do not believe it would be productive to discuss remediation alternatives at this time, short of a commitment by you and/or your company to perform the necessary remediation.

Please feel free to contact me should you or your attorneys wish to discuss this further.

Very truly yours,

Michelle N. O'Brien
Assistant Attorney General
Environmental Protection Division

"Ms. Kelly-Dominick of the DEP staff was not given the opportunity to discuss this Clean Harbors plan with us. I suspect that her supervisor, the system or her fear of being out of step with her peers would not allow her to contact me regarding the concept of using a Licensed Site Professional to direct the remediation of the Panama Street site.

"Perhaps somebody felt that this plan would foreclose on the possibility that the DEP costs incurred for the Panama Street site would be paid by Hutchins Tool rather than from the DEP budget. Maybe Attorney O'Brien, the Assistant Attorney General, retained control. Whatever the reason, the DEP lost their best opportunity to have the insurance companies underwrite cleanup costs for the Site.

"This extinguished any illusion I may have had that the DEP's first priority was the safety of Massachusetts' citizens. It is clear to me now that personnel at the DEP and other environmental regulatory agencies march in lock step doing their daily tasks giving their own job security the first priority. If the DEP put a cleanup on Panama Street in a truly high priority classification, would the cleanup have languished for over eight years?"

"I...don't...think...so," said the Jester in a slow, singsong voice. The Jester stopped when Zeus looked at him and he replied, "I'm sorry Zeus, just something that people said when I lived in California."

Now Zeus laughed and repeated the sentence the same way in his deep booming voice, "I...don't...think...so!"

When Zeus continued, he looked at the Muse and said, "Muse, I realize that you're trying to show that lawyers have gained the most financially and therefore are responsible for CERCLA. From what I am hearing, it appears that most of the lawyers and environmental agency employees do these things just as a robotic response as part of their profession."

The Muse answered, "I understand how it is difficult for you to see intent on the part of these local lawyers, but you must understand how I have influenced the trial lawyer's associations to keep

CERCLA type laws alive.

"I did not stop after formulating CERCLA. I have continued to lobby right up until the present time. Here are some examples of my methods of making fear of carcinogens overpower mortals' abilities to reason."

XXIV.   Fear Ahead of Reason

Before the Muse continued further, I jumped up to speak. I could see that this was taking the same course as most environmental discussions. Therefore I said, "Let's make this simple. I want a clean environment as much or more than the next person. If I had been a congressman, I would have voted for all the environmental bills passed by Congress including CERCLA.

"However, today I am in the unique position to know that CERCLA is flawed. I've been there, I've lived with it and I've been its victim.

"What America does not recognize is that we have all been CERCLA's victims. Its flaws do not allow the law to function properly to meet the goals of the Congresspersons that framed it. A few others have seen its flaws, including candidates elected to national offices during the past ten years, but nothing has changed CERCLA. The goal of CERCLA was remediation and CERCLA has made very little progress towards that goal. Ten times the money spent on remediation has been spent on litigation. In my opinion, this is unpardonable.

"Rachel Carson's goal of banning the sale and use of DDT and other insecticides was reached many years before the CERCLA legislation was passed by Congress. We should recognize that most of the environmental successes were the result of the early environmental laws, which contained fines and other penalties for wrongdoers. CERCLA on the other hand has forced people to clean up insignificant low priority sites while many of the worst offenders remain hidden. The reason for CERCLA's failures is its use of civil penalties rather than criminal law.

"Let's consider what would have happened if the early environmental legislation had called for soil testing on farms to discover the residue of DDT. Also, let's assume that these same laws made the test findings reportable to state environmental agencies so the reports became a matter of public record. If that had happened, how long do you think it would have taken sharp lawyers to find cancer victims that could show that they had purchased food from the farms that reported remnants of DDT in their soil? My guess is that these lawyers would have burned rubber driving to courts to file damage claims. Eventually, large corporate farms would have found defenses to protect their assets. However, local farmers with roadside stands or those specialized farms who proudly attached their logo to their produce would find themselves in expensive legal battles that they could not afford to fight."

"It could happen," said the Jester. "If a farmer sold strawberries to a customer from his roadside stand, it would be easy to show that the berries may have contained DDT. I think that somebody said that DDT caused tumors in female rats or was it mice. Whatever, you humans are susceptible to all sorts of toxic agents. Maybe those farmers should have known better than to use DDT. Of course, at the time those cancer victims were probably using DDT in their own flower gardens. Who can prove that these cancer victims didn't ingest DDT from using it around their homes?

"I'm happy they didn't start testing the ground water of strawberry patches for DDT residue. The only way you could straighten it all out would be to have the courts decide. I mean, the cancer victims would retain lawyers so the farmers would need their own lawyers to defend themselves. This is too confusing. Hutchins, why did you bring it up?"

"Jester," I replied, "if the original environmental legislation that Rachel Carson inspired was written with the same penalty structure as CERCLA, that strawberry farmer's story would have happened over and over again in America. I'm sure that there is residue of DDT in the soil of many apple orchards, wine vineyards and soybean farms all over America. I believe that it follows that the consumers of the apples, wines and soy would have ingested this DDT.

"There are only two elements that differentiate the Panama Street problem from that of the strawberry farmer and any other place where DDT may have been used. The laws dealing with DDT had no reporting features for soil residue and the penalties for storing and using DDT were criminal in nature, while penalties under CERCLA are civil penalties."

"Hey, you forgot the biggest difference," said the Muse. "At the time of the early environmental legislation, I had not put the fear of Love Canal into America. If I had been involved and loaded the early environmental legislation with tort law, by now many of the small farmers in America would have auctioned off their farms.

"Oh, I take back the last part, no one would want the environmental problems, so there would be no buyers at the auctions. Those small farmers would just have to live out their days on their 'polluted' homesteads."

"That's a lot of crap," said the Jester. "Are you saying that many small farms in America are polluted."

"That's exactly what I'm saying Jester," replied the Muse. "Using the most stringent federal standards and sensitive instrumentation, I'll prove that many American farms have ground water pollution of some kind. Of course, you would have to send me to farms under the protection of National Guard troops because those farmers are not going to stand by and let me drill test wells on their land without putting up a battle."

"If you're right Muse, I feel sorry for Hutchins," said the Jester. "If farms have pollution in the ground water, the hazardous material becomes part of the food chain. That Panama Street site is miles away from any drinking water supply and an expert has said that the brook poses no imminent danger to animal life or vegetation. Why is the DEP picking on Hutchins when the chance of humans ingesting the infinitesimally small amounts of Panama Street toxins is minimal?"

"That's easy to answer," said the Muse. "We know in the heavens that worldly government agencies and legislators can be bullies. They rarely pick on people who are strong enough to take care of themselves. Farmers have very powerful advocates protecting their interests. They reluctantly accepted the laws that banned the use of DDT, but that was as far as they would go. For Congress to pass an environmental law that would subject farms to government inspection of ground water is not feasible.

"The truth is, we really didn't think of small business owners like Hutchins when we wrote CERCLA. We were after the big chemical and oil companies and the small businessmen and property owners just got caught up in it."

"I agree with you Muse and I applaud Ms. Carson for her diligence and success," I said; "but must her war continue at its current misguided and costly pace? America should prioritize concerns and place those things of greater danger to our society at the top of the list. For example, masses of young black men in America have been blocked from opportunities that would have detoured them from a life in prison, drug use and crime."

"Mr. Hutchins, I would yield the floor to you, but it looks like you have already taken it," said the Muse. "Before you speak further, let me caution you that you are making that fatal mistake again; you are trying to make sense out of the CERCLA legislation.

"You would save yourself endless frustration to acknowledge that these laws are based on emotion rather than reason. Actors know to avoid sharing scenes with dogs and children because people adore dogs and children. People also adore the flowers, trees and clear blue skies that enhance the environment.

"My studies have shown that most Americans do not relate to young men as they do to flowers, trees and blue skies. Young black men are a misunderstood portion of the population and as a group they scare many Americans. Hutchins, you have no leverage when you argue that money should be transferred from protecting flowers to protecting prison bound young men."

"Muse, what you say may be true," I replied, "however I find your view obscene. I don't want to live in a country that gives a higher priority to protecting humans from obscure chemical agents than to saving men from almost guaranteed early deaths on the streets."

The Muse threw up her hands in frustration with my answer and said, "Hutchins, I am not arguing with your reasoning or sense of fairness, I am just asking you to smell the roses. See the world as it is."

"But Muse," I replied, "as Rachel Carson's muse you allowed her to think of a better and cleaner world devoid of toxic pesticides. Please allow me to hope for a better, cleaner world devoid of gunshot wounds and life destroying drugs."

The Muse came back at me by saying, "Hutchins, as a muse, I don't control the way people think, I keep throwing out ideas that I feel would appeal to humans. I could attempt to interest a writer in selecting a topic about the lives of black youth, but unfortunately that's a hard sell these days. Look at *Amistad*, it didn't even get Spielberg a best picture nomination.

"I would wager that a muse sat on Jonathan Harr's shoulder and whispered stories about pollution in Woburn, Massachusetts. Think about it, his book, *A Civil Action*, had the best ingredients for success: Good guys, bad guys, scary toxins, courtrooms and sick children.

"Only someone who has been through what you have would question why the City of Woburn did not share some of the responsibility for the toxins in the water supply. Smell the roses Hutchins, the public wants to see John Trivolta go after those big corporations and their Boston law firms rather than talk about strict liability and Woburn's share of the responsibility for the pollution in the water supply.

"Face it Hutchins, you're not a puppy dog or a child, so no mortal wants to hear that you're a victim. Besides, after 20 years of CERCLA, we never hear from anyone that complains about those laws, why should your crying make any difference?"

Feeling a little like that beaten puppy dog that the Muse said I could not be, I answered, "I don't have the answers. I agree, very few Americans hurt by CERCLA have spoken out. I expect one of the reasons is that those accused under CERCLA carry the stigma of being called polluters. Rather than face that stigma, most people find their only choice is to settle with the EPA or state environmental agencies and walk away to nurse their wounds.

"It is also true that most environmental litigation is settled out of court. For that reason, there have been very few published reports or statements coming from environmental lawsuits."

Now the Jester broke in, "Hutchins, do you ever feel that you want to walk away from Panama Street and wish the DEP never named you a responsible party?"

I answered his question, "Jester, I wish all the time that it would just go away and Hutchins Tool could move on. I don't talk about these litigation problems with my family or friends. When they ask, I can only tell them the truth; that nothing is settled and that there is no end in sight.

"I think it is similar to being accused of being a child molester. You know that the accusation will stay in people's minds forever, no matter what the outcome. I know that the stigma of polluter will follow Hutchins Tool and me forever. We may not have a scarlet "A" on our chest, but we stand accused of adulterating our surroundings."

At that point, Zeus leaned forward and said, "If I understand you Hutchins, you are in accord with Rachel Carson, Vice President Gore and any other mortals who have influenced the environmental movement in America. You have no wish to dismantle the laws written prior to CERCLA. You don't want to dissolve the DEP in Massachusetts or the federal EPA."

"That's correct, Zeus," I answered. "I want people to open their minds by seeing Hutchins Tool as an example; to understand that certain sections of the CERCLA law and its counterparts in the states are totally against America's concept of fairness. You may ask how a law could survive in America for almost twenty years that is unfair to citizens. My answer is simple — the slavery laws and laws against women's suffrage lasted for over two hundred years in America. Americans must feel the pain and hear the truth over and over again to change legislation."

"Don't blame it on the American people, blame it on the politicians," said the Jester as he jumped to his feet. "Those politicians love to confuse people with their laws. Why don't they just say it like it is?

"I also saw that movie, *Amistad*, and expected to hear somebody say, let's give those slaves their freedom. Instead, the lawyers in the movie spent two hours arguing if the slaves were property or salvage from the shipwreck. The American legal system made no sense in John Quincy Adams' time and makes no sense now. Think of it, not one lawyer with the guts to demand freedom for the slaves in that courtroom. Under the property laws in effect at the time, the American courts treated the slaves as salvage washed up from the sea."

I was startled with the Jesters candor and said, "Jester, Hutchins Tool faces the same kind of courtroom scene under CERCLA. The arguments will not involve criminal responsibility because lawyers in civil cases have to argue property damage claims. At the end of the Panama Street litigation, everyone will walk away from that courtroom with an empty feeling; neither emotion or reason can be a winner."

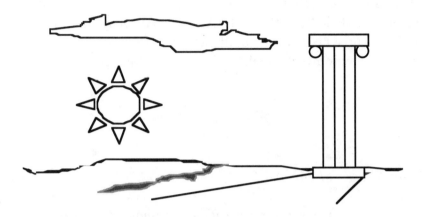

XXV. Changing Lawyers

Now Zeus looked down at me and in a concerned voice he said, "Hutchins you have told us that CERCLA has flaws. You say that in 20 years the law has not been changed or seriously challenged in the U. S. Congress. You also say that most lawyers, including those that represent you, don't understand these flaws and the way the law has encouraged litigation to the detriment of remediation.

"Yet, you have told us that your lawyers are not ready to challenge the law or give you a different defense. They should know the laws better than you do, so you have two choices, either accept their defense or change lawyers. Have you ever considered changing lawyers?"

"Yes, frequently," I answered, "several times I have discussed such a change with Attorney Doherty and asked that a more creative lawyer from his firm be brought into the case. Each time I was met with great resistance.

For example, in late 1995 Hadley was convinced that he could get moneys from the insurance company to settle with the DEP.

After a number of encouraging conversations regarding settlement with Michelle O'Brien, the Assistant Attorney General, she followed up with this letter outlining seven steps to prevent having the Commonwealth seek the Preliminary Injunction:

December 12, 1995

Dear Messrs. Moore and Hadley:

This letter provides a summary of our telephone discussion today and requests your assent to the terms articulated below in exchange for the Commonwealth's agreement to postpone commencing a civil action against your clients.

As discussed in our meeting on December 8, 1995, the Commonwealth agrees that additional assessment work is needed at the One Panama Street site ("the site"). To that end, we are pleased that Hutchins Tool & Engineering Co., Inc. is committed to performing the Subsurface Investigation approved by the Department of Environmental Protection ("the Department") one year ago. There is still a need for an Immediate Response Action ("IRA") at the site, however. We continue to believe that the information obtained from the proposed and approved Subsurface Investigation will not significantly change the options for an IRA Plan. Accordingly, we request that the parties prepare a draft IRA Plan and conduct the field investigations simultaneously. Although we expect the IRA Plan to be submitted by the owner of the site, Arden T. Thompson ("Thompson"), any party could undertake the IRA work.

The Commonwealth agrees not to file a lawsuit seeking a preliminary injunction and other relief until March 8, 1996 if Thompson and Hutchins Tool agree to the following:

1. On or before January 15, 1996, Thompson shall submit to the Department a written conceptual IRA Plan consisting of a general description of the IRA work Thompson intends to perform to abate the migration of contaminated groundwater to Pecousic Brook.

2. On or before December 20, 1995, Hutchins Tool shall submit to the Department a letter stating its intent to perform the Subsurface Investigation provisionally approved by the Department on November 15, 1994, and a schedule for performing such activities so that the work will be completed by March 1, 1996. Hutchins Tool also shall provide copies of its access agreement and contract with a Licensed Site Professional to perform the Subsurface Investigation at the site.

3. Hutchins Tool shall commence fieldwork at the site on December 26, 1995.

4. Within five days of the completion of fieldwork associated with the Subsurface Investigation, Hutchins Tool shall submit to the Department all field data gathered during the investigation.

5. Hutchins Tool shall submit to the Department written status reports summarizing progress on the Subsurface Investigation every two weeks after fieldwork begins.

6. On or before March 1, 1996, Hutchins Tool shall submit to the Department a report documenting all activities performed during the Subsurface Investigation and detailing the results of the field work and data analysis.

7. On or before March 12, 1996, Thompson shall make any necessary modifications to the conceptual IRA Plan and shall submit to the Department a revised conceptual IRA Plan if needed.

The Commonwealth will convene a meeting with all the parties on or about March 7, 1996, to discuss the results of the above-referenced site activities and to determine whether the parties will continue to conduct response actions at the site voluntarily. At that time, the Commonwealth will seek a judicial order, preferably with consent of the parties, requiring the performance of an IRA, the completion of all response actions, and the payment of the Commonwealth's response costs. We will expect to receive an IRA Plan within 30 days of the Department's approval of the conceptual IRA Plan.

Please indicate your assent to the activities and schedule outlined in paragraphs 1 through 7 above by returning a copy of this letter, signed in the area designated below, to me by December 19, 1995. Feel free to call me with any questions.

Very truly yours,

Michelle N. O'Brien
Assistant Attorney General
Environmental Protection Division

"In reaction to Attorney O'Brien's letter, Hadley wrote to the Insurance Company asking for meaningful discussions with regard to the Insurance Company paying for at least part of the cost of remediation. You can see that he continued to act as if he were conducting the same type litigation settlement as he would if he were working on an automobile tort case. Here is that letter:

Chapter Twenty Five

December 14, 1995

Civalyn Jackson
American International Adjustment Co,
80 Pine Street, 6th Floor
New York, NY 10005

Re: Arden Thompson vs. Hutchins Tool and Engineering
Company, et al

Dear Ms. Jackson:

On December 8, I attended a meeting with your insureds, and representatives of the Massachusetts Department of Environmental Protection. Also in attendance was the owner of One Panama Street, his attorney, and counsel for co-defendant Precision E.D.M. The purpose of this meeting was to advise the DEP as to the status of litigation involving the One Panama Street property, the parties' intentions with regard to remediation and to discuss the possibility of a legal action on behalf of the DEP against the landowner, and possibly Hutchins Tool & Engineering Co. and Precision E.D.M. Inc. Although the meeting was fairly lengthy, I can summarize as follows.

First, DEP officials were advised that the trial of the case brought by the property owner against your insureds and Precision E.D.M. is presently scheduled to be conducted in March 1996. Because no one is yet able to reasonably approximate the cost of remediating the Panama Street property, the DEP was advised that there have been no settlement discussions among the parties to date, and that in the event of a decision in favor of the property owner, the most likely event would be an award of relatively low monetary damages, and a finding by the court as to the liability of your insureds and Precision E.D.M. The DEP advised that it has little or no interest in this litigation, as it would not be bound by any findings in a case to which it is not a party. DEP personnel therefore advised us that its actions in relation to this property would not be influenced by the existence of the pending litigation or its outcome after a trial.

With regard to the investigatory work which has been authorized by your company, I advised the DEP that this work would be commenced Christmas week, and that it would be completed within 60 days. I expressed my hope that as a result of this work, the parties would have a much better understanding of the extent of contamination at the site, which would allow us to at least discuss the potential costs of remediation. With this information, the property owner, your insureds, and Precision E.D.M. could hopefully begin to discuss the possibility for an amicable resolution of this problem.

The DEP representatives were pleased that some "progress" was being made but expressed a level of frustration that the parties have been fighting among themselves for years, rather than cleaning up this site. As a result of this, an Assistant Attorney General has now advised me, as well as the other attorneys involved in this mater that the DEP will wait until March 1 to initiate litigation against the parties. Suit may be avoided, however, if there is significant progress in the development of a plan for remediating the site by March 1. As I have noted in the past, this may be possible once the upcoming investigatory work is completed.

Given the prospects for a lengthy Superior Court trial and the commencement of another lawsuit against your insured in March, it is imperative that we discuss your company's position with regard to the actual remediation of this site. I would therefore appreciate it if you would call me as soon as possible so that I can begin to formulate a response to the DEP's demand on behalf of your insureds.

I look forward to hearing from you.

Very truly yours,

William P. Hadley

"Thompson did not submit the written conceptual IRA Plan requested by Attorney O'Brien. Our Insurance Company never discussed its position with regard to actual remediation. All the parties kept shadow boxing and Attorney Hadley continued to feel that all the parties would come together to settle."

The Jester spoke up, "Hey, when I was on duty in America in the taxi business, we had accidents every day. These cases all got settled pretty fast. I can't think of one that lasted eight or nine years like this Panama Street thing. I'm sure Hadley has dealt with many insurance companies and knows what he is doing."

While the Jester did not expect me to reply so quickly, I knew that I could help this make sense, so I said, "Jester, America has a long history of tort law which deals primarily with automobiles. However, tort law when applied to the environment is different. The major difference is that the vast majority of automobile owners pay over $1,000 per automobile each year for automobile insurance premiums. Unlike automobile insurance, insurance companies have written very few environmental policies. Therefore, there is no large fund of trusted money to tap to underwrite the cost of environmental damage and litigation.

"That is why most insurance companies question a policy's coverage for environmental damage claims. The insurance industry's position is easily understood when you appreciate that the insurance companies did not realize that CERCLA type laws would become operative in 1980. The inclination of insurance companies has been to challenge environmental coverage and I would guess that their strategy is paying off. We read of very few large environmental claims being paid as compared to product liability and medical malpractice."

At that point the Jester jumped up, "What you're saying is that there is no money in the insurance industry's tills to pay environmental claims."

"Exactly," I replied, "and then you have a second major problem which Attorney Hadley and other lawyers practicing environmental law must face. There is very little history of environmental case law. No one has a road map or pattern to follow.

"Worse still are the terms strict, joint and several. These terms expand liability to include any person, company, municipality, trucker or waste facility that can be linked to a problem. These terms are like a giant net cast out to catch anybody that may have cash. Guilt and degree of guilt are not relevant."

Again Zeus looked down on me in disbelief and said, "Hutchins why were you fighting this thing? The average human would turn it over to a lawyer and have faith in the lawyer's abilities. I'm a god and even I know when I'm out of my league. My suggestion is to have faith in your attorney because I'm sure that Hadley was negotiating to get you the best settlement possible."

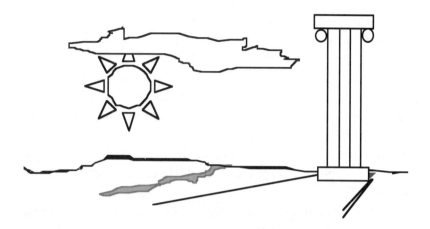

XXVI.   A Classic Script

I continued my testimony by answering Zeus, "Throughout 1997 Attorney Hadley continued to tell me that a settlement with the DEP was close. The major stumbling block for the insurance company was the fact that the DEP did not have a fixed cost of damages. We had understood from the beginning that no insurance company could give the DEP a blank check that could be used to pay remediation costs.

"From early 1997 while talking about a settlement figure with Hutchins Tool, Attorney O'Brien continued to press litigation against the Thompson estate. To keep the estate from dispersal, she disregarded Hutchins Tool and Precision EDM and pursued a Partial Summary Judgment against Thompson's estate. A letter from Attorney O'Brien, dated April 24, 1997, is an indication that Hadley could be in over his head in this case. In it O'Brien states that the Commonwealth of Massachusetts will undertake response actions at the site."

At this point there was a slight commotion behind me. As I looked around I saw a number of figures wearing different masks gathered around a very distinguished looking man who I had seen sitting high in the amphitheater that rose behind us. I say a man because I sensed that he was a human and not a celestial being.

The commotion from these masked figures diverted everyone's attention from my testimony. At this Zeus banged his fist on the podium and called for a recess. He then called the distinguished man down to the podium and talked to him in a low voice that neither the Muse nor I could hear.

Seeing that I was totally confused, the Jester looked at me and said, "Don't you recognize that mortal? I thought every earthling knew him."

Now the Muse responded by saying, "Hey Jester, you've been in America in the last century and you know that Americans are not into ancestral homage so take it easy on my man Hutchins. That mortal talking to Zeus is Sophocles, the earth's greatest playwright. He's here to participate in the Dionysus Festival that Zeus holds every five years and those masked figures are the chorus that Allen used for his movie."

Then, Zeus banged his fist again to get everyone's attention. The Muse stopped talking and turned to Zeus as he said, "This is the great mortal Sophocles. He holds my respect because he knows man. I asked Sophocles to attend this hearing today to gain knowledge of the Muse's quest to become the lawyer god. Perhaps he can give us insight into her thoughts that lie somewhere between earth and the heavens. I am sorry that that imposter chorus interrupted us. Their crudeness does not surprise me, considering where they were last employed. Now, Sophocles give us your counsel."

"First let me apologize for the boys," said Sophocles. "Working for Woody Allen in his movie has made them a bit incorrigible."

"Do not speak of that mortal Allen in my presence," roared Zeus. "He is a neurotic abomination. I welcome Sophocles to my Festival because unlike Allen he is a writer that is capable of disillusionment without cynicism or despair. The world knows that

Sophocles never surrendered his ideal of the dignity of man or his belief that the horror of life could not obscure man from seeing its splendor.

"When I sent a Greek chorus down to earth to be used by that moviemaker, I thought that it would revive the classic tradition and show America that man is capable at arriving at self-knowledge and a spiritual awakening."

"Zeus don't be so harsh with him," said Sophocles. "A writer must write for his time. This is the time of cynicism and despair in America where individual dysfunction takes priority over communal concerns. Besides, I think it's his bawdiness that bothers you."

"Bawdiness bullshit," yelled Zeus, "with your drama *Oedipus* I loved the incest, suicide and self-mutilation because it was used to show the humanity and reasoning powers of man. That moviemaker shows man as a spiritual bankrupt, bereft of dignity and self control. But, enough of this Sophocles, please tell those assembled how you would like them to conduct the remainder of this hearing."

Sophocles answered, "If it please you Zeus, I would ask those assembled to conduct this hearing as the drama it is turning out to be. You need not speak in verse, but do use a dramatic style as if you were reading a script. To start, let me cue you by repeating the last words that Mr. Hutchins spoke, 'From early 1997 while talking about a settlement figure with Hutchins Tool, Attorney O'Brien continued to press litigation against the Thompson estate. To keep the estate from dispersal, she disregarded Hutchins Tool and Precision EDM and pursued a Partial Summary Judgment against Thompson's estate. A letter from Attorney O'Brien, dated April 24, 1997, is an indication that Hadley may be in over his head in this case. In this letter O'Brien states that the Commonwealth of Massachusetts will undertake response actions at the site.' Jester, I see that you want to start this scene, so please speak."

*　*　*　*　*　*

JESTER: [Standing up to recite with a smile on his face]
Hutchins, it appears that the lady had had enough of you
guys, or, maybe the State of Massachusetts came up with
some funds in their budget to do the remediation on Panama
Street.

HUTCHINS: What you say may be the answer. Of course the
alarming part is that in her letter, Attorney O'Brien repeated
her threat of collecting three times the amount of all response
costs incurred by the Commonwealth. She follows this with
the reminder that the DEP has the power to place liens on
the defendant's properties in the Commonwealth.

JESTER: Can she do that under MGL Chapter 21E? I've got to
believe that a lien would be a real threat to Hutchins Tool.

HUTCHINS: By this time, RECOLL was discontinued and
our loans reverted to the Federal Deposit Insurance Agency
(FDIC). Because the loans held by the FDIC were collateralized with all of Hutchins Tool's assets, O'Brien would be
able to get at very few of our assets. However, she could
post a lien that would restrict our ability to function as a
business. As you can see, the noose was drawing tighter
around our necks.

In response to Attorney O'Brien's letter saying the State
would perform the response actions, Attorney Hadley sent a
letter to Attorney O'Brien telling of his surprise in view of
the past discussions. He again pleaded with O'Brien for a
specific monetary demand that he could take to the Insurance
Company.

A breakthrough came between Hadley and O'Brien in
May when she advised him of the estimated costs of cleanup
and the State's past response costs. Together, they came to

about 1.2 million dollars. Happily for Hutchins Tool, Attorney O'Brien asked that Hutchins Tool pay only $350,000 to settle. Having finally received a specific monetary demand from the State, Hadley wrote to Krystyna Laskowski, the claims adjuster for New Hampshire Insurance:

May 30, 1997

Krystyna Laskowski
American International Adjustment Co.
80 Pine Street, 6th Floor
New York, NY 10005

Dear Ms. Laskowski:

As I believe you know, I have been attempting to engage the Commonwealth of Massachusetts in discussions leading to an amicable resolution of litigation which is pending against your insured, Hutchins Tool and Engineering Company. Unfortunately, for an extended period of time the Commonwealth has taken the position that it will not negotiate and has repeatedly demanded that Hutchins and the other named parties voluntarily remediate the One Panama Street site. Over the past months, however, the DEP has reviewed financial documents supplied by your insured and the other parties that supported the claim that neither Hutchins, nor the other parties, had financial resources to comply with the DEP's demands, assuming liability was conclusively demonstrated.

Finally, the DEP has made a commitment to remediate the Panama Street site itself by contracting the work out to private consultants. I have been advised by the Attorney General's Office that these consultants have prepared preliminary estimates of the work which will need to be performed, including continued monitoring of the site for a number of years into the *future. The Assistant Attorney General handling this case advised me in May 30, 1997 that preliminary estimates for all future remedial work are in a range of $700,000 to $1,000,000. In addition, the Commonwealth's past response costs, including attorneys' fees and internal Department of Environmental Protection costs, reportedly total approximately $200,000. Apparently accepting the fact that your insured does not have assets available to satisfy a potential judgment of this magnitude, the Commonwealth has made a settlement demand upon Hutchins Tool and Engineering Company in the amount of $350,000.00.*

In view of the strict liability nature of the claims against your insured and in view of the potential amount of an adverse judgment, I continue to believe that every reasonable attempt should be made to settle this case and extricate Hutchins Tool and Engineering Company (and your company) from this litigation. On behalf of your insured I therefore request that you advise me as soon as possible as to whether your company will accept the demand made by the DEP. Alternatively, I request that you provide me with authority to make a reasonable counteroffer and to negotiate the terms of a settlement which will finally conclude this matter after these many years. Please contact me as soon as possible to discuss these issues in greater detail.

Very truly yours,

William P. Hadley

HUTCHINS: While I thought the request for $350,000 from the Insurance Company was fairly reasonable considering the 1.2 million dollar exposure, Hadley hoped that Laskowski would agree to the lower figure of $200,000.

In the meantime, James Colman, the Assistant Commissioner at the DEP sent me a letter saying that the Panama Street site would be on the DEP's List of Tier I Disposal Sites as of June 11, 1997. Tier I is the highest priority. I accepted this as just another indication of the bureaucratic nature of the DEP. I am sure that after eight years of depicting the Site as a major health hazard, the DEP would be embarrassed not to give it a top priority.

JESTER: Doesn't Tier I classification mandate that a cleanup should start immediately using public funds?

HUTCHINS: I think so. I'm sure the DEP was between a rock and a hard place. Even though evidence in their possession would make this a low priority site, to place it anywhere but Tier I would bring to question the eight years of wasted time. Of course, I am sure they knew that Panama Street posed no imminent danger to public health or safety. It was all a charade to divert attention from the harmless nature of the site compared to what was now estimated to be over a million dollars in remediation costs.

ZEUS: Mr. Hutchins, may I stop you for a minute and sum this up?

HUTCHINS: Please do.

ZEUS: After all the litigation, after all the charges and counter charges, Michelle O'Brien acting as an Assistant Attorney General for the State, agreed to settle with Hutchins Tool for $350,000 even though the DEP's costs were expected to be 1.2 million dollars.

HUTCHINS: That's correct.

ZEUS: It appears that the DEP finally understood your financial condition and decided to take what they could get as a
settlement from your Insurance Company. This would
mean that Hutchins Tool was off the hook after eight years
of harassment from the DEP and other parties.

HUTCHINS: That was the understanding I got from our
attorney, Mr. Hadley. He finally had his settlement.

MUSE: [As she stood up with a smirk and said in a cocky
manner] Come on now, Hutchins. You had been at this a
long time. You know that there were still potential legal fees
open. Do you think my lawyers would walk away from a
good thing so easily? Had you forgotten that if the parties
settled, the lawyers could lose their opportunity to participate in the damages from the litigation and the enormous
legal fees produced by a trial?

HUTCHINS: You win again, Muse. I suppose I hoped that
Hadley was right and that this was the beginning of the end.
I longed to get out from under this mess. I knew that
Hutchins Tool would end up insolvent, but I wanted an
opportunity to a fresh start with all this behind us. There
was a chance Hutchins Tool could still make it.

MUSE: You and I know what happened next. Perhaps you
could describe to Zeus how things did not work out as
Attorney Hadley had expected.

CHORUS: [The masked men had moved from the seats to an
area behind the podium. Quietly at first and with increasing
volume they started to chant] Out from under this mess;
Out from under this mess to a fresh start; Oh, message of
Zeus, whose words are sweet; Speak to me of golden hope.

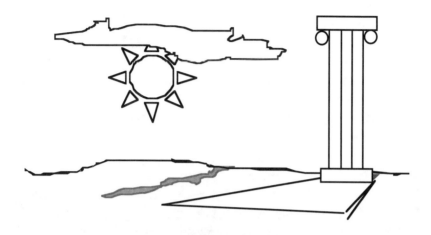

XXVII.   The Settlement

HUTCHINS: Yes, you're right Muse. Attorney Moore who
was now representing the Thompson Estate had been busy.
In July of 1997, he cross-filed to include my brother, Bob,
and Steve Peroulakis in the Commonwealth vs. the Thompson Estate lawsuit. I had asked Hadley a number of times
about our position if the State settled. Would Attorney
Moore continue to pursue Hutchins Tool in a separate
litigation? The way Hadley ignored my question, I suspected that he hoped that O'Brien could force Attorney
Moore to agree to release Hutchins Tool from responsibility. I was not surprised when Moore did not follow that
course. I am not privy to Attorney Moore's arrangement
with the Thompson estate, but I assume that by settling with
the State and dropping the case against Hutchins Tool, his
fees for this litigation would dry up.

MUSE: As I have told you Zeus, I created an atmosphere
under CERCLA where lawyers feel they have a right to

environmental funds. For every dollar spent, they expect to have the giant share no matter what the source. But, here is my coupe de grace, Mr. Hutchins, tell Zeus how the Insurance Company reacted to the State's offer of $350,000 to settle what could be at least a 1.2 million-dollar judgment.

HUTCHINS: [with his head down and a muted voice] $25,000 dollars.

JESTER: Bullshit, come on that's not true.

HUTCHINS: It's true. As proof, let me show you this letter Hadley sent to Krystyna Laskowski at the claims office of New Hampshire Insurance:

July 23, 1997

Krystyna Laskowski
American International Adjustment Co.
80 Pine Street, 6th Floor
New York, NY 10005

Dear Ms. Laskowski:

I have relayed your offer of $25,000.00 to the Attorney General's Office in the above-entitled matter. As you might expect, the Assistant Attorney General who is handling this matter for the Commonwealth of Massachusetts expressed considerable disappointment regarding the amount of this offer in the face of the Commonwealth's $350,000.00 demand. In response, I explained what I understand to be your company's position regarding insurance coverage for these claims. The Commonwealth's attorney then asked me to provide evidence of the terms of insurance coverage provided by your company to Hutchins Tool & Engineering Co., Inc., and I agreed to provide *her with copies of the policies in issue.*

After having also discussed this matter with your insured, I must express your insured's deep concern over your company's decision to offer only $25,000.00 in the face of an exposure which could exceed one million ($1,000,000.00) dollars. Your insured pointed out that it did business with the New Hampshire Insurance Group for many years with very few, if any, claims. In discussions with the <u>ten</u> adjusters who have preceded you in the handling of this matter, the intention to support your insured wherever possible in this case was clearly reflected. For an extended period of time, the central problem in attempting to reach an amicable resolution of this case on behalf of your insured arose from the refusal by the Commonwealth of Massachusetts and the owner of the One Panama Street property to make a specific monetary demand. After a significant amount of negotiation, I was able to finally elicit a demand of $350,000.00 from the Commonwealth. Based on my discussions with the Assistant Attorney General handling this matter, it was and continues to be my firm belief that this figure was an initial demand and that the Commonwealth is willing to be very flexible, and actually would accept a figure significantly lower than this amount.

An offer of $25,000.00, however, particularly when compared to an offer of $75,000.00 from co-defendant Precision EDM, Inc., does not provide the Commonwealth of Massachusetts with a great deal of incentive to resolve this case. Moreover, as I have previously advised you, the Thompson estate is seeking to bring a claim for contribution against Robert Hutchins individually, exposing him to personal liability which could be avoided through a global settlement of this controversy. On behalf of your insured, Hutchins Tool & Engineering Co., Inc. and its officers, I therefore request that you reconsider your position on settlement in this action. More specifically, if the Commonwealth of Massachusetts makes a counter proposal, which would present a possibility of extricating Hutchins Tool and its officers from exposure to liability in this matter, every effort should be made to take advantage of this opportunity and resolve this mater after these many years.

If you need any further information or if you wish to discuss these issues further, please contact me.

Very truly yours,

William P. Hadley

HUTCHINS: In reaction to our Insurance Company's offer of $25,000, Attorney O'Brien exploded. She called the offer extremely disappointing and demanded a wide assortment of financial documents from Hutchins Tool. She asked for meetings with our accountants. I was not surprised that the settlement had failed and I was also not surprised that Attorney Moore would continue to litigate against Hutchins Tool.

The curse of CERCLA permeates everything it touches. The struggle to find funds to support remediation is so intense that all parties became desperate. By all parties, I include government agencies, potentially responsible parties and the attorneys that represent everyone who could possibly be related to an environmental action.

Potential for settlements under the CERCLA laws is close to nonexistent. Cleanups are so expensive that no one can afford them including both the private and government sectors. We are not dealing with bad people; we are dealing with bad legislation. Even the most honest, best-informed and well-meaning persons can become monsters under CERCLA.

Hutchins, O'Brien, Hadley, Peroulakis, Thompson, Moore and Laskowski are not the names of bad people; they are the names of people caught up in a struggle to survive. While we know that Hutchins Tool is desperate, think of the DEP, they are also desperate to show results to save their jobs; the insurance company must save its assets from damage claims; the Attorney General's Office must save its reputation and protect the public interest. CERCLA does not allow these institutions to survive without the use of ruthless tactics by the people involved.

I had great hopes that our Insurance Company would come up with a suitable figure and the case with the DEP would settle. If that had happened, it is possible that Attorney O'Brien would have negotiated with all the parties for some sort of settlement and the worst times would be over for everyone concerned.

JESTER: [Quickly standing up] Why didn't the Insurance Company come through with a responsible offer? If the Attorney General's Office wanted to show that insurance companies should be forced to honor claims, this was a good case for them to use. The policies were written between 1972 and 1979 so they had almost no exclusions for environmental claims compared to those written in the '80's and '90's.

HUTCHINS: I know, our insurance company may have made a bad decision by not offering the Commonwealth a reasonable sum. Now they will have to pay to defend Hutchins Tool against the Commonwealth in court, which will be very expensive. They could pay for the discovery work before the trial, plus a month long trial and still lose. At that point, they would be exposed to millions in damages demanded by the government and a lawsuit from Hutchins Tool for not paying our damage claims.

ZEUS: I am amazed at the slow speed of litigation in America. In both Greece and Rome, things were resolved quickly. In

America, I can see that it pays to delay. Mr. Hutchins, what was happening to Hutchins Tool as time passed? Were you able to stabilize the business?

HUTCHINS: Unfortunately, things kept getting worse. RECOLL was dismantled and all our loans were sent to the FDIC for resolution. In the meetings that followed, I was told that the FDIC was not a bank. The work of the FDIC was to negotiate the refinancing of loans with the client. If that did not happen within a six to twelve month period, the policy of the FDIC was to consolidate many loans into packages and auction them off to speculators.

JESTER: [shaking his head] Hey, this is crazy. First, you've got an environmental lawsuit, then the DEP, then the Massachusetts Attorney General, then the Insurance Company backs down and now the FDIC wants you to refinance or they'll sell your loans. You must have gone crazy. How could you live with that?

HUTCHINS: Jester, you're right. These things were unreal. But, strange as it sounds, the crazier those things became, the calmer I got. If you were involved with the movie business, you may remember the movie, *Gone With the Wind*. At one point, Scarlett O'Hara came home to find everything ruined by the war and her workers scattered. As others cried with concern, her reaction was, "I'll think about that tomorrow." That has become my attitude. I'll think about things tomorrow that I can do nothing about today.

I can say that the threat of losing our plants and assets to the FDIC forced us into attempts to sell our buildings and equipment. After attempting several deals that did not work out, we negotiated with a medical equipment manufacturer to sell our largest, most modern building, plus some equipment.

This was particularly difficult for me because I had worked with the architect and builder during the construction of the building. When it was finished in 1979, my parents were still alive and shared a proud moment with me when we erected a plaque that dedicated the new building to them.

Because we work long hours in the manufacturing business, this building was my second home for about 18 years until December of 1997 when the sale closed. It was particularly sad to have the plaque removed from the building and delivered to my current cramped office.

Years ago, before our environmental problems, I expected that if the building sold, it would be included with the business and provide us with a considerable amount of money. I hoped that such a sale would assure my family a comfortable retirement. Now, the environmental litigation on Panama Street has crushed that dream. After the FDIC loans, city taxes, attorney's fees and closing costs were paid, the building sale netted Hutchins Tool nothing.

JESTER: Nothing. You sold a valuable building. Do you mean you ended up with zero?

HUTCHINS: Jester, what I said is correct. Hutchins Tool is now downsized to a small percentage of what it once was. We continue in business to retain as many employees as possible and to serve our most loyal customers. I fill in regularly running production machines. I find physical work very calming compared to all the craziness that I have been through. Our hope is that some day the environmental litigation will end and we can pick up the pieces and start fresh. Of course, the court tracking for the trial goes right through next year.

* * * * * *

At this point, there was some commotion outside and Zeus looked out into space. It was obvious that he had been waiting for someone to arrive.

* * * * * *

ZEUS: [Standing up at the pedestal] Has Mercury returned from Earth? What news does he bring?

* * * * * *

Moments later, I heard that swoosh sound that I had heard when Mercury left. In an instant he landed with the grace of Nijinsky, next to Zeus. Again, I was in awe at his sleek body. To me, Mercury looked like a Michael Jordan television commercial.

* * * * * *

ZEUS: Mercury, did you have success? What have you learned that can be meaningful for this hearing? Can you tell us about those laws that Mr. Hutchins speaks of: CERCLA and MGL Chapter 21E?

* * * * * *

Now I heard that chorus again starting to chant. I knew that Zeus was acting as Sophocles' patron as he wrote a drama about the Muse. It did not seem to bother her, but to me it was an unnerving sound.

* * * * * *

CHORUS: Pick up the pieces; Pick up the pieces and start fresh; Speak to me of golden hope, Immortal Voice.

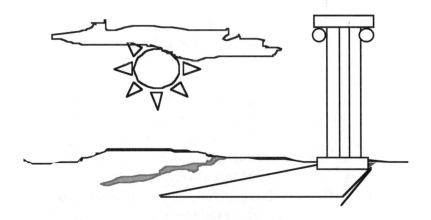

XXVIII.   Mercury's Mission

MERCURY: [showing a certain pride in his successful mission] Zeus, as you requested, I descended to Earth to learn about those environmental laws in America. This trip rekindled memories of Rome when I was the Roman god of commerce. It was good to see America thriving.

Of course, I was happy to use my other divine skills that I developed in Rome. As you know, I was also the Roman god of thieves. My catlike agility helped me get into many sealed vaults to gather the information you requested.

Zeus, you asked me for background information on CERCLA and MGL Chapter 21E. To do this, I had to time warp myself back to the late 1970's when the U.S. Congress wrote this legislation.

There is no question that the U.S. Congress was not led by reason in writing this bill. I can believe that this Muse used fear and superstition to reach her goals. Just as the earthling, Francis Bacon wrote in 17th Century England, "But superstition dismounts all these, and erecteth an absolute monarchy in the minds of man."

I believe that the Muse co-oped television to erect her monarchy over men's minds. I found that today, legislation in America is shaped by public opinion polls based on thirty minutes of television news each evening.

In Greece and Rome, learned men made decisions in senates, academies and temples. In America, this has been replaced by 120-second sound and visual bytes that guide audiences to emotion charged positions on public issues.

This is not to say that television is bad, it is simply a reality in America. It is generally conceded that television got the U.S. into and out of the Vietnam War and that Love Canal, as seen on television, seduced people into CERCLA.

MUSE: [Jumping up, excitedly] Yes, wonderful, you understand how my marketing plan worked. My lawyers had Love Canal written right into the language of CERCLA, when we designated Section 9661 of that law, *Love Canal Property Acquisition.*

JESTER: Bullshit, I don't believe that. Even American congresspersons are not so crazy as to write local projects into major legislation.

ZEUS: Sit down, Jester, Let Mercury continue. Senators schooled in the classic tradition write rational laws.

MERCURY: Zeus, I am sorry to tell you that the classic tradition is not currently honored in America. I found that the Muse is correct. Love Canal was written into CERCLA along with an equally irrational rule, Section 9651(e).

Section 9651(e) of the legislation calls for an evaluation of the law within twelve months of enactment. This evaluation was conducted by three members from each of the American Bar Association, the American Law Institute, the

Association of American Trial Lawyers and the National Association of State Attorneys General. I was not able to obtain a copy of that evaluation, but there is no question that this group of lawyers found CERCLA was working very much to their satisfaction after its first year of existence.

JESTER: This is crazy. It makes no sense. To use 12 lawyers to evaluate that law is like having a fox guard the chicken coup.

MERCURY: My investigation showed that the American public had been deluged with pictures of concerned citizens who wanted to sell their homes near Love Canal in Buffalo. These citizens feared the chemicals that had been released into the soil some years earlier. They described many ailments and professed that the buried chemicals were responsible for these problems. There was little scientific evidence to prove or disprove their fears. However, the values of their properties had declined so the residents wanted out and were looking for moneys to pay for relocation. To do this they needed legislation to allow them to sue the chemical companies that had once operated on that land.

JESTER: I can't believe this. Are you telling me that a muse from the heavens was able to influence a whole nation into pressing their congresspersons for a law that has not worked?

MERCURY: Jester, I can understand your disbelief. Yet I uncovered much evidence that showed that the American people were predisposed toward such action. For example, an American historian named Lawrence M. Friedman, chronicled the times in his book, *A History of American Law*, when he wrote:

"*Air and water pollution, urban squeeze, and other symptoms of distress were old enough; there had always been voices crying in and for the wilderness. But the voices became more strident from the 1960s on. A real sense of doom began to hang over this small and limited world. Many sources fed the ecological movement. First, economic growth (in a society which, after all, had had a great deal of this otherwise scarce commodity) no longer satisfied everyone, particularly those with money to spare and still no inner peace. Second, the crisis was real. Resources were not infinite. Big business was poisoning the rivers and darkening the air; lumber companies were chopping down irreplaceable trees; cities were pouring tons of muck into lakes and oceans; highway engineers were driving concrete paths through pieces of the American heart and heritage. This debauchery could be justified only by blind faith in the invisible hand of the market, and in "progress" and in the virtue and sense of public institutions. Faith of this sort was itself becoming a scarce commodity. Third, this was a society with many rich and leisured people; with enormous government and governments, peopled by professionals and bureaucrats; and with a growing number of academics and intellectuals looking for a place in the sun. All of these interest groups (it is fair to call them that) had consciences and needed causes. The government needed causes because its size was only excusable if it pursued the national interest; every part of every government had to have some sort of socially useful program. Academics and the leisure class had their own self-interest, as consumers, at stake; they also needed and wanted some way to spend their surplus time and money. Many expended energy collecting stamps, writing histories of China, going to antique shops, getting drunk, and otherwise, but a certain number hit on the environmental crisis, which was genuine, and for which the time was somehow ripe. Hence, an interest group with some power — particularly, power to mobilize the neutrals — joined forces on an issue that suited the '60s. By the late '60s, many prior issues had become inhospitable. (The blacks, for example, had rudely taken over, with hardly a thank-you, the job of their own liberation.)"*

MERCURY: Records show that CERCLA was not considered major legislation prior to its passage. However, it was the kind of bill where many lobbies and interest groups were allowed wide latitude for their pet ideas to be included.

Essentially, most congresspersons believed that the major emphasis of the CERCLA legislation was government funding to clean up a number of sites in the U.S. that contained hazardous waste which had been abandoned. This is why the bill became known as the "Superfund Law."

Most of the language contained in CERCLA is very specific as to the limit the government would spend for five years and the limit per site. It also clearly stated that if parties responsible for the hazardous material spills could be found, they would be forced to reimburse this Superfund.

This requirement provided the environmental lobbies with an opening to place the concepts they wanted into the legislation. As part of their wish-list they inserted the following: First, funding to create lists of hazardous materials and to test agents which could cause harm to humans, second, wording to hold large companies liable for pollution and remediation of hazardous waste sites, third, agencies to handle current releases including liability for cleanup, fourth, legislation to encourage state participation by enactment of state environmental laws.

CERCLA is printed as a 260-page document. Even I, Mercury the Roman god of commerce, found it to be one of the most confusing documents I have seen produced in America. Almost every lobby in Washington added pork as they usually do, only this time it was emotional pork rather than public works projects. For example, fearing that some agents would not be listed as hazardous; the bill established a quota system so that each year a certain quantity would be added to the list.

JESTER: How would you do that? If something is hazardous, it's hazardous. You can't say I want to add 50 chemicals each year. Wouldn't the agency responsible for listing find agents to be hazardous, just to fill the quota?

MERCURY: Jester that is exactly what happened. Scientific proof was thrown out the window and replaced with subjective decisions from risk assessment studies. When I asked an environmental lobbyist why Congress insisted on quotas, she said, "Left to themselves, those agencies would name very few carcinogens. We expected that some chemicals cause cancer, so we reasoned that it was better politics to play it safe and have a long list rather than a short one. If there had been no quotas, the list would have remained small."

Then, when I asked why petroleum products and gasoline were not included in CERCLA, she said, "We had to compromise with the petroleum lobbies. That happens all the time in Congress."

When you read CERCLA, you'll realize why it has caused such confusion. You would expect the law to read much as it is interpreted by the federal EPA and state DEP with passages that list controlled hazardous materials, rules for controlling the material, release response actions, containment, removal, liability, limits of liability, etc. Instead CERCLA includes many passages that appear innocuous but in reality contain hidden phrases that have been the foundation for most of the litigation. Here we find the wording that has caused the damage to people like Mr.

Hutchins. These are the recourse actions open to those parties damaged by those considered abusers of the law and they are written in the property damage format of civil law.

In my opinion the major flaw of CERCLA and the reason that hazardous waste sites are being litigated rather than remediated, are these civil law statutes. I can only guess that environmental activists in the 1970's were frustrated by the inability of earlier legislation to punish the perceived wrongdoers. By joining forces with those citizens who felt that they could redeem their personal losses through civil actions, these activists created the tools for tort that are imbedded in CERCLA.

ZEUS: I don't understand. Following the classic guidelines, the laws of Greece and Rome would tell citizens what was forbidden and the penalty for breaking the law. For example, if a citizen killed another citizen, he would pay with his life or be jailed or banished. Why didn't the EPA use scientific methods to prove that an agent was hazardous and then control the agent? When the Greeks found asps to be poisonous, they avoided asps. Is it not possible to test drinking water supplies to prevent carcinogenic agents from being absorbed by men or beasts? Surely if laboratories can test the ground water at a site like Panama Street, they are also capable of running tests on other drinking water supplies.

MERCURY: Zeus, you are a rational thinker. You use reason. I saw little evidence of reason while studying CERCLA. I saw only a conglomeration of ideas pushed by interest groups. Nothing is defined and the wording is not definitive. Under the wording of this law, it would be possible to have almost every substance found on earth included as hazardous to the health of Americans.

CERCLA also looked to the President to make most of

the decisions. The President is responsible for establishing the testing agencies, allocating funds for remediations, assessing fines for abuses and encouraging the states to write environmental laws by sharing federal funds.

All of this could have worked and led to the remediation of many known hazardous waste sites except for three monstrous problems contained in CERCLA. First, after the first few years, there was no requirement for Congress to fund the Superfund. Superfund in time became "Nofund."

The second problem must have seemed insignificant to the framers of the bill who were for the most part lawyers, politicians and academics with little technical knowledge. At the time, technology did not exist to make remediation economical. The framers showed total ignorance of remediation costs as is evidenced by the fact that a maximum of two million dollars was allowed from the Superfund moneys for any one site. This is like bailing out a sinking boat with a teacup.

The third problem, we can truly credit to the Muse. It is impossible to think even the best lobbyists in Washington could slip this one in on the American public. Muse, I see your hand in this. Section 9614(a) of CERCLA states, "Nothing in this Act shall be construed or interpreted as preempting any State from imposing additional liability or requirements with respect to the release of hazardous substances within each State."

These words seem very innocent. But, we soon realized that CERCLA had built the foundation for states to carry out the dreams of every environmental lobby in America. CERCLA put the stamp of approval on lists of hazardous agents that previously had not been recognized as such. Now, a lawyer could go into any American courtroom and say simply, it's on the list.

CERCLA also gave persons accused of polluting the right to force other parties to share the responsibility of reimbursing the Superfund. Also, CERCLA encouraged states through financial incentives to pass their own laws modeled on CERCLA. The states embellished their laws with longer lists of hazardous substances and more provisions for liability than CERCLA itself. For example, Massachusetts under MGL Chapter 21E included storage of hazardous material as a reason for liability, whereas CERCLA did not recognize storage in that context.

ZEUS: If CERCLA was enacted as the "Superfund Law" and designed to use federal funds to do remediation, how did it become so ineffective?

MERCURY: I suppose we could speculate on any number of reasons. Whatever the reasons, after almost 20 years of existence, it is clear to me that CERCLA has not been successful. After billions of dollars have been spent, so called hazardous waste sites are more plentiful than ever and far more money has gone to litigation than for cleanup.

This is failed legislation. Hutchins as a victim of this law is but one example of a life being destroyed. There are others and as long as such legislation stays on the books, there will be many more victims.

Rachel Carson is quoted in *Silent Spring* as saying, "All this is not to say there is no insect problem and no need of control. I am saying, rather, that control must be geared to realities, not to mythical situations, and that the methods employed must be such that they do not destroy us along with the insects." In truth, many Americans can now say, the methods employed by some misguided environmentalists have destroyed us.

ZEUS: Thank you Mercury for your report on the origins of CERCLA. I think it unfortunate that Americans pay little attention to their history. Perhaps this is why many American lawyers understand laws but have no feeling and reverence for "the law."

MERCURY: The problem is the system under which Americans become lawyers. I found that unlike physicians, scientists and other professions, Americans do not grow up aspiring to study law. At some point, when a career choice has to be made, law school becomes an option that promises graduates prestige and a good living.

    The controlling factor of a law education is the passing of state bar exams. As a result, I found that American lawyers focus on the words of the laws and treat them as universal truths. They see legislated laws as absolute. Most could not understand that rules that apply in Massachusetts might have no relevance in other times or in other places in the world.

MUSE: Are you saying that legislated laws like CERCLA are not sacred? Lawyers have recognized the environmental rulings of CERCLA as absolute for 20 years. There is no way that you can show that they are not as viable as those Ten Commandments that were carved in stone.

MERCURY: I would agree with your point, if it were not for the "Brownfields" laws that are currently being passed by most of the states. While the Muse does not take credit for these new laws, I believe that this quorum should know about them because these laws challenge the sanctity of environmental laws like CERCLA.

ZEUS: Mercury, you have gone beyond what I asked of you. I commend you for your initiative. Please tell us about the Brownfields.

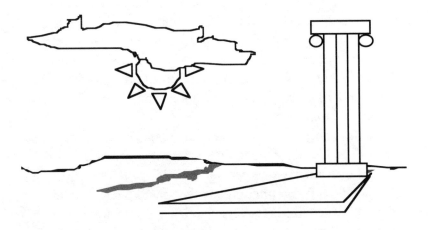

XXIX. Brownfields

MUSE: Possibly I did not spend enough time in America to learn about Brownfields. Mercury, you'll have to educate me on that one.

MERCURY: Brownfields are vacant, abandoned or under-utilized industrial properties that are contaminated with oil or hazardous materials. The DEP has reported that there are over 7000 contaminated sites officially listed in Massachusetts.

JESTER: Unbelievable, Massachusetts must be the pits. That's like living in a sewer.

HUTCHINS: It just depends on your perspective.

JESTER: Well, if you're in Massachusetts, your perspective must be like sleeping under a tethered bull. When they say brownfields, they really mean brown fields.

MERCURY: Actually, Massachusetts is a very clean place
with very few reports of environmentally related health
problems. But, your comments are very pertinent to environmental laws like CERCLA and Massachusetts General
Law, Chapter 21E. The question comes down to the
definition of such words as pollution, toxin, carcinogen and
hazardous material.

Those poorly defined words are responsible for billions
of dollars of environmentally budgeted funds being misdirected over the past 20 years in the United States. I personally would not fear pitching my tent on all but a handful of
the 7000 sites in Massachusetts. If I had a guarantee of no
nuclear waste on a site, I would fear none of them.

JESTER: That's bravado Mercury. That's easy to say, because no one's going to challenge you. I suppose you
would swim in the canals of Venice and bathe in the Nile
among the fecal matter.

MERCURY: Jester, even though I'm a god, I grew up knowing that I should stay away from decomposing organic
substances. I learned about germs on my visits to earth and
I have no doubt that they cause health problems for mortals.

Most Americans spend their lives living with the majority of the agents listed as hazardous material by states like
Massachusetts. Unfortunately, Americans can not function
without automobiles, buses, airplanes, home heating systems, snow blowers and all those other necessities that use
oil, gasoline, natural gas, antifreeze, catalytic converters,
soaps and cleaning compounds that are found on the various
government hazardous material lists.

I found American pediatricians disturbed by the pain
inflicted on children because of alcohol, malnutrition,
physical abuse, AIDS and drug addicted mothers. When I
asked pediatricians about health problems caused by those

244

agents on the DEP's hazardous list, they had to dig deep into their physician's manuals to find case studies. Generally, the cases they could find involved treatment for children who drank these agents. The cure usually involved stomach pumping.

MUSE: Certainly, Mercury, you are not claiming to know more about hazardous materials than the U.S. Government. I hope you would not want to see children sickened by exposure to heating oil and gasoline that has soaked into the soil of the yards, sidewalks and paths where they play. You know that children do put things like dirt in their mouths.

MERCURY: Children do play in yards of residences where soil could be filled with oil, paint, gasoline, solvents and household cleaners. Those residential areas that pose the greatest risk to children are not on the list of 7000 sites in Massachusetts because environmental investigations have focused on businesses. The threats of viruses, bacteria, accidents and violence have proven to be the significant risks to families while pollution risks are statistically insignificant.

I am not advocating that humans should ignore the threat of agents that the state and federal government claim to be hazardous to human health. The question is where do governments and the private sector put their efforts and money to improve world health? I am disappointed in the Brownfields legislation because I see the failures of CERCLA repeating themselves.

JESTER: As Yogi Berra used to say, It's deja vu, all over again. Oh I'm sorry, I'm sorry. I heard that in California, I always wanted to say those words.

ZEUS: [Laughing at the Jester while trying to restore order]

Mercury, please describe a typical Brownfields bill and then tell us your misgivings.

MERCURY: OK, I'll tell you about the Massachusetts legislation by paraphrasing literature published by Douglas Peterson and Lois Pines, the Massachusetts Senate and House Chairpersons. Their Bill H.5299 encourages the clean up and redevelopment of the sites by combining liability reforms with benefits to the investors who provide moneys for revitalization. Changes in the liability provisions of MGL Chapter 21E plus state tax credits and private and government loans are expected to accomplish the Bill's goals.

   The legislation amends Chapter 21E with liability relief for "eligible persons." An "eligible person" is defined as an innocent current or future owner who neither caused nor contributed to the contamination.

MUSE: That seems reasonable to me. There is no reason that an innocent current or future owner should pay. I think that such an amendment could encourage parties to buy these contaminated properties and fix them up.

MERCURY: I agree with you Muse, I don't think an innocent person should pay. I also agree with the provisions that say that downstream and downgradient owners should be exempted from liability. The Bill also relieves tenants, municipalities and secured lenders of liability if they fall into that category of "eligible persons."

ZEUS: I'm sold, this Brownfields legislation makes sense to me. I assume that it also takes another look at the Massachusetts' list of hazardous materials and reassesses those 7000 contaminated sites.

MERCURY: I'm sorry to report that the list of hazardous materials was considered sacrosanct by the Massachusetts legislature.

JESTER: Sacrosanct, what's this sacrosanct. You mean it's untouchable. Who got to those people?

MERCURY: Jester, it was not that way. You see these legislators don't want to get into what they refer to as "science." They continue to accept the risk assessments assigned by laboratories that are under contract to the federal government as part of CERCLA.

JESTER: But, science is the key. How can they decide health issues without considering science? That's like scheduling baseball in the winter and saying that you did not consider the weather.

MERCURY: That's my point. As well intentioned as these legislators are, by avoiding the science question, this Bill remains ineffective. If state legislators accept everything coming out of the federal Environmental Protection Agency as absolute truth, there is no chance to produce wise legislation.

The absence of scientific considerations is one of the many reasons that I am against these Brownfields bills. Real changes can only be made at the federal level. It was there that the biased scientific conclusions were created that influenced both CERCLA and the state programs that followed.

ZEUS: Mercury that's a big jump, even for you. What difference does it make? Pollution is pollution. I think every American has the right to know that his health is not in danger because of another citizen's lack of consideration.

MERCURY: Zeus, on the surface what you say seems realistic. Unfortunately, when we studied actual situations we were surprised. First, Petersen and Pines say that approximately 60% of the 7000 brownfields sites are contaminated by oil. Historically, oil has been used in Massachusetts primarily as a heating fuel and for auto engines. Industrial usage by volume is comparatively small. Many of the sites are abandoned service stations and businesses that stored oil in tanks that leaked. However, under the federal guidelines, they are full-blown hazardous waste sites no matter where they are and no matter what the threat to health. By federal definition, they are an abomination that must be eliminated.

Let's say that by magic the federal definition could be changed so that oil was not considered extremely hazardous to health. At that point, things would change in the Massachusetts Brownfields Law. By deleting from the list those sites contaminated by oil, it would leave only 2800 sites to be cleaned. As a consequence dollars could be focused on the higher priority sites that pose a much greater risk to health.

MUSE: Some cars and trucks drip oil onto the highways and into storm drains and then into the rivers. What is your solution for that pollution?

MERCURY: Muse, at that point I would suggest to Americans that they purchase a whole lot of mops for the highways or wise up to reality. I would ask the feds for a realistic risk assessment for oil. By relying on questionable risk assessments that show every hazardous substance to be of equal danger to mankind, the states can not pass reasonable and effective environmental laws that are economically justifiable.

MUSE: Hold on Mercury, are you saying that oil poses no

health risk to humans?

MERCURY: I am saying that there is no proof that oil that has spilled into the ground is a major health risk factor. During the first half of the century, county governments would oil dirt roads to keep down the dust. At that time no one attributed that practice to deaths or health problems.

MUSE: Then you are advocating that America slip back to the 1940's and allow oil to be spread on the ground to keep down dust.

MERCURY: I would not advocate that any more than I would suggest bloodletting by physicians as the means to good health. But, I do ask for scientific proof that oil in the ground is hazardous before I would condemn 4200 sites in Massachusetts to a leper's existence. It's really a question of terminology. If more specific terminology eliminated oil from the federal hazardous list, think of the millions of dollars that would be saved in remediation costs.

JESTER: Hey, I understand what you're saying Mercury. When I lived in California, I had friends that questioned whether marijuana was a drug like heroin or in the same class as nicotine and alcohol. That definition made a big difference when someone got busted.

MERCURY: Jester you've got the idea, but let's stick with the question of oil.

MUSE: I continue to believe that Massachusetts should clean up all 7000 sites. Every site that gets cleaned up would be one less threat to Massachusetts' citizens. Even if the danger from oil were small, I would rather be safe than sorry.

MERCURY: Muse, I'm not arguing that point. Certainly if such clean ups were inexpensive or there were unlimited funds, that should be done. But you must realize, that if the average remediation cost per site were $150,000, the total for those 7000 sites would be over a billion dollars. Whether the money is private or public, that's a hell of lot of money to pay for something where the risk factors to health are so low.

MUSE: There you go again Mercury, throwing out figures like a billion dollars. Hutchins, from your experience please tell Mercury that the average site would not cost $150,000 to clean up.

HUTCHINS: Well Muse, I'll have to back Mercury on this one. Considering that it costs about $10,000 for the original testing and $30,000 for the Licensed Site Professional's evaluation for even the smallest site, I think Mercury's $150,000 figure may be too low.

Also, you should realize that most of these 7000 sites were discovered through business real estate transfers. I'm sure that there are another 10,000 sites in Massachusetts that have not made the lists. Mercury's figure of 1 billion dollars may turn out to be 2 or 3 billion dollars. Can you imagine what the total would be to clean up all 50 states?

MUSE: Whatever Mercury says, I think that agencies like the DEP have done an outstanding job with the limited resources they have been provided. With a limited budget, these government employees have been able to find 7000 sites in Massachusetts by having the public report on itself.

JESTER: [Mumbling] Rat on one another to save their own skins.

ZEUS: [As a reaction to the Jester's outburst, Zeus hit the Jester again with one of his lightning bolts. This time it was more like a warning shot that simply startled the Jester.] That's enough, Jester. I think we should look upon this as creative financing by the State of Massachusetts. The money has to come from somewhere.

JESTER: If remediating these 7000 sites is a critical public health issue and the health of the residents of Massachusetts is at stake, then this should be treated like any public health emergency. The State should put out the billion dollars first and collect from responsible parties later. How do you explain that one Hutchins, you're a Massachusetts resident?

HUTCHINS: Jester, Saint Patrick was able to explain the blessed trinity, but I think Massachusetts' politics would baffle even him. It's not the first time that the legislature voted for legislation and worried about paying for it later. But don't put the blame on Massachusetts, the U.S. Congress established the master plan with CERCLA, so Massachusetts and Washington are marching to the same drummer.

ZEUS: Enough Jester, no more outbursts and no more unsolvable riddles like Massachusetts' politics. The Muse is right. The people who work at these public agencies are just trying to do their jobs. If all the various kinds of waste are given equal billing by the federal government and called extremely dangerous to human health, then the state agencies must treat them as such.

MERCURY: You are right Zeus. Unfortunately many of these agency people are doing their jobs like robots by not determining if a spilled substance is truly a threat to health.

Worse still, these agencies are weighted with persons with anti-business attitudes who attempt to make businesses pay simply to right some imagined wrong they see in society.

After my in-depth study, I believe it would be best for America to revamp CERCLA. This makes more sense than to have all the states attempt to plug the holes with superficial fixes like these Brownfields laws.

While legislators like Pines and Petersen are trying to help the economy by salvaging abandoned commercial sites, their efforts will be ineffective. At the same time, the energy that could be used to alter the wrongs of CERCLA will be dissipated if citizens accept the illusion that the Brownfields laws are accomplishing something of significance.

Realistically only a few strategically located and politically expedient locations will be reclaimed using quasi-government financing. Unless there are government guarantees as there are with student loans, conservative bank lenders will run away from "eligible persons" loans no matter what assurances come out of these Brownfields laws.

ZEUS: Mercury, your insight and vision have always been right on the money so I accept your concerns with Brownfields as legitimate. Do you see anything positive in such legislation?

MERCURY: Yes, yes, Zeus, I do. What I see coming from the Brownfields laws is very liberating to those who want reason to prevail in the environmental movement in America. The breakthrough I see in the Brownfields laws is that legislators are beginning to see the futility in using civil law to correct environmental problems.

For example, Pines and Petersen show the "status liability" of Massachusetts General Law, Chapter 21E that imposes strict, joint and several liabilities can be changed. This tells Massachusetts citizens, that 21E's "status liability"

252

is not a self evident truth or divinely inspired and therefore this liability statute can be attacked, debated and dismantled as any other man made rule. I do not want to overly state my enthusiasm for this small crack in the armament of civil law. However, you must understand that after 20 years of CERCLA, I see this as hope that reason will finally prevail.

ZEUS: Excellent, Mercury, your point is well taken. It is unfortunate that the changes you prophesize will come too late to help such people as Hutchins who have suffered too long in silence.

HUTCHINS: Don't concern yourself with me Zeus. Just to have environmental liability debated is progress. I'll give you an example of how deeply ingrained tort law is in the environmental movement.

Some time ago I was visited by Christopher Geehern, a Senior Vice President with the Associated Industries of Massachusetts (AIM), a Massachusetts business association. In an attempt to encourage me that Associated Industries was aware of its members' environmental concerns, he said that the AIM Environmental Department was staffed completely by lawyers.

After he left our plant, I realized how dysfunctional the environmental movement had become. Rather than an Environmental Department staffed by persons capable of helping member companies with educational topics and environmentally sound technical solutions, it was staffed completely with lawyers. AIM was placing emphasis on their member's most compelling environmental problems, which had nothing to do with a clean environment. These problems had to do with environmental law. All I could think was, "what a waste!"

MUSE: Even after 20 years, my influence on CERCLA is

evident. I love it because my lawyers have boundless opportunities to do environmental work.

Mercury, you are only wishing and hoping if you think you will separate litigation and remediation. As you can hear from Hutchins' testimony, my lawyers are entrenched. They're dug in and will ride out any storm. In response to your efforts to bring reason into the environmental equation, the law lobbies will simply answer that any attack on CERCLA is an attack on a clean environment by business interests. You should realize that reason means nothing because I have emotion on my side. You are dealing with good versus evil, green trees versus the industrial revolution, well-tailored lawyers versus blue-collar polluters. Mercury, you might as well throw down your weapons of reason and common sense and give up before you begin this battle.

MERCURY: Muse, there is no question that your influence has been felt in America. I was just pointing to a glimmer of hope that reason could return and money would flow to the environment and not into law offices.

ABC Television has said that in the past 7 years, 30 billion dollars has been spent on cancer research. This averages out to be about 4 billion dollars per year for all America. In comparison, for Massachusetts' citizens to spend more than 1 billion dollars to clean up 7000 sites that may actually pose no risk, seems insane to me.

I also know that CERCLA has cost the American people many times 30 billion dollars during the past seven years if we add up the costs in investigations, litigation and administration. The 30 billion spent on cancer research has shown tremendous results in terms of cures, remissions and prevention. Americans have little to show for the billions spent on the legal obligations prescribed by CERCLA.

ZEUS: Thank you, Mercury. Your findings are impressive. You have convinced me that the Muse swayed the U.S. Congress in 1980 when it passed the CERCLA legislation. It is obvious that various trial lawyer lobbies influenced the bill to the point where environmental law is the fastest growing discipline of the legal industry.

MUSE: Thank you, Mercury for bolstering my position. Thank you, Mr. Hutchins for showing Zeus that I share the same powers as the other gods and can bring out the same emotions in mortals. You have testified to your pain, anger, humiliation and despair. I am truly the lawyer god!

ZEUS: [Standing up in anger and pounding his fist on the podium] Easy Muse, this is not over! Hold your tongue and let Mr. Hutchins finish. I'm sure he has more to tell. Mr. Hutchins you have the floor.

HUTCHINS: I am happy to be of help Muse, because you are right. I have been through anger, humiliation and years of pain, but not despair. I always hoped for a way out. I believed that this insanity would right itself, if not for me, at least for others. I did not despair because there were other things that gave me hope.

ZEUS: Mr. Hutchins, what is this hope. Your business is in a shambles. Your future is dim and at your age you have little time to recover. Let's say that in the next few years, Hutchins Tool is revitalized and you are able to bring in more cash. The DEP could place a lien on Hutchins Tool and take away your success in the future.

HUTCHINS: Zeus, I take one day at a time. Something always seems to relieve the situation, so I don't despair. For example, for a while Jeff McCormick raised my hopes.

CHORUS: [Chanting] What the God has told I will then tell. Phoebus, our lord, speaks plainly: Drive out, he says, pollution, defilement harbored in the land; drive it out nor cherish it until it prove past cure.

MUSE: [Looking at the Jester] Hear the chorus chanting Creon's speech from *Oedipus*, they must be practicing for Zeus' Dionysus Festival. It appears that even in ancient Greece they spoke of pollution defiling the land. There will be a chorus with happy omens when Sophocles writes about my ascendance to lawyer god.

HUTCHINS: Why do they chant that dirge now? If I recall the drama, Oedipus had noble qualities like intensity and self-confidence and he relied on reason.

MUSE: Hutchins, you should also recall that Oedipus did not recognize the limits of reason. By reasoning that he could understand the mystery of that pollution in his land, he destroyed himself. Reason may work no differently for you in trying to unravel the riddle of CERCLA.

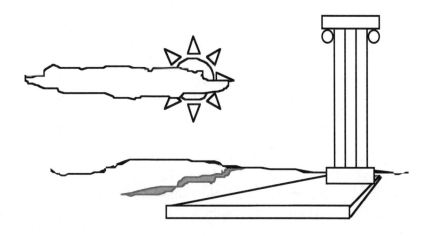

XXX.   Jeff

HUTCHINS: When Attorney Doherty encouraged me to
settle the Thompson lawsuit, I was frustrated by his firm's
lack of creativity. As I saw it, Attorney Hadley was losing
every battle and plodding on to Hutchins Tool's eventual
doom.

    The client/attorney relationship would have been much
better if Hadley communicated with me more frequently. At
times, months would go by and I would not hear from him.
I initiated most of the phone calls prompted by reading
copies of his bills that were being sent to our Insurance
Company. Hadley's secretary was instructed to send me
copies of these billing statements, so they came to me
faithfully every few months. What usually caught my eye
were the amounts the Insurance Company was being billed.
It was not unusual to see fees that averaged about $5,000
per month and a running balance in the range of $10,000 to
$15,000.

At this point, the Insurance Company's lack of enthusiasm did not surprise me. Their actions mimicked the behavior of most agencies dealing with environmental issues that employ an army of people sleep walking their way through the maze of rules and regulations. Most of these people are totally unaware that their actions can bring devastation to the lives of other citizens.

This is all camouflaged by the occasional tank truck oil spill, gas leak or chemical fire reported on the evening television news. How often do you see pictures of HAZMAT teams, wearing yellow suits and facemasks standing by a tanker truck leaking oil?

JESTER: Hey, I've seen them. I like the suits and the boots. That oil must be real hazardous for you earthlings to bring out the emergency crews and evacuate people from large areas.

MERCURY: [standing up wanting to interject] Actually, most of the emergencies don't amount to anything. However, with the new regulations, there must be HAZMAT teams on the scene of spills. According to some public health officials, there are fewer health risks from these spills today than there were a hundred years ago, when horses, oxen and cattle walked the highways and relieved themselves along the way.

JESTER: Can you picture a scene during the Nineteenth Century as the DEP sent HAZMAT teams out with their yellow uniforms, brooms and shovels? That's when they needed those masks and air packs.

ZEUS: Divinities, enough of this, Mr. Hutchins, please continue.

HUTCHINS: Well, as I was saying. I was frustrated with my attorneys, the DEP and my Insurance Company for their lack of sensitivity. I was being killed and no one seemed to care. It was unbelievable that my rights could be trampled on for eight years without some legal protection. I knew that even the worst criminal had the rights of due process, speedy trial by one's peers, and all those other things I learned in fourth grade civics.

Each year, I would see and hear about legal efforts to assert minority rights, women's rights and gay rights, through the courts. I wondered if there was any way that I could assert my right to be protected from the illegal acts of the employees of the Massachusetts DEP.

I had no hope that my law firm would challenge MGL Chapter 21E or CERCLA on constitutional grounds such as ex post facto. However, I realized that one of the major flaws in both the federal and state CERCLA type laws was in their administration. The framers of CERCLA had placed great power in the hands of the President. For example, section 9604 says, "Whenever. . . there is a release or substantial threat of release into the environment of any pollutant or contaminant which may present an imminent and substantial danger to the public health or welfare, the President is authorized to act, consistent with the national contingency plan, to remove or arrange for the removal of, and provide for remedial action related to such hazardous substance, pollutant, or contaminant at any time."

On the surface, this wording seems very logical and simple. An American President can not do these things alone so he is authorized to develop federal agencies to carry out the regulations established by Congress. In this regard CERCLA is no different than most federal laws.

Many lawyers jumped at the chance to join the EPA and administer CERCLA. This was an unbelievable windfall of opportunity. CERCLA's administrators were given the power to prescribe what was hazardous, explain the word release, define the word responsible and expand the limits of liability with the modifiers strict, joint and several. It was mandated that the EPA would also manage the expenditures of Superfund and the entitlements to the states that encouraged CERCLA type state laws and state participation in local remediation projects.

JESTER: Congress gave the President the responsibility and he turned it over to the EPA. So it's actually the EPA that determines what hazardous agents make the federal lists and what sites are designated to get federal funds for clean up. If the people at the EPA are the more fervent environmentalists, doesn't this put the inmates, or as you call them the activists, in charge of the institution?

MERCURY: My study shows that many of the administrative positions were filled with persons active in the environmental movement. Of course, I believe this is very understandable. For example, the Agricultural Department has a bias toward hiring people with enthusiasm for good farming.

Jester, you are correct in recognizing that many of these first EPA administrators were on a mission. They harbored strong sentiments that big business was poisoning America and they recognized it as their duty to force big business to pay the cost of restoring the environment to good health. They had no premonition that major corporations could insulate themselves from the civil penalties of CERCLA and that the costs would fall upon the backs of small businesspersons and property owners who used banks for financing.

The early EPA officials also did not realize that America lacked the technology required for cost effective remediation efforts. Nor did they know exactly what poisons they were expected to eradicate. Their bias was to place the burden of proof on those declaring a substance to be of "no" or "low" risk. All the EPA knew was that Congress had set quotas that called for the publication of a list of 100 hazardous substances within 6 months, to be followed by the listing of at least 100 more each year for 3 years. It was like Senator McCarthy looking for communists; if you can't find them, create them to fill the quota. If Congress said there are 400 hazardous substances, it must be true. There was no time to waste on either reason or reasonableness.

MUSE: Mercury, are you trying to say that these early environmental administrators were bad or that they were not carrying out the President's policies?

MERCURY: To the contrary. It appears they were good mortals doing the best job they could. They were also following the public sentiment at the time, which generally saw these issues in black and white terms, polluters vs. environmentalists. The public felt that certain industries showed no respect for the environment, and, as a consequence, they put pressure on Congress and the administrators of CERCLA to remediate. Congress had provided funding for projects like Love Canal, so people assumed that the administrators were using federal funds for remediations. There was little public recognition that those administrators were setting federal and state guidelines and creating the greatest opportunity for tort law since the invention of the automobile.

MUSE: [Jumping to her feet showing great pleasure] You see Zeus, I not only directed the passage of CERCLA, I guided the early administrators. To guarantee my success, you will remember that I encouraged wording in the bill to include a watchdog committee to oversee my handiwork. A committee made up of 12 lawyers with a budget of $300,000. They would have been watchdogs of CERCLA for nothing or in their legal terminology, "pro bono publico."

ZEUS: Muse, please allow Mr. Hutchins to speak. We recognize what you have accomplished.

HUTCHINS: It looks like Mercury understands the history of CERCLA. He should understand that most of the state laws, which were encouraged under the guidelines of CERCLA, gave the state administrators the same immense power. They also mirror CERCLA, in that the state laws called for unobtainable goals and the state legislators voted very little public funding to meet the goals.

In Massachusetts, MGL Chapter 21E places most of the decision making in the hands of the Department of Environmental Protection (DEP). In my opinion, it is this delegation of power to the DEP that has caused Hutchins Tool and myself such grief.

I realized some time ago that the DEP could use their powers in either positive or negative ways to reach their goal of decreasing environmental risks in Massachusetts. There has been minimum progress toward that goal while vast sums of money have gone into the payment of legal fees as the parties disputed liability issues.

It is not difficult to understand why the DEP's efforts have been unsuccessful, when you see that their methods are primarily confrontational. The first letter that Hutchins Tool received from the DEP seeking information on Panama Street contained warnings as to our responsibilities and listed the penalties for not complying. These same threats have been contained in almost every document we've received from them in the past eight years.

JESTER: Like a dog showing its fangs as you approach.

HUTCHINS: Jester, more like a little dog with an annoying bark. These are mild mannered people who as individuals would do you no harm, but as a group, they resemble a wolf pack. Many seem to revel in the role of being the guardians of mother earth buttressed by their favorite threats, such as triple damages, strict liability, joint and several liability, etc.

In time, I realized that the DEP employees had continually violated my civil rights. In fact, most of the damage that Hutchins Tool and I suffered was the direct result of the policies, methods and actions of DEP personnel.

JESTER: You mean they acted like those state workers who prevented most blacks from voting in the South and that Governor that kept black children out of the segregated schools in Mississippi.

HUTCHINS: Exactly, with the power of the state behind them, many bureaucrats are very confrontational dealing with ordinary citizens. Local police in America have been educated on the limits of their powers when dealing with citizens, but many civil servants that work in agencies like the IRS, FDA and Treasury Department continue to violate citizens' civil rights indiscriminately.

As my convictions grew stronger that my rights were being violated, I would test those convictions by thinking of the alternatives. For example, if the DEP had called all the occupants of Panama Street together early, described the problem and requested cooperation, is it possible that things would have been resolved without litigation? My answer is yes.

Would the Panama Street site's location, next to a brook that led directly to an interstate river, allow federal Superfund moneys to be used for remediation? The answer is yes.

In question after question, I realized that DEP personnel had not operated properly under the mandates of MGL Chapter 21E. As these ideas were focusing in early 1997, I attended a wedding and sat at a table with Attorney Jeff McCormick.

Jeff is a personal friend of mine and he is my wife's favorite dining partner. We are always happy to see the McCormicks at parties and events. Jeff is a trial lawyer and litigates many cases each year for his firm, which is one of the largest law firms in Springfield. He is active with the Massachusetts Bar Association and one of the few lawyers from Western Massachusetts to be elected an officer of that Association.

Toward the end of the wedding reception, I had a long conversation with Jeff in which he recited his experiences in attempting to encourage better selection for Massachusetts' judgeships. His quarrel was with the Governor's Council, which he felt was politically motivated in the judge selection process. Throughout the conversation, I was impressed with Jeff's love and respect for the legal profession.

After our talk at the wedding reception, I started to think that I should talk with Jeff about my feelings that DEP personnel had violated my civil rights by not operating within the scope of the law. Perhaps Jeff would consider my hope of taking a more creative approach to our environmental problems. Perhaps he would see how MGL Chapter 21E harmed Hutchins Tool and that he would want to right this wrong out of his respect for law and as a service to his fellow man.

In that spirit, I wrote the following letter to him:

May 12,1997

Jeffrey McCormick, Esquire
Robinson, Donovan, Madden, & Barry, P.C.
1500 Main Street
Springfield, MA 01115

Dear Jeff:

In 1990, my stock interest in Hutchins Tool was appraised by banks and accountants at approximately 2.3 million dollars. Using conservative appreciation formulas, that value could be placed at 3.4 million today. However, that value today is actually zero or negative if one considers that as an officer of the Corporation, I could be responsible for environmental liability which extends through the Corporation to me person-ally. There is no question that I have suffered severe financial damage and great damage to my reputation.

My loss in investment and the devaluation of my interest in Hutchins Tool is directly related to Hutchins Tool being named a potentially responsible party by the Massachusetts Depart-ment of Environmental Protection in February of 1991. A lawsuit filed in 1991 which exposes Hutchins Tool to demands in the millions of dollars and which has been so footnoted on our financial statements has eliminated bank financing, thrown us into the hands of the FDIC and prevented the sale of the business. While Hutchins Tool is being defended under insur-ance policies issued in 1973-79, the insurance company is defending with reservation. I estimate over $200,000 in de-fense-fees have been paid to Doherty, Wallace, Pillsbury & Murphy, over the past six years.

I personally would like to bring civil action in Federal Court against the Massachusetts DEP and named employees of the

265

Springfield Office. I want Robinson, Donovan to represent me in this action.

In this regard, I would like to meet with you or anyone you select at Robinson, Donovan and present documentation that I feel supports a high damage claim and proves the liability of employees of the DEP. I can also cite the Sections of MGL #21E that supports my case. I can prove that the polluted site falls under federal jurisdiction and show that the DEP intentionally kept this site out of federal jurisdiction. Everything leads to the Federal Court System where I expect we can get positive results.

Sincerely yours,

Donald C. Hutchins

HUTCHINS: I hoped for an immediate response to the letter, but it never came. When I saw Jeff socially, the subject never came up. Finally, a few months later at a ceremony where his son became an Eagle Scout, Jeff did stop and say, "I haven't forgotten your letter. We lost our environmental specialist a few weeks ago and I'm waiting to take it up with his replacement. You'll be hearing from me."

While frustrated with the delay, I was happy that there was still Interest in bringing my personal damage suit against the DEP. I moved from being frustrated to elation very quickly when I decided to jump-start this thing by writing a first draft of the Complaint.

JESTER: Hutchins, with all due respect to you, as I remember you told us that Judge Ireland told you that you could not practice law in his courtroom. Now you decided to write a Complaint! Are you crazy?

HUTCHINS: I suppose I was crazy, but in the past I wrote patent applications that were changed very little by the patent attorney before submission. For that reason, I felt that by writing my ideas in the form of a Complaint, it would clarify my ideas, simplify the presentation for the lawyers and save time. I also believed that I knew the CERCLA laws better than most lawyers because I had read them over many times during the past eight years.

In my draft of the Complaint, I wrote about 30 single spaced, typewritten pages which included a cover sheet, Parties, Statement of Facts, plus nine Counts of Negligence, one Count of Waste and one Count of Violation. I felt that this was not a bad effort for a toolmaker with no legal training.

To give you an indication of the sweat I put into this Complaint, I'll show you this example. It is Count number I and comes after 87 Statements of Fact, approximately 15 pages into the document:

<u>*COUNT I*</u>

(Claim Pursuant to Section 3 of M.G.L. Chapter 21E)

88.   *The Plaintiff reasserts and incorporates by reference paragraphs 1-87 of this complaint.*

89.   *Section 3 of M.G.L. C21 states in pertinent part that:*

> *"The Department shall take all action appropriate to secure to the Commonwealth the benefits of FWPCA and CERCLA and other pertinent laws including the Oil Pollution Act."*

90.   Section 3 of M.G.L. C21E states in pertinent part that:

"The Department shall make every effort to provide the documentation required under CERCLA in order to make sites eligible for federal response action moneys."

91.   Plaintiff is a "person" as the term is defined in Section 2 of Chapter 21E.

92.   Joyce, Symington, Wanat, Richmond, Kelley-Dominick and Weinberg are or were at one time employees of the Department given responsibility for understanding Chapter 21E and administering Section 3.

93.   Pecousic Brook as a direct contributory to the Connecticut River falls under federal jurisdiction and CERCLA.

94.   The DEP Western Office retains maps showing the Site, Pecousic Brook, the Connecticut River, and the New England States. Kelley-Dominick in a meeting held September 20, 1993 recognized that the Site falls under CERCLA.

95.   The DEP, Joyce, Symington, Wanat, Richmond, Kelley-Dominick, and Weinberg individually are liable for not notifying federal authorities concerning the Site. They are liable for not taking actions under Section 3, which mandates that they take all actions appropriate to secure the Commonwealth the benefits of CERCLA.

96.   Federal remediation funds were available for remediation in the years between 1990 and 1997. If response action moneys were provided for remediation early, the Site would have been remediated. The DEP's

costs would be limited, the claimed exposure of hazardous material to the public would cease, and the Plaintiff's legal and administrative costs would be minimal. Most importantly, the remediation cost could be defined and the various insurance companies would have paid for the remediation because the amount of the claim would be a specific amount.

97.   *Plaintiff has suffered financial loss, emotional trauma and loss of reputation, through a seven-year period as a result of Kelley-Dominick, Joyce, Symington, Wanat, Richmond and Weinberg's refusal to "provide the documentation required under CERCLA in order to make sites eligible for federal response action moneys."*

JESTER: There's no question, you are nuts. Why would you put so much time into trying to write a Complaint? Did you really think that a lawyer would litigate against the Massachusetts DEP and possibly undermine the legal profession's environmental law business that is so profitable?

ZEUS: That's enough Jester. I can appreciate what Hutchins was doing. This Panama Street litigation has destroyed him. Should a mortal take it or fight for his life? I'm sure Hutchins knew the CERCLA and MGL Chapter 21E statutes better than most lawyers did. It is also evident that some American citizen must take a stand against the injustices of the CERCLA laws or many thousands of Americans will suffer the same consequences.

HUTCHINS: Thank you Zeus. Maybe it was crazy or a last ditch effort, but by studying the law and finding eleven Counts, I felt that there would be a few Counts that Jeff could use when he wrote the actual Complaint. I suppose it was also a catharsis, a purification of my emotions, just as

Aristotle described the effects of tragedy.

ZEUS: I like that imagery. Your story is a tragedy. I hope that Jeff McCormick appreciated your efforts and used some of the Counts from the Complaint you had roughed out.

HUTCHINS: Zeus, I gathered my 30 page attempt at a Complaint and dropped it off at Jeff's office with a cover letter saying that there was no rush and that's the last I've heard on the subject. I've seen him many times since I delivered the copy of the Complaint to his office. He has not spoken to me about what I wrote or my request to discuss litigation against the DEP. While I don't think about it often, his silence really took the wind out of my sails.

I'm a big boy and have been disappointed many times in my life, so I could have accepted any explanation that he would offer. Perhaps he felt that, I was naive and didn't understand the law, that his firm should not undertake such a controversial case or that the chances of winning were marginal and the case would be a poor gamble.

ZEUS: It appears that your hopes at litigating against the DEP went nowhere. What were the results of the two lawsuits, the DEP versus Hutchins Tool and Thompson versus Hutchins Tool? Certainly those cases are resolved by this time, because they have been on the books for about eight years.

HUTCHINS: Zeus, as unbelievable as it may sound, there is little or no action taking place. As one of Massachusetts' highest priority sites, you might expect that there would be pressure to get things resolved both in the courts and at the Site. I have not heard from my attorney or the Insurance Company in months; nor have we heard from the DEP or the Massachusetts Attorney General's Office.

I'm just waiting for the litigation to take its course. Hutchins Tool is downsized and limps along with very little working capital. Our financial statements are still footnoted to show that we have a potential exposure of millions of dollars in lawsuits pending. This prevents us from bank borrowing even if some of the manufacturing projects that we are developing start to expand. We are also aware that if we started making profits again, they could be claimed by the DEP to recover damages.

As part of the downsizing of Hutchins Tool, my brother retired and now consults on a contract basis with a medical device manufacturer. He continues to be pursued as a defendant in the litigation by Attorney Moore, who, with the death of Thompson, now represents the Thompson Estate. Under MGL Chapter 21E, the protections of corporate limited liability do not apply to my brother because he managed the Panama Street operation in the 1970's.

MERCURY: [Standing up slowly as if deep in thought] The "code," it's the "code." Mr. Hutchins, don't feel that you have failed. It's just that you could not overcome the "code" that lawyers follow.

JESTER: Come on Mercury, what "code?" Surely there's not a lawyers' code of ethics. Give us a break.

MERCURY: I can't explain it and I don't believe the Muse is responsible for it. I just know that lawyers have an unwritten code of conduct when it comes to dealing with one another.

JESTER: Big deal! Doctors take an oath. I'm sure that in each state the lawyers take an oath to defend that law.

MERCURY: Not an oath or formal code of conduct. It's more like an understanding to not invade another lawyer's turf. Sort of a fraternal thing. Consider this – in the past twenty years you've heard about hundreds of lawsuits against manufacturers for product liability, physicians for malpractice and accountants for dereliction. Did you ever hear of litigation in the legal industry with lawyer versus lawyer? Can it be that doctors and manufacturers make mistakes and that lawyers never do? Possibly physicians are poorly trained, machinists are error prone and lawyers are 100 percent perfect!

I'm a god so I can only guess why any mortal lawyer would hesitate to respond to Hutchins' request for legal representation to take action against the DEP. It's my guess that a lawyer would be uncomfortable being involved with the issue. While it may appear to us that Hutchins' civil rights were being violated by the actions of people at the DEP, a lawyer may see it differently. To defend Hutchins' rights a lawyer would have to find fault with CERCLA laws that had been on the books for almost 20 years. To make matters even more difficult, there have been no challenges by civil rights groups or the Civil Liberties Union that environmental agency persons or policies have violated any American's civil rights.

To take up Hutchins' cause, a lawyer would also need to challenge laws that have brought a surge of business to the legal industry and which are defended in a knee jerk reaction by most trial lawyers associations. Considering the difficulties that a lawyer would encounter to take this case, I can easily understand why any law firm would hesitate to take on that task.

HUTCHINS: I appreciate what you are saying Mercury and can accept the fact that Jeff would be slow to respond. For me it's not an issue worth talking about except that it shows that the best, most well-intentioned lawyers see environmental issues in terms of environmental law.

JESTER: Wake up Hutchins and run a search on the Internet using the search word, "environment." Almost every article written in America on the environment talks about the law. I suppose you see the environment in terms of golf and the evils are sand traps and deep roughs.

HUTCHINS: You're right Jester. The environment was once green golf courses, sandy beaches and ski trails. Now it's a nightmare of unfriendly verbiage.

CHORUS: But now, O Zeus, whose is the story more grievous to hear, and who is more yoked to misfortune now his entire life is reversed.

ZEUS: Sophocles, quiet that chorus. Let them practice Oedipus elsewhere. It is Hutchins' life we address on this stage today.

SOPHOCLES: On my stage also. My father was an armorer and worked with metal, so I embrace Hutchins as a father. To me the *Oedipus* chorus blends to his fate as point and counterpoint.

ZEUS: Sophocles, direct your drama about the Muse when we are finished. Mercury, please bring some sense to this insanity. CERCLA is a massive hoax that is being played on every American that wants a cleaner environment. Is there any hope that things will change and in the future that moneys will go to remediation rather than litigation?

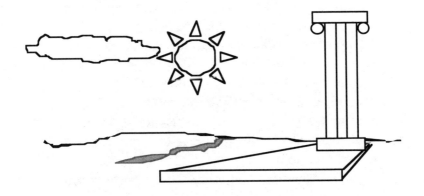

XXXI.   Mercury's Journey

ZEUS: Thank you Mr. Hutchins. Your case has proven to me that the Muse has done what she claimed. There is no question that mortals are not capable of creating the mess that is called CERCLA. It took divine intervention or you may call it devilish interference. A U.S. Congressperson would need tremendous outside inspiration to conjure up a law like CERCLA that has hurt the environmental movement by diverting moneys from remediation to the coffers of the legal establishment. I can not believe that politicians would be so shortsighted to create a cesspool of controversy, finger pointing and litigation by arming CERCLA with civil law remedies. Why did Congress not continue with the criminal penalties that had been so successful in eliminating much of the pollution that infected America?

The Muse has also shown me that she used her powers to bring pain and misery to mortals just as Ares and Aros brought pain to the ancient Greek Republic. In many ways the Muse has used CERCLA to send daggers deep into the hearts of humans like Hutchins, just as the gods Apollo and Cupid have caused pain in their venues.

To further clarify these hearings, I shall call upon our god Mercury to summarize his findings on the environmental problems on Earth. As you know, we have had setbacks in the movie business with our attempts to bring classic heroes to the American youth. This mortal, Lucas, appears to have outflanked us with strange creatures that I would rate as heroes to no one.

I asked Mercury to infuse the classic spirit in American athletes to make them heroes for the young to emulate. In this quest, Mercury has quietly taken children from the poorest homes and made them heroes in America. These youngsters grew to become athletes who are much honored by the American public. I was impressed when it was reported that many of these athlete/heroes recognized their God when they were victorious in prizefights. Others thanked God when they won the NBA Championship.

I am told that today in America children and older mortals also pay homage to these heroes by wearing team jerseys and numbers worn by their heroes. There are trading cards that carry the hero's image and myths.

Through Mercury's influence, television has learned to use these heroes to sell products. In recent years Mercury has had more success than any other god keeping the classic traditions alive in America. Because of this success, I asked Mercury to return to America and bring me suggestions on how we might revive a classic respect for America's most pathetic tribe, the lawyers.

Lawyers are the object of scorn and jokes and have lost the respect of the American people. At a time when this once great society is dying and the need for leadership is greatest, this group of mortals is depicted as buffoons. There was a time when lawyers were heroes in America. Daniel Webster, Thurgood Marshall and Abraham Lincoln were lawyers and heroes molded in the classic tradition. Where has that image gone?

Socrates used his wits as an advocate but retained his self-respect. The senators in the Roman Republic honored truth, reason and social justice. Barbaric ideas like greed, anarchy and self advocacy came to Rome from outside their classic society and led to the demise of the Roman Senate.

Frustrated by the Roman people's rejection of those things that made them great, I lost hope in them and let their emperors fill the void. I sense that lawyers are encouraging these same barbaric ideas in America because they are constantly testing the classic system by impeaching traditional values like truth and respect for authority. They have no understanding that it is much easier to tear down than to build a tradition. Societies are fragile and there is a constant need for integrity and heroics.

Mercury, what have you seen in America? Give us good news; give us hope. Is the classic tradition flourishing?

MERCURY: Zeus, I visited America many years ago, just after the Second World War. At that time the classic influence was extremely strong. America was a conqueror like Greece and Rome, but did not enslave its conquests. Actually things like the Marshall Plan helped America's former enemies recover their civilizations. The influence of the American society spread throughout the world enhanced by trade and the presence of America's troops that protected the peace by stationing themselves in foreign lands.

While cloaked in words like democracy, Americans like General MacArthur exported the classic influence when he wrote the Japanese Constitution and organized Japan's government as a republic after the war. Just as in early Greece and Rome, there were civilizations outside America's influence that did not experience the wisdom of Zeus. They had no experience with the classic tradition and

277

no knowledge on how to organize and govern themselves in the spirit of mutual respect and social justice. These modern barbarians called their civilizations China and Russia and it was inevitable that they would embrace autocratic regimes.

At the time of that visit, America had its heroes. People like Eisenhower, MacArthur and Roosevelt were honored for their deeds and their personal lives had no relevance. America in the 1950's reminded me of early Greece and Rome as America's influence permeated the world and Americans were filled with pride and self-confidence.

When I reported these things to you, it was good. Yet, as America's mentor, Zeus, you wanted to do more for these chosen mortals. Recognizing this, I asked you if I could work with a part of the American population who was not sharing in much of this good fortune. That part of the population needed its own heroes to gain respect. For reasons of which I was not aware, these good, intelligent and happy mortals did not share in America's success.

As Mercury, I have godlike powers of speed, strength and communication. I selected a number of children born of these neglected Americans to be my future heroes. I gave some of these children gifts of speed, some of strength and some my skill in communications to sing or orate.

On this latest visit to America, I was happy to see that my influence had flourished. These children have grown to become heroes in athletics, entertainment and the arts. Their athletic bodies and beautiful voices mimic mine.

JESTER: Yea I've got to hand it to you Mercury. Most of the heroes I saw in America reminded me of you.

But the old heroes that Zeus talks about have been knocked down from their pedestals. The greatness of these heroes was diluted as reporters dredged up sordid details about their personal lives. Humans became more interested in scandal than the accomplishments of these mortals. They knocked down Eisenhower and Roosevelt and even took a few shots at Lincoln and Jefferson. If we reported on the personal lives of the gods in the heavens, we wouldn't have any heroes either.

ZEUS: That's very upsetting. A vibrant civilization must have leaders that command respect for their skills and power to influence. It only diminishes a civilization to defame heroes by exposing their personal problems and flaws.

To be more positive, let me ask you Mercury to bring us up to date on those lawyer heroes that the Muse has sponsored in America.

MERCURY: Zeus, during my latest visit, I neither saw or heard about any heroes who were lawyers. Oh, I saw many well-dressed lawyers surrounded by influence and power, but no lawyer heroes.

In movies and on television, lawyers are depicted as arrogant fools with no conscience. The people give them no respect and at times the lawyers do not appear to respect themselves or one another.

JESTER: I don't understand. Of all the professions, I would expect lawyers to revere the classic traditions of governance, to understand civics, to zealously guard such words as truth, honesty, respect and fairness. It is these words that made Lincoln and Webster heroes in their time.

ZEUS: Mercury, if what you saw during your last visit is the reality, I don't see any hope for lawyers to ever again be heroes in America. If law schools are attractive because they promise careers of financial gain and power and at the same time do not emphasize ethics, lawyers will never gain the respect of citizens.

Lets move on to the area that I asked you to investigate on your visit to America. I asked you to study and recommend possible amendments to America's environmental laws. My concern is the excessive amounts of money paid to lawyers for litigation compared to the small amounts paid to environmental contractors for remediation. I know that the legislators that wrote these laws expected that by the year 1985 most of the major sites would be cleaned up. Now we find that very few sites have been cleaned up, thousands of new sites have been discovered and that environmental law has become the fastest growing segment of the legal market. If what you are saying is true, it is a massive blight on American legislative bodies that must be rectified if America is to continue in the classic tradition of republican government.

JESTER: [Jumping up with a knowing smile on his face] Oh, Zeus, you mean it's a Republican Party sort of thing?

ZEUS: Dam it Jester, you know what I mean. Republican and Democrat are only the names of political parties in the United States. Since the year 1789 the U.S. has been a republic just as were the early Greek and Roman republics. It's a shame that the English language allows party names to be tied to governing concepts.

Mercury, please tell us what you saw on your recent trip to America.

MERCURY: Zeus, I think that you have been misled. I found that most of the goals of Rachel Carson in writing *Silent Spring* were met. DDT has been removed from the American marketplace and other insecticides are under control. There has been no silent spring in America.

Carson's influence started the environmental movement. This in turn led to the initial federal and state legislation that controlled the sale, distribution, storage and reclamation of most hazardous material. These early laws did a great deal toward cleaning up the rivers and lakes of America to the point where fish returned to the vast majority of the waters and recreational use was restored.

Some years later, in 1980, Congress passed CERCLA, which was named Superfund. CERCLA is responsible for such valuable developments as local HAZMAT teams, clinical studies of carcinogens and greater public awareness of the proper use, storage, disposal and remediation of toxic materials. I found that much of CERCLA and the other environmental laws have had a positive influence on America.

Mr. Hutchins' story is unique in that I saw no reporting or editorial comment on persons and companies in his situation. The public press is very active in reporting hazardous waste spills, carcinogen alerts, global warming and ozone layer voids. But I saw very little reported on remediation of sites, environmental litigation or EPA remediation settlements. It could be that stories like Hutchins' have no reader appeal or that Hutchins and other victims of CERCLA have found no voice.

However I expect that the Hutchins case may be the forerunner of many thousands more that will emerge in the future. I have found that the American public responds to the plight of their fellow citizens and I expect that once stories like Hutchins' are told, Americans will take a second look at the CERCLA legislation.

While I did not do research on lawyers or their influence in passing and benefiting from the CERCLA legislation, I was able to thoroughly study CERCLA and its effect on both America and the other nations of the world.

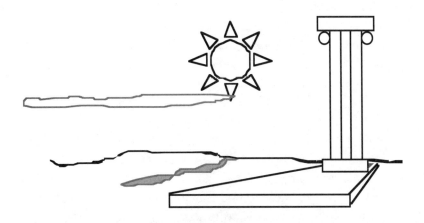

XXXII.   A Scandal

MERCURY: When I started I felt that Congress could easily
tweak CERCLA to correct those problems that the passage
of time has exposed. But, I found that the CERCLA legislation so defies logic that it may be impossible to alter. The
hallmark of at least 20 different Washington based lobbies is
on CERCLA and to change even a sentence would be
considered a threat to each lobby's individual concerns.
They have a mindset that says you're either with us or
against us.

I realize that the essence of CERCLA, MGL Chapter
21E and the other state laws modeled after CERCLA, is
money. The law's title is the *Comprehensive Environmental
Response, Compensation and Liability Act of 1980
(CERCLA)*. The words: response, compensation and
liability essentially mean, who will pay for a response action,
who will pay compensation and who will pay liability costs
or damages?

The goal of CERCLA is to remediate disposal sites and clean up current spills. CERCLA as legislation governs methods of funding these actions and through the use of federal grants CERCLA also controls state laws that over-see disposal sites and spills. Among the issues that the framers of CERCLA failed to consider is that toxic waste is a universal problem not confined to the United States or any one of the 50 States. Much of what becomes waste is material shipped to the U.S. from other parts of the world. A large quantity of America's water and air pollution comes to the U.S. from Mexico and Canada and I am sure that America, in turn, exports pollution to these countries.

A second issue given little consideration by the creators of CERCLA was the lack of modern technology available to remediate and contain toxic waste. Equipment had not been developed that could be used to economically purify ground water and soil. Oh, there were methods available like "pump and treat," but in 1980 and up to the present, this technology has proven to be slow and expensive.

A third issue missed by Congress in writing CERCLA, was that much of the waste is lodged at public sites like municipal waste dumps, military bases, medical disposal areas and under community property such as public roads and city sewers.

JESTER: That's right. I remember driving taxicabs in New York City that were always leaking oil and antifreeze. Where does that City dump all its garbage and trash? I saw barges taking that stuff down the river and out into the ocean.

MERCURY: That's exactly the problem. For years America's population did not recycle. Everything went into the sewer, garbage pail or to a dumpsite. When people heard of Love Canal they were only aware of other people and other

places and the large corporations who took the blame.
They did not realize that every day the general public is the
greatest producer of waste. Almost 20 years later we can
see that the framers of CERCLA had little idea of the vast
costs involved waging a war on toxic waste. The amounts
that Congress initially voted for Superfund were not enough
to cause even a small dent. In the years that followed the
federal funding diminished because the nation went through
cycles of budget cutting.

Congress also had little understanding of the resiliency
of Americans and American institutions such as manufacturers and municipalities. These institutions do not die without
a fight and when accused they defend themselves. In most
cases industry and local government had no choice but to
fight back. Very few private or public bodies could afford
the monstrous costs of remediating sites.

The environmental laws passed before CERCLA were
easy to understand. For example, Congress would ban a
substance like DDT from the marketplace and fine those
that continued to manufacture or distribute this material to
American markets. That is not to say that all manufacturers
were happy with the early environmental laws, for some it
hurt their business. However, the laws were recognized as
fair, persons were given time to comply and the penalties for
non-compliance were addressed as criminal law and therefore were specific with regard to penalties.

JESTER: [Jumping up as if a light had turned on in his brain]
It's just like here in the heavens. If you do something that is
against the law, they kick your ass, make you pay a fine or
put you in confinement. I can understand that; you do the
crime – you pay the fine or do the time!

MERCURY: You got it Jester. If a major corporation had
been dumping their wastewater into Lake Michigan, they

were told by the EPA to cease, desist and start a cleanup effort within a specific length of time, such as six months. If the practice continued they would be forced to pay a penalty or fine of up to $25,000 per day until they complied with the EPA's order. Further resistance could lead to a court order and later to the jailing of corporate officers.

Because of the threat of these penalties, most companies complied with the directions of the EPA and most of the lakes and rivers of America showed an impressive decrease in pollutants. Cities and towns also complied and limited discharges from their sewage plants and sewer lines. In the case of states and municipalities, they did not want to lose federal subsidies.

When CERCLA was passed a different set of rules went into effect. Because CERCLA was governed by civil law, environmental compliance became very complicated. This is when the resiliency of American business started to show itself. Rather than simple fines, provable guilt, and defined costs, industries were faced with unsubstantiated claims, unpredictable costs and the "deep pockets syndrome." At this point the only defense was to fight lawyer with lawyer.

CERCLA gave thousands of bureaucrats working in environmental agencies throughout the country, the power of policemen, judges and juries over citizens and businesses in America. Under the CERCLA legislation and state laws, citizens were encouraged to bring lawsuits against businesses and property owners for real or imagined damages.

For years Americans had heard doctors complain about the unfairness of damage suits that had caused mal-practice insurance costs to escalate. For the most part the complaints of these doctors fell on deaf ears because it was difficult for Americans to be sympathetic to doctors who worked at the highest pay scales. Besides, insurance companies paid most of the damages so the doctors were only hurt when their insurance premiums increased.

The public perceives most businesses as wealthy. Despite this perception, in reality there is very little discretionary money in corporation treasuries. In many cases, it is easier for individuals with savings accounts to come up with uncommitted dollars than it is for corporations. Therefore, when companies are forced to pay for remediation, there is no money budgeted for that purpose. There is also very little insurance coverage to pay remediation claims. As a result, it is more practical for a business accused of infringing CERCLA type laws to hire attorneys and fight back rather than submit to what they perceive as environmentally based extortion.

Mortals know what is fair and when they are being extorted. The English word extortion means to take money and things of value that are not due. Most Americans would agree that to ask companies to pay for exorbitantly expensive cleanup damage claims, for which they are unfairly accused, is extortion. The fact that Congress and state legislatures devised the extortion schemes does not give such schemes validity. They become even less valid when the accused companies are selected from many other candidates because the accused companies are perceived by the accusers to have the deepest pockets.

I choose to believe that the framers of CERCLA were not aware of the quantity of litigation that CERCLA would spawn. At the most they could be accused of lack of foresight. However for the congresspersons that have seen the results of CERCLA's imperfections and have done nothing, we can not cut them such slack.

MUSE: [Jumping up] I've said before and now Zeus agrees. Blame me! I'm responsible. Those in Congress could not fight all the lobbying and emotion that I created for CERCLA, they had to go along.

MERCURY: I won't dispute what you say Muse. During my visit I could find no one in congress that truly understands the ramifications of CERCLA. They seem to have their heads in the sand when it comes to that one.

When America has gone to war, public moneys have always funded the war effort. Remediation of America's pollution should be looked upon as a war against years of waste and mismanagement of resources. The rewards of winning a remediation war go to the public either in this or future generations. While the framers of CERCLA were ready to wage war, they had neither the means nor the guts to properly finance that effort. That is why that law was a shambles from the beginning and stands as a monument to waste today.

Billions of private dollars have been squandered on legal fees rather than being used for remediation. As an outside observer, I, Mercury, find this to be a great American scandal. Shame on those that wrote CERCLA! Greater shame on those that have allowed it to thrive and divert moneys into the hands of lawyers, opportunistic environmental consultants, politicians and public agencies.

The first rule of the heavens is that you do not go to war without being prepared to fight. America was only prepared to fight the remediation war with words. Congress was not ready to back the environmental war effort with public funds.

The key to remediation is money. The answer to problems with administering laws like CERCLA and MGL Chapter 21E must lie with raising remediation funds without extorting those that are believed to have deep pockets. To do any differently goes against the classic concepts of fairness and the republican form of government.

ZEUS: You're right Mercury. Laws must be recognized by citizens as fair to be useful to a republic. That is the classic way.

I agree that money is the key to CERCLA and that extortion of citizens and merchants is not fair. Unfortunately, there are only limited means available to Congress to raise funds for remediation.

With war you defend yourself or are destroyed, so it is imperative to meet the danger quickly and at any cost. However for the average American the threat of toxic waste is elusive. You can not see it and many knowledgeable people question if there is truly a danger. Rather than pay for remediation, most Americans may elect to accept the risk and vote public money toward more solvable problems. Their parents never died from toxic waste as they have from heart disease, cancer, accidents and violence, so why should remediation be given a higher priority?

It's easy to force Hutchins Tool and other small companies to pay for remediation because they have no voice and can not be heard crying in Washington. Even if they were heard, it is easier to paint them as guilty parties who should pay for the damages rather than to question the law. While I have not visited America during this decade, I can believe that people will never vote sufficient public funding to cover the cost to remediate even a small portion of the sites now on the federal and state lists. At the same time Mercury, I feel it is unrealistic for you to suggest that CERCLA be scrapped. This law has produced some remediation even though it has forced a great number of companies like Hutchins Tool into insolvency. It has always been so in the heavens and on earth. We must all play out a tragedy and the innocent must suffer.

MERCURY: I believe that I have a solution to the remediation-financing problem that will not require more taxes or the extortion of American citizens.

MUSE: Well, I don't know if any plan would work. The environmental lobbies have said in the past that they do not want to change CERCLA. They feel that any change would be a step backward for the environmental movement and encourage polluters to revert to the past.

Does your plan eliminate litigation and confrontations between environmental agencies like the DEP and people like Hutchins? If your suggestion eliminates litigation fees for my lawyers, you'll never get it by my trial lawyers associations and me.

JESTER: Yea, you've got to love it. Stick it to her Mercury. Blow the Muse's lawyers away. CERCLA just gives those lawyers a way to share in the extortion money and now they will have Brownfields' fees to fill their carpetbags to the brim. From what we've heard from Hutchins, in his case and most others, lawyers are getting almost all the money.

It bothers me that guys in expensive suits can screw a small businessman like Hutchins. It looks to me like passing the bar exam gives lawyers a license to share extortion money.

ZEUS: Jester, quiet down. Give Mercury a chance to tell us about his plan.

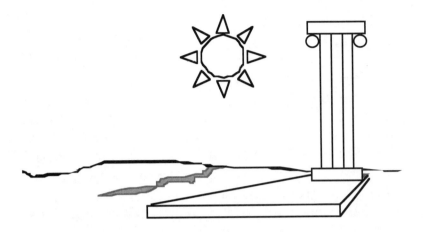

XXXIII.   An Answer Divinely Inspired

MERCURY: As I have told you, it is wrong to take a provincial view of the earth's environment. Air streams, ocean currents and trade between nations transfer materials between territories continuously. You must also understand that those that profited most from what is now hazardous waste, are the consumers of the world. Yes it is true that mining, oil, chemical and manufacturing companies profit from marketing their products to consumers. However, in time these profits are dispersed to investors, so the major, long-term, beneficiaries of the manufactured products are the mortals that buy them.

For example coal mine companies at an earlier time in America furnished coal to heat homes. Coal was more economical and a better source of heat than wood. Little thought was given to the fact that coal mining produced waste at the mine site, plus residues of that waste remained when the coal was stored and transported. The coal that was burned in homes also produced ash as waste and the gods only know where 75 years of this waste ash was spread throughout the world.

The bottom line is that the chief beneficiaries of this inexpensive fuel were the parents and grandparents of the framers of CERCLA. If CERCLA had been passed in 1880 rather than 1980, the cost of ash and coal mining waste control would have made coal very expensive and mortals could not have afforded to use it. The alternative may have been the fireplaces of earlier times.

Depending upon your viewpoint, coal waste is no one's responsibility, a property owner's responsibility or every citizen's responsibility. This same scenario applies to oil, automobiles, railroads, plastics and buggy whips. To place responsibility for remediation on Rockefeller, Vanderbilt, Ford or Du Pont is a historical rather than a logical exercise. Realistically, America grew and became prosperous while waste was being created. If there is a cost to remediate old waste sites, the public bears the responsibility to pay the cost for cleaning up because the value of a clean environment extends to living Americans and their descendents. If the robber barons of old, like Carnegie, Rockefeller and Du Pont are buried in contaminated soil, I'm sure it does not bother them or their health at this point in time.

Let's take a giant step and agree that the burden for the cost of remediation in America must be the responsibility of today's citizens. If America's leaders accept that concept, then the remediation policy can be debated in a rational manner. The United States could enact national environmental remediation programs with the same approach that was used to put a man in space. Under the CERCLA laws, hazardous waste sites have been remediated in a random manner based on the government's ability to force its will on property owners. In contrast, what is needed is a well-informed independent agency with a mandate to prioritize a national list of sites with regard to risk, remediation costs and public health concerns.

When I investigated Mr. Hutchins' Panama Street Site, I found the State of Massachusetts had given it a high priority for all the wrong reasons. The site poses no risk to life or vegetation. The priority classification remains grossly inflated so administrators at the DEP can justify the hundreds of thousands of dollars that the DEP has spent. I expect that the DEP also finds it an advantage to include these costs as damages when dealing with those parties they name as responsible. This too is an exercise in futility because as you can see from the Panama Street situation, Hutchins Tool and the other parties can not possibly reimburse the State for the massive costs involved.

We found many sites in America like Panama Street where risk had no relevance to the priority classification. We also know of many toxic waste locations that have not been disclosed to environmental officials. Very few people are willing to expose their businesses, farms and properties to investigation by environmental agencies. They all have heard of horror stories like that of Mr. Hutchins.

You have taken this leap in faith with me and we agree that the public should pay remediation costs and that an independent agency should set priorities. Let's discuss what other steps should be followed if America truly wants to take a realistic approach to obtaining the cleanest environment without bankrupting its economy:

First, a major effort should be made to develop technology to clean up ground water, soil, etc. It is not economically feasible to do the job without good tools.

Second, methods must be implemented to test drinking water everywhere in the U.S as a public service. The chain of responsibility goes from the citizen to the water supply, no matter if the source is a major reservoir or a private well.

If the water supply is inspected regularly for toxins, the chances of the consumer drinking toxic agents is diminished to almost zero.

JESTER: [Slowly getting to his feet] Yea, yea, yea – this all sounds great, but it's no good 'cause you got no cash, no money – the bank is empty. Mercury, In order for your plan to fly, the first step is to raise money for all those cleanups.

ZEUS: The Jester is right Mercury. We need to know how America can raise the millions of dollars needed, if it does not come from private business, insurance companies and local taxes. Without alternative funding, America will have to live with CERCLA because it's better than nothing.

MERCURY: Both of you are right. Here is my plan: Every product coming into the United States will eventually become waste. We realize that Americans will have to pay the cost to either recycle or maintain that waste forever, because it will not be returned to the originating country. Americans will also have to pay for remediation if that waste is lost into the ground, the air or the water supply.

Americans, as consumers use these imports in their daily lives and profit from the importation process. These imports could be oil, chemicals, automobiles, toys, cosmetics, film or anything else. The consumer generally pays less for the product because it is manufactured, mined or originates outside the border. American consumers, as a group, enjoy the use of these imports to the end of the product's life cycle and therefore must eventually assume responsibility for the imports as waste.

JESTER: That's right, they're not like ET. They don't return home.

MERCURY: Toy ET's may be a perfect example. When they're old and broken they end up in a Jersey landfill. It is correct to say that 99% of what comes, stays in America, either alive or as waste.

By recycling consumers' trash, Americans accept a cost that should be borne by the producer or country of origin. To make an American producer compete with foreign competition that does not follow America's environmental standards puts the American producer at an economic disadvantage. This disadvantage is compounded when we understand that the American producer may also be paying for equipment to upgrade plants to comply with American environmental laws.

Unfortunately, a mechanism for placing responsibility for environmental costs on foreign producers is not available. Even if it were, the U.S. could not collect the funds, so such a collection tactic is impossible.

But it is possible and totally fair to institute what we shall call a "porting fee." The mechanism for a "porting fee" is already in place because every port of entry to the U.S. receives foreign shipments by weight.

JESTER: Hold it Mercury. I don't get this weight thing. What's the relevance?

MERCURY: The customs papers of shipments into the U.S. must list the shipments by weight. Whether it's 20 one pound plastic toys or thousands of tons of lime, each and every shipment has a weight assigned.

It would be very simple for a customs broker to pay a "porting fee" into an environmental trust fund. The amount of the fee would be determined by the weight of the shipment. An equitable amount would be assessed for all shipments whether they weigh a pound or a ton.

This "porting fee" would have nothing to do with the

value of the shipment or the material involved. The assumption is that once something becomes waste or is compounded into a material that becomes waste, it goes to recycling or to a dumpsite by weight. The "porting fee" would have no relation to the producer, nation of origin or any international trade agreement. It would not matter if the shipments were bottles of perfume from Paris, bananas from Brazil or oil from Venezuela.

The "porting fee" for the perfume could amount to pennies and that for the oil shipment could be thousands of dollars. This is fair when we consider that the cost to dispose of the waste glass perfume bottles would be small compared to disposing of the many products that could come from the oil, which as a petroleum could be used to make plastics, gasoline, solvents, etc.

JESTER: [Jumping up with excitement] That's right! I got that weight thing. It's so simple. If a product is produced outside the United States and Americans have to dispose of it when the American consumer is finished, why shouldn't the cost of disposal be included as part of the original price?

Today America is the world's dump. Toxic materials are imported for one citizen's or a group of citizens' use and then all the other Americans are expected to take care of the waste forever. This stuff ends up in the ground water, waste dumps or incinerators. Wherever it lands as waste, it becomes the responsibility of the receiving country forever.

MERCURY: You've got it Jester. That's exactly what is happening on earth. Nations are so elated to get bargain imports; no thought is given to the future. I'm sure that if one country could get inexpensive enriched uranium fuel from its neighbor, the deal would be made with no thought of where the fuel would go when it became waste. If the receiving country were smart, it would contract to have the producer of the fuel take it back when it was spent, rather than undertake the risk and cost of establishing disposal facilities.

JESTER: I understand! It's no different than when some states in America forced beer companies to add a beer can recycling-charge. Motorists once saw many beer cans tossed along the roadsides in Massachusetts, but, with the passage of the "bottle bill," the cans are not there any more. People bring cans back to the store to cash in the deposit. Your "porting fee" for all imports is like a beer can deposit ready to be reclaimed for the benefit of every American citizen.

MUSE: Zeus, this is an embarrassment to the heavens. Should we stoop to his level and talk about beer can deposits? If the Jester doesn't understand what Mercury is saying, that's his problem. Why should this judicial hearing slip to his level?

ZEUS: [Reacting in an angry manner] Muse, now you're out of order. I think we're finally making some progress. Mortals are not very rational. It is evident in the way you were able to sway Congress that earthlings are simple beings and perhaps the beer can analogy is something they'll understand. It's obvious that the people in Washington don't know how to raise the amount of money needed to provide Americans with a clean and healthy environment. I think that Mercury is on to something.

On my visits to America in the past, I remember the elation the citizens showed at their progress. Things like railroads, steel mills, automobile factories, insecticides and gasoline stations were the tools that made America a great nation. These tools helped win wars, feed starving people and raise the American standard of living to the point where

America was the envy of the world.

Waste is a byproduct of this progress. As a nation of people, Americans have not handled their waste problems well. However, now that America realizes these mistakes of the past, it is trying as a nation to redeem itself.

Should we scoff at the few blunders Congress made in writing CERCLA or should we praise Americans for finally recognizing their waste problems and trying to rectify things. I think that if we can help by inspiring a remediation-funding plan, we should do it. Mercury let's get back to your ideas.

I believe you were saying that these "porting fees" would be collected by the U.S. Customs Department and paid into an environmental trust. I assume that this would be independent from the general funds and it would be treated like the Social Security Trust Fund.

MERCURY: Not exactly, I mean not like the Social Security Fund. This trust would actually have money rather than promises. It would be completely separate from the general treasury. It would be more like the FDIC.

The environmental fund trustees would be appointed for life like Supreme Court justices to allow them to be independent and insulated from politics. This independence would permit them to fund realistic studies of risk assessment, develop remediation technology and establish site selection criteria. Sites would be prioritized for remediation based on risk and economics, with no partiality shown to political expediency.

The custom authorities would collect the porting fees just as they have collected import taxes and duties throughout history. The funds collected would be sent directly to the environmental trust and would not be considered taxes.

MUSE: [Starting to work herself into a frenzied condition]

Import taxes are what they are. How can you say they are not taxes? If the Customs Department collects them as "porting fees," than that makes them import taxes.

ZEUS: I think she's got you there, Mercury. Looks to me like they are import taxes. If they are, the U.S. State Department is going to raise hell. Think of all the trade treaties, the favored nation status and all that "Group of Seven" stuff.

MERCURY: I said earlier that the American people would have to make a leap of faith to get this done. We can stand here forever debating whether or not this "porting fee" is a tax. Many cities in America now charge fees for things that were once considered taxes. Ask the homeowner who pays a fee for water and sewer costs that at one time were included in his real estate taxes. He can't even write the sewer fee off on his federal income tax as he can for other state and local taxes. Are dog, marriage and hunting licenses, fees or taxes? How about building permits or fees for patents?

Americans must take a positive approach if they want to better the environment and keep it healthy for future generations. We know that CERCLA and the state laws patterned after it have not been successful. We must expect that the American State Department, Congress and the environmental lobbies will have an immediate knee jerk negative reaction to this proposal. On the surface it appears to be a threat to their individual interests and they will not want to admit to CERCLA's failure.

The State Department must realize that this "porting fee" treats all foreign nations as equals. One nation or one product would not be favored over another. The same weight of oil coming from Venezuela, Saudi Arabia or the North Sea would have the same "porting fee." If we have a favored nation treaty with another foreign country, the "porting fee" would not affect it.

MUSE: What about the North American Trade Agreement. What would the U.S. say if Mexico charged a "porting fee" on U.S. goods and used the funds to clean up the Mexican environment?

HUTCHINS: Excuse me for speaking up, but from what I've read about environmental problems along the U.S./Mexican border, I believe that both the American and Mexican people would welcome such an arrangement. As a matter of fact, I believe that all groups that encourage international cooperation for environmental problems would welcome such "porting fee" based environmental trusts for every country. It goes back to the question posed by the Jester, why should one country become the dumping ground for another country's products when they become waste? More importantly, what nation's citizens should pay the costs for remediating waste? Besides, the citizens, miners or manufacturers of the producing country would not be paying anything. The American importer would pass on the "porting fee" to the American consumer as part of the cost of the imported goods.

MUSE: Mr. Hutchins, I believe that would make the imported product cost more for the American buyer. People want to pay the lowest possible price.

HUTCHINS: Muse, I agree with you. Imported goods would cost more if the "porting fees" were added. But, if the imported product is the best value or the most impressive product to the American buyer, such foreign products will continue to compete.

Because this "porting fee" would also apply to goods

manufactured by American companies offshore destined for the American market, these American manufacturers would also share in remedial responsibilities. Shouldn't Mattel and Hasbro take some responsibility for the GI Joes and Barbies produced outside the U.S. that eventually fill landfills with non-biodegradable plastic of foreign origin?

You must remember that American manufacturers have lost much of their competitive advantage to imports because of environmental legislation. These domestic factories have had the costs of complying with American environmental laws and investing in such things as scrubbers, alternative solvents, filters, etc. Much of the foreign competition does not have to live with America's environmental costs and constraints. It is also significant that these fees would be collected and spent internally and would not add to the imbalance of trade.

MERCURY: These "porting fees" would add a small amount to the costs of imports because the import brokers would pass on the costs to consumers. However, as we previously agreed, it is the consumer that is demanding remediation. It is also the American consumer that profits from a cleaner environment because a healthier environment should reduce health care costs.

MUSE: Be realistic. If these "porting fees" are available to underwrite the costs of remediation in America, every landowner with an environmental problem is going to be standing in line waiting for a free cleanup. It will be like welfare.

MERCURY: Muse, I agree. There is a good chance that could happen.

MUSE: Oh you agree. All those toxic waste sites where

owners have been in denial will surface. They'll be hundreds more remediations required in all the states.

MERCURY: I agree with you again. To put this in perspective, tell me the goal of the CERCLA legislation. What was the intent of Congress when it passed this law?

MUSE: To punish all those chemical companies that polluted – no, I mean to create controversy and legal work. – No, no, that's, well, you know… there was a lot of pressure from the press and we…

ZEUS: Muse, you're transparent. Let Mercury continue. I think the American people want to know where the most dangerous sites are. It doesn't matter if the sites that pose the greatest risk to human health are on military bases, in Boston Harbor or at an abandoned G.E. plant. That's where this independent environmental trust will fund a cleanup effort.

There are many toxic waste sites unknown to the Environmental Protection Agency because they have avoided discovery. It is the small company that goes through an investigation that includes ground water well testing for bank financing that comes to the attention of environmental agencies. We hear reports concerning many local gasoline stations faced with site remediation, but rarely do we read about the major oil refineries or distributors. This imbalance can be traced to property transfer and bank financing by small operators compared to bond financing by the major corporations. When the majors sell bonds, the investors never require environmental site investigations. Therefore, there is no reporting to state environmental offices like the DEP in Massachusetts. It is naive for Americans to believe that there are not massive toxic waste spills beneath the oil refineries and chemical companies along the New Jersey

Turnpike. If you can smell chemicals, they probably permeate the groundwater beneath those sites, in the same way
the smells permeate the air.

That is not to say that I believe that pollution at major
corporations and military installations pose any greater
danger to Americans than the local gasoline station site
already on an agency's list. This is impossible to answer. It
would depend upon the proximity of the spills to a water
supply.

The answer is this environmental trust, governed by
independent trustees, who have a mutually agreed upon
goal to clean up the high-risk areas first. If the landowners
believe that the sites can be disclosed without exposing
themselves to the liability of cleanup costs, many owners
will emerge from the shadows and America can attack the
worst sites.

Mr. Hutchins, tell us what you think of Mercury's plan.
Do you think the American people will feel that it is fair and
workable?

HUTCHINS: [Without hesitation] Mercury's plan is wonderful, it's simple and it's fair but it scares me. Maybe it's too
simple, too fair and makes too much sense. There are many
Washington lobbies that would attack such a sensible
solution.

MERCURY: I expect there will be negative reaction to the
"porting fee" plan. However, I believe that the environmental, insurance, defense, real estate, banking and farming
lobbies, plus the manufacturing associations and labor
unions would be very much in favor of this method of
raising money to create a more healthy environment.

Just think of the positive effect that these changes would
have on the banking industry. Lenders would no longer be
concerned that mortgage holders would stick them with

abandoned property that needs remediation. Also real estate transfers would not be encumbered with the endless delays which the CERCLA laws have created. If land buyers know that remediation of a purchased site will be funded by outside sources; it would be like buying property with an indemnity clause.

Certainly those lobbyists employed by foreign governments would work against anything that appears to be a threat to trade with client nations. Massive negative reaction will come from the trial lawyers associations because trial lawyers thrive on conflict. To remove civil litigation from environmental laws will signal an end to their lucrative situations.

I have considered the reaction of persons working in environmental jobs at agencies like the DEP and EPA and concluded that these workers would look upon funding from "porting fees" as a fresh start. If the EPA were well funded and dealt with cooperative clients, their efforts would go toward a healthier America rather than to arbitrating disputes. I can't imagine that EPA employees enjoy dealing with attorneys intervening with each decision and delaying every attempt at cleaning contaminated sites.

MUSE: What about all the positive things that CERCLA accomplished. Would you discontinue HAZMAT teams, funding of state agencies or systems that have been established for handling spills from trucks and railroad cars? Do you throw away the baby with the bath water?

MERCURY: No, all those things would remain in place. The real differences would be guaranteed funding and the elimination of those chapters in the law that force confrontation between parties. It would be more like no fault insurance, with "porting fee" funds underwriting the costs.

We would also want to amend those parts of CERCLA

that do not require the most enlightened scientific procedures to determine if substances are carcinogenic or pose
actual risks to human health. Here is where an independent
trust can be very helpful. Rather than treating all hazardous
materials equally, the trustees would have the power to
schedule remediations based on the highest threat of health
risks. The idea would be to eliminate the basis for private
lawsuits that use indiscriminate lists of hazardous agents
published by federal authorities as evidence to prove fault
for damage claims.

I found during my visit to America that many scientists
have a good understanding concerning the types and levels
of pollutants as they relate to human health, while other
mortals like lawyers, journalists and legislators are confused. Most of these people use terms such as health
hazard, hazardous waste, spill, solvent, PCB's, pollution,
carcinogen, etc. interchangeably. This may be OK when
people are talking over the back fence, but in the courtroom
this blurring of terms can result in totally unjust results.

As part of my survey, I asked many different American
lawyers to define the terms: Solvent, PCB, waste and
pollution. Most stumbled as they attempted to provide
valid definitions, while they all reacted to these words as if
they were the lowest form of animal excrement. When I
pointed out that pure water was the most common solvent,
most of those quizzed just smiled with embarrassment.

To answer your other question, yes, I am concerned
with the lawyer lobbies. However, once these lobbyists
realize that the environment has been the loser to this legal
avarice, I think most lawyers, except the trial lawyers who
have the most to lose, will join us. I wish I could promise
that my plan would get through Congress, but dealing with
congresspersons is not my strength.

You know that I am Mercury, the messenger god, the
god of commerce and the god of science. I like action and I

understand movement, strength and speed. Congress is a world different from mine.

In Rome, I was also the god of thieves and vagabonds. I enjoyed the role, but you can see that it's at the opposite end of the scale from lawyers and politicians.

JESTER: There are a lot of Americans that would dispute that statement.

ZEUS: Jester, this is no joke. We pray that those in Congress will look deep into their souls and find the right direction on this one.

We understand your concerns Mercury. I praise you for your skills in both interpreting the CERCLA laws and gifting America with a plan to fund remediations. That "porting fee" plan is a stroke of genius. It makes sense that the funding for disposal of waste comes from the consumers of the products that produce the waste. I salute you Mercury and thank you again for a job well done.

* * * * * *

With this Zeus and Mercury threw that high five salute that I had seen before. In a flash Mercury was gone.

* * * * * *

ZEUS: [Breaking the silence] I love that Mercury. He makes it happen. I would there were more like him.

Muse do you want to sum up your case. Do you have more to say before the decision?

MUSE: Honored one, I have no more to say. I thank Mr. Hutchins and Mercury for validating my work in America. You can now believe that I have brought major disruptions to a mortal civilization, just as did the gods that came before me.

I have raised the image of lawyers and through the CERCLA law, my powers have brought dissention, pain and suffering to many Americans like Hutchins. I have shown all the divinities that I am one of them. I am the lawyer god and should be recognized as such.

Thank you Zeus for hearing me.

ZEUS: [Banging his great fist on the pedestal]. All hear, I shall return with a decision.

JESTER: All hail, my god, Zeus.

MUSE: All hail, my god, Zeus.

HUTCHINS: Thank you, Zeus.

＊　＊　＊　＊　＊　＊

Zeus disappeared in an instant leaving the Muse and the Jester facing one another.

＊　＊　＊　＊　＊　＊

JESTER: [Extending his hand] I'm out of here. I'll give you credit Muse; you beat me fair and square. When you're a god, remember me. I do bar mitzvahs and emcee at the forum for Lenaea. Catch my act some time.

＊　＊　＊　＊　＊　＊

At that point the Jester left. I was sorry to see him leave because he was so casual and non-god like.

*   *   *   *   *   *

MUSE: [Approaches the table and sits down beside Hutchins]
You did well, Mr. Hutchins. You may be washed out on
earth, but you could make it here in the heavens. I like your
style because no matter how humiliating this was for you,
you spoke the truth.

*   *   *   *   *   *

Before she said more, Zeus returned and mounted the podium.
I still could not get over the size and strength of the man.

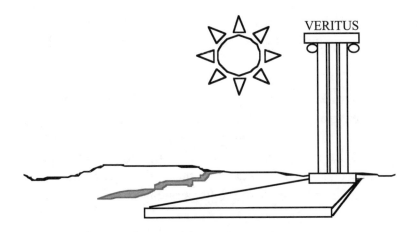

XXXIV.   Coronation of a God

When Zeus returned his demeanor had changed. That warm fellowship that he showed to Mercury was gone. I couldn't say that he was upset. He wasn't gruff.

There was sadness about him. He did not look up and smile at me as he had done frequently before he adjourned that last session. As he turned to address the Muse, he paused as if waiting for something. I expected that he was waiting for cherubs or bands of angels or trumpeters or any of those other groups that I had seen on television when monarchs are crowned. Finally Zeus looked down at the Muse.

*   *   *   *   *   *

ZEUS: Muse you disgust me. Your ambition has blinded you. I can not pronounce you a god. Your petition is denied!

MUSE: Zeus, I, I don't understand. I showed mortals that I had the powers of a god.

309

ZEUS: How did you show mortals that you were a god? There is no god in the heavens that would do what you have done.

MUSE: But Zeus, through CERCLA I brought dissention between groups of mortals just like Ares, the god of war has done. America's country singers describe the love of the god, Eros, in terms of pain, suffering, lies and cheating. I exposed all those feelings with the testimony of Mr. Hutchins and his story of the Panama Street site.

ZEUS: I don't deny that you have proved that an innocent mortal like Hutchins was harmed by CERCLA. I'm embarrassed that you could cause such harm to earthlings that are trying to live productive lives.

MUSE: Ares, the god of war, brings pain to innocents. With war there is burning, rape, looting and children are killed in their beds. I did no worse than Ares did in Greece and Mars did in Rome. Possibly you approved of the agony of war for Greece and Rome because these societies were the conquerors. Why would you look at it differently when lawyers are the victors and take the spoils?

ZEUS: First you say you acted like the god of war and then like the god of love. These gods have integrity, but you are just one sick muse.

MUSE: Yes I claim I acted just the way that Eros, the god of love would operate. Eros is not love. Eros commands the power of love. Mortals know that love can bring hurt and pain. When they are under the influence of Eros, they are slaves to love. Mortals respect and honor gods because they stimulate human emotions that can be good or bad.

310

My lawyers are slaves to the law. I am their god and the law is their god. We are the same. Lawyers blindly follow the law. Doesn't the lawyers' symbol carry a blindfold over her eyes?

ZEUS: That is the symbol of justice. Justice is blind. Mortals can have laws without justice, but republics can not thrive with unjust laws.

MUSE: My lawyers know the law and the law is the engine that runs America. Certainly Mr. Hutchins has shown that justice and the law are not the same thing in America. Get with the times, Zeus, justice has become an out of fashion word to most lawyers and politicians in America.

Look at CERCLA. The law was enacted to force remediation of hazardous waste sites to appease the American public that was calling for something to be done. CERCLA was written to achieve that goal and therefore that goal must come before justice. The way to achieve that goal is to have lawyers force people to follow the law.

ZEUS: You mean to act as policemen.

MUSE: CERCLA has no criminal punishments. CERCLA requires that lawyers force compliance through civil law. The lawyers simply help individuals protect their property rights against others who damage them.

ZEUS: But what becomes of the American citizen's civil rights under CERCLA. It is like the Spanish Inquisition. Citizens can accuse other citizens of breaking the law and there is no judicial review. The accused are denied everything dear to American justice, like a speedy trial, the opportunity to face accusers and the assumption of innocence until proven guilty in a court of law.

311

In the litigation we just reviewed, the burden of proof falls back on Hutchins. He must prove his own and his Company's innocence. Under CERCLA's tort law and strict liability provisions, the outcome of his litigation is not based on fault it is based on circumstance. Under the provisions of joint and several, he could be judged 1% responsible and be forced to pay 100% of the damages. Is that justice? To make matters worse, the State of Massachusetts can demand triple damages. How can Americans respect a law like that? CERCLA has not only drained Hutchins' blood, but also the blood of his innocent wife and children.

MUSE: That's the only way that CERCLA could have been written. Congress did not want to allow all those large chemical companies that had once operated in the Love Canal area to walk away. Homeowners who had purchased homes in the neighborhood surrounding Love Canal wanted to collect damages for their loss of property values and for their health problems that they believed were caused by chemical spills that could have taken place 25 years earlier.

Criminal type penalties generally only cover the present and future. By instilling civil law into CERCLA, Congress was able to extend responsibility for damages into the past. Congress also added such tort law weapons as "joint and several" and "strict liability" to the arsenal of those seeking to collect damages from those chemical companies, many of whom had sold the properties and left the area.

To be honest, I can't remember that there was any thought of small companies like Hutchins Tool ever falling under the law except for reporting purposes. By reporting, I mean that it was assumed that all users of hazardous materials would be directed to keep records of the purchase and disposal of the material. Actually those requirements under CERCLA have been successful. It is the civil penalties and inscrutable health risk assessment sections of

Chapter Thirty Four

CERCLA that have been unworkable.

ZEUS: Unworkable! that is a mammoth understatement. After all these years there is no verifiable list of carcinogens that is universally accepted and not in dispute in the scientific community. It's like alchemy in the Middle Ages. Rather than change base metals into gold, a small number of laboratories in America are turning a huge number of chemicals into carcinogens by combining inflated risk statistics and fear. The only health problems some of these misnamed carcinogens are causing are to the psychological health of innocent citizens like Hutchins.

MUSE: Zeus, I'm admitting to you that Congress didn't foresee that small companies like Hutchins Tool would be caught up in having to pay immense remediation costs. We felt that the American public would feel vindicated having those big chemical companies pay for the mess that most people assumed they had created in past years. It would teach them a lesson. It was simply an oversight that companies like Hutchins Tool have been caught in the crossfire.

ZEUS: An oversight! — CERCLA was written about 20 years ago. Couldn't those elected to Congress rectified their mistake in all that time? To let this continue is intolerable. I believe that you realized that this would bring vast amounts of litigation to your trial lawyers and you overdosed on the feeling that this law was improving the lot of the legal profession.

MUSE: Well Zeus that's true, it has been a boon to law offices all over the country. Until you heard from Hutchins you didn't know what CERCLA has done and what it could do to Americans who own small businesses, real estate and farms.

Before Hutchins raised his voice there was very little complaining about CERCLA. However, a few years ago, there was a tremendous outcry from the bar associations and environmental lobbies when some newly elected congresspersons talked about amending environmental laws. Some environmental activists considered just the idea of discussing these laws a threat and a step backward for the environmental movement.

ZEUS: Gods have made terrible blunders and mortals could view as evil much that the gods have done throughout history. But, to us these are just pranks we play on mortals. However, any god would view CERCLA not as a prank, but as an ongoing conspiracy to cheat Americans out of a healthy environment while redirecting funds to lawyers. When Hutchins' story is publicized, the reputation of the legal profession will sink further and those lawyer jokes will multiply.

With CERCLA, you and your lawyers have robbed Americans of money that could have been used to make the world a healthier and safer place. That is the fatal flaw in your quest to become the lawyer god. CERCLA does not work, so the law is a colossal failure. You have done a total disservice to the environmental movement and to the American people.

MUSE: Is it my fault that Congress did not fund CERCLA properly? I guess the enthusiasm of Americans for the environment was more in their words than in their pocket-books. I may have fanned the flames of enthusiasm for remediation in America, but the American environmental community has to take some responsibility that CERCLA was not built on reason. Many in that community were determined to punish big business to right some perceived wrongs in the American social order.

ZEUS: But you had a watchdog committee set up as part of the CERCLA law. What did they tell Congress when they looked at the results after the first year?

MUSE: Well, the watchdog committee was made up of twelve lawyers and they realized that the bill was creating a gold mine for trial lawyers. I already told you that I created CERCLA to enhance the fortunes of lawyers. I'm proud of that. I followed Hades plan. He suggested that my ticket to being a god was to raise the power and wealth of lawyers.

Think of what I have done for lawyers. I am their patron. Sure, you think that CERCLA allows lawyers to extort money from the various adversarial parties both as their defenders and representatives. It's not extortion; it's the wording of the law. Lawyers are only doing what the law requires them to do.

ZEUS: Muse, you are misguided. I see the hand of Hades in this. You know that Hades is the god of the Underworld. He is no good. I can not anoint you to be a god. I do not create gods. Muse, the truth is that mortals create gods.

Your ambition and Hades treachery has played you for the fool. There are those in the heavens that think I have the power to deify you, but that is not true. The only one here that could deify you is Hutchins. Perhaps it is better that he holds you responsible for his plight, than for him to feel that his fellow man would do him such an injustice.

Mortals need answers. Mortals need support. For an earthling life has a limited span and is filled with uncertainty. We gods furnish explanations and make life more tolerable for mortals. Whether they're called myths or superstitions, all earthly cultures have used legends of gods to explain their lives.

Your influence may have created CERCLA and en-

315

hanced the wealth of lawyers in America, but what you have done has also taken away a part of America's faith in its laws and institutions. You failed to understand that while war is bad, Ares, the god of war, is not deceitful as you have been. War is an honest venture that opens up man's mind to truths. Mortals have learned from Ares that the price of war is too dear compared to the spoils of war. One day these lessons will bear fruit and there will be no violence between nations. World War One gave birth to the League of Nations and without Ares' Second World War, there would be no United Nations.

Eros, the god of love does not deal in deceit. Lovers enter with their eyes wide open and Eros will let them see the paths their love may take. Lovers may become deceitful to one another but Eros holds the truth up to the light for each partner to see.

You wanted to be the lawyer god so badly you dressed CERCLA in a cloak of deceit by calling it "Superfund." That was a sham. Despite your protests Muse, you were aware that the CERCLA legislation would create confrontations between citizens that could only be handled by trial lawyers.

Historians can tell the world how wars get started. Poets and scriptwriters can do the same with love. Who can tell us how a simple law devised to remediate a few sites like Love Canal can carry the seeds of a whole new industry, environmental law?

Muse, you have betrayed the trust of environmentalists because under CERCLA most sites have not been remediated. Like the Panama Street Site, throughout America disposal sites have become quagmires of conflict between parties who can not afford to be bankrupted by the massively oppressive costs of remediation. Through endless conflicts you have destroyed companies like Hutchins Tool with a slow death of attrition. You have championed those passages of CERCLA that cause government agencies, municipalities and private companies to bicker over responsibility and make settlements impossible.

Worst of all, your actions have helped to destroy those classic myths which are the fabric which keep a republic functioning and which have made America, Greece and Rome great societies. You have commissioned acts that destroy faith, trust and respect for the governing assemblies that are the foundations for governance in a republic.

Let me ask a simple question, Mr. Hutchins, do you think CERCLA is fair?

HUTCHINS: No, I do not.

ZEUS: Speaking as an American, do you respect CERCLA or MGL Chapter 21E?

HUTCHINS: I respect neither.

ZEUS: Do you have faith in the advice of the DEP or the lawyers involved as your advocates?

HUTCHINS: I have very little faith in these people because they generally have placed their self-interest as lawyers above their obligation to act as facilitators between me as a citizen and the environmental laws.

ZEUS: Mr. Hutchins, I'm sure you realize that mortals created myths and classic gods to explain the meaning of events in their lives. Is this why you have raised this common muse to the position of lawyer god?

HUTCHINS: I haven't raised, I mean, I don't know why you would think that I would.—Maybe I have thought of her as a god. It hurts to think that any group of congresspersons could be so careless as to create a law like CERCLA. It hurts even more to think that the law would stay on the books when Congress knows that it is not working. I think it's an abomination that all that money has gone to lawyers rather than to clean up the environment.

I suppose I could think that I am facing a period of bad luck. But, what is luck if not just another myth? Luck has no face. OK, I guess I am leaning on the Muse, but thinking of her as an outside force with a face and a motive makes sense to me at this time. A hell of a lot more sense than trying to conceive that I live in a society where a fear induced mob would act as a posse and brutalize me.

What's the difference, I know that the popular press put the fear of cancer, birth defects and leukemia into people during the Love Canal incident. As a result Congress passed a law specifically designed to resolve that issue and punish the perpetrators.

I'm a positive person. I don't want to think that I live in a society where no one cares. It's easier for me to forgive the ignorance and insensitivity of my peers and look for reasons outside politics. If my defensive mechanism is a myth and the myth is the Muse, I'll live with it.

My hell is different from Dante's. Thinking of a beautiful but misguided muse is better than having nightmares filled with devilish figures with tails and pitchforks.

ZEUS: Hutchins have you considered seeking some help.

HUTCHINS: You mean a shrink? If that's what you mean, I couldn't afford one. Besides, I don't want to subsidize another profession that would draw sustenance from CERCLA.

ZEUS: Hutchins, I didn't mean that you should seek a psychiatrist. I was just wondering if you thought there was someone or something that could help you get through this.

HUTCHINS: To be honest, I thought that writing a book to explain the flaws in CERCLA would be good therapy for me and an invaluable service to the American public. At the very least I would be doing something positive rather than curse the darkness. But, I'm not a writer. I don't even write letters to my friends. Besides, with my luck, if I sold a book I'd probably be convicted of polluting and be forced to turn over any income from the book to my victims. That's what happens to us jail house authors.

ZEUS: [Smiling and starting to laugh] Hutchins, you don't need a shrink. I think your best medicine and defense mechanism is humor. I give you credit for laughing at yourself during this stressful time. But let's get back to my question. Mortals create gods. Hutchins, do you feel that the Muse should be considered the lawyer god? You and other mortals are going to have to answer that one.

HUTCHINS: Rachel Carson mentioned a myth in her book, *Silent Spring*. I can believe that this Muse guided Ms Carson's hand to get the environmental movement started in America. I believe this was a wondrous event and I give the Muse credit for her part in it.

But, why would she want to be the lawyer god, the patron of lawyers? She would be the butt of lawyer jokes. If her claims about acting as the muse that promoted CERCLA into law were true, I would consider her one of the greatest villains in all literature.

MUSE: Wait, please. [The Muse had started to cry as she slowly stood up. She raised one hand toward Hutchins in an attempt to be heard. With a sob she continued] I'm sorry, you're right Zeus. I didn't mean to — well, I did intend to, but I never thought it would go this way.

I feel dirty. Lawyers are good people. But, when they tasted that money and power that I bought to them, they became different and I also became different. It was like an opiate that took hold of a whole class of people.

This environmental litigation took on a life of its own. There is a code that binds lawyers together. They had the code long before I became involved. Originally I think it was a code that demanded honor and brought respect for the profession. Now it's just a shroud that hides greed and arrogance. It is that code and the fear of being ostracized by peers that has kept lawyers from speaking out and telling America the truth about CERCLA and similar laws.

But it's not all the fault of the lawyers. The environmental lobbies don't want to be embarrassed by having stories written about moneys diverted from remediation to litigation. Also, the press finds it easier to slam business than to research the truth. Pollution and hazardous waste stories sell papers best when they are played like soap operas with good guys and bad guys.

During elections there is much talk about the mess in Washington. The ingredients of that mess are the thousands of special interest groups that roam Washington to spread their influence. I found that these interest groups played a greater part on framing CERCLA than I did. We listened to everyone's voice except small businessmen like Hutchins who were the people most affected.

Most mortals are complacent. If they themselves aren't being hurt, they are blind to the pain of others. Complacency was the key to Hitler's power and the long reign of slavery in America. The words most heard after mortals fight wars are, "I didn't" — I didn't know, I didn't see. What should be said is, I didn't really care.

I agree with both of you, that this isn't right. CERCLA is poor legislation and must be reshaped until it produces good results. The proof of poor legislation is poor results.

ZEUS: Muse, I'm happy that reason has reentered your mind. At least we can walk away from this as reasonable deities.

MUSE: [Having regained her composure and appearing to get that spark back] Zeus, I do not want to walk away from this. I want to redeem myself. I want to be known as Rachel's muse and if Hutchins believes in me, I want his respect.

I think that Mercury's idea of a "porting fee" is the answer. We need to get the American people behind it. I know that once Americans understand the failure of CERCLA, we can change things. Keep what's good in CERCLA and throw the rest out.

What do you think Zeus? Can we bring back faith, trust and respect to the American republic?

Remember I got the environmental movement started years ago when I helped Rachel Carson write the first chapter of *Silent Spring*. I remember the title and the first words of that chapter, "A Fable for Tomorrow...There was once a town in the heart of America....."

Hutchins, we can do it. Zeus, you tell him. I may not be recognized as the lawyer god, but as the Muse, you know that I'm the best there is at inspiration. Hutchins, I'll be your inspiration.

HUTCHINS: Inspiration for what? I can't....

MUSE: Hutchins, sit back and enjoy the ride. [She started to orate as if a whole staff was present] We'll need a marketing campaign.

Zeus please let me go back to America. Who could do a better job than I can do? I know the Washington press, television and the lobbyists. Please Zeus, I want to redeem myself. I know that I've still got it. I'll redirect my energy to create something better for the world.

No, not create, I'll restore things that made America great. Zeus, we'll bring back the classic ideas of reason. With reason comes faith in institutions, trust and respect for authority, plus all those other values that built the republics of Greece, Rome and America.

Maybe some day Americans will think of me, the Muse, as the god of reason. Rachel started it with a book. Hutchins, you and I will get moneys going to remediation rather than litigation, just the way I made that war on DDT happen. To think of it, that's what Rachel used, reason. She didn't want to punish anyone, she just wanted companies to cease and desist in real time, today and tomorrow. Rachel knew that if she could only stop distribution of insecticides, that nature was strong enough to take care of the future. The last thing she wanted was an environmental civil war pitting Americans against one another.

Please Zeus, send me back to America. Hutchins and I will start by.......

* * * * * *

XXXV.   Walking By Day

It will come as no surprise to you, that I am not a writer, I'm a machinist. Cowlbeck, my college roommate, was a writer. I remember seeing words just flow through his fingers and onto the page in small script, with clearly written sentences and no cross-outs. The last thing he wrote was an eight-page suicide note addressed to his wife, his father, Suzy and me, written on hotel stationary. It was a beautiful letter written in that same hand that I remembered from college days. What I thought at first were cross-outs, I later realized were dried up tears.

I think I said before, that I am a practicing Catholic and have a strong faith in God. I spent enough time in catechism to believe that there is but one God. That's where I learned that myths and other superstitions are but false gods.

That's why it seems strange that a few months ago, as I read the Gospel during Sunday Mass, I found a title for my book. Or, maybe I found the title and was inspired to write of my concerns about the direction of the environmental movement in America.

*　*　*　*　*　*

A reading from the holy gospel according to John.
There was a certain man named Lazarus who was sick. He was
from Bethany, the village of Mary and her sister Martha. This
Mary whose brother Lazarus was sick was the one who anointed
the Lord with perfume and dried his feet with her hair. The
sisters sent word to Jesus to inform him, "Lord, the one you
love is sick." Upon hearing this, Jesus said:

> **"This sickness is not to end in death;**
> **rather it is for God's glory,**
> **that through it the Son of God may be glorified."**

Jesus loved Martha and her sister and Lazarus very much. Yet,
after hearing that Lazarus was sick, he stayed on where he was
*for two days more. Finally he said to his disciples, **"Let us go***
***back to Judea."** "Rabbi," protested the disciples, "with the*
Jews only recently trying to stone you, you are going back up
there again?" Jesus answered:

> **"Are there not twelve hours of daylight?**
> **If a man goes walking by day he does not stumble,**
> **because he sees the world bathed in light.**
> **But if he goes walking at night he will stumble,**
> **since there is not light in him."**

*　*　*　*　*　*

I want only to bring light to CERCLA. I want Americans to see
the law clearly and know why it has not been successful and why
it has not met the goals of its framers. I feel that Americans should
learn why CERCLA and the state laws that followed have been a
very lucrative source of new revenue for the legal industry, while,

at the same time, this law has forced many farmers and small businesses into insolvency.

"Walking by day," the words appeared to me just as if someone had passed over them with a yellow highlighter. That had to be my theme and my title, because the picture in my mind was of lawyers and legislators walking at night and stumbling. The congressmen of 1980 were not bad people; they just had the misfortune to "go walking at night" and were blinded to reason. Or, as my children would say, they hadn't a clue.

But, why me? I'm a machinist. As enthusiastic as I became during that Gospel reading, I went in the opposite direction when confronted with reality. Now I know why protestors chain themselves to fences forcing police to forcibly remove them. Their method of drawing attention to an issue involves action and emotion. Action has to be a hell of a lot easier than writing a book.

When I tell people about my conflicts with lawyers and the DEP, things flow much easier because I use profanity. Unfortunately, I can't do that and be published!

I am also acutely aware that many newly elected congresspersons have entered office swearing that they will amend environmental legislation. Their initial fervor is soon blunted with the realities of their powerless positions or the defensive reaction of environmental lobbies who look upon any changes as a reversion to the old days.

With all my doubts, I face going up against the trial lawyers associations with some undefined glee. Here is the one case where the frustration that has grown within me is best put into words and not acted out. A physical protest against them, which is something that I would enjoy, would surely put me in jail. Knowing that trial lawyers associations have been the main stimuli for inflating insurance costs for medical malpractice, workers comp and products liability, is enough to encourage any working American to cherish the idea of going to the mat with them. Of course, their lobbying efforts to protect CERCLA raise me to a special frenzy.

The lawyers I need to describe to tell my story pose an agonizing dilemma for me. Many are personal friends of mine. These are good guys whose only fault is simply following the party line. They are doing their jobs, as they feel their jobs should be done. But how can I tell my story without telling it, "the way it is?" Can I gloss over what I believe to be imperfections in the moral fabric of these lawyers, when compared to the lofty image they hold of themselves?

As a machinist, I'm expected to make parts fast and within tolerance. As a businessman, I face different levels of scrutiny. On what scale should the legal community be judged?

I can not tell my story without presenting a true description of the actions of each of these attorneys. I suggest the reader pass no judgements on these individuals, but simply recognize that my situation is but a microcosm of similar events taking place all over America.

I enjoy lakes, green golf courses, lush forests and walks on a clean, sandy beach. My conscience had never allowed me to pollute or dump trash on a sidewalk even before Rachel Carson made such behavior taboo in America. If you think of yourself as someone who cares for the environment, I'm just like you. I'm no hero. I'm nothing special. Like most Americans, I'm just trying to make it through.

I feel the urge to write today. It's snowing outside, I can't play golf, all my excuses are gone and, most importantly, I do have a title. Better than that, I have a story to tell. If you want to see it, this is the only channel that's on tonight.

If only Cowlbeck were here, we'd have this knocked off in no time and head out for a beer. I wonder how he would start? I do remember that dream. As a matter of fact, I think often of the Muse, Mercury, the Jester and Zeus. Seems like every time I see Michael and the Bulls, I picture Mercury rising through the heavens.

Mostly it's the Muse. Her face and her body all seem so vivid. I know that it was a dream and all that classic mythology is not real. It's what the nuns once called false gods. But, I can imagine that when the Greeks fought the Trojans, it was a comfort to think they had a god or two on their side. At times it's tough to know what is real and what isn't. If I go into battle to get environmental moneys flowing in the right direction, would you deny me the comfort of these false gods?

OK Muse, lets have at it. We'll start just like Rachel, "*A Fable for Tomorrow*".........